Complete
Guide to
Roses

Meredith® Books
Des Moines, Iowa

Complete
Guide to
Roses

The Story of Roses 6

Selecting the Right Rose 24

Using Roses in the Landscape 46

Planting Roses 64

Caring for Roses 84

Pruning Roses 104

Protecting Roses 116

The Pleasure of Roses 132

Creating and Multiplying Roses 152

Gallery of Roses 168

The Story of Roses

The roses grown in today's gardens have a complex and intriguing history. For thousands of years, people around the world have reserved a special place for these exquisite flowers—in their gardens and in their art, literature, and music. Thanks to the efforts of rose breeders through the centuries, roses now exist in a variety of colors and forms.

Rosa damascena semperflorens, the twice-blooming Autumn Damask rose, dates at least to 500 B.C.E. Some historians believe it was cultivated on the Greek island of Samos as early as 1000 B.C.E.

Prehistoric evidence

Throughout history no flower has been so loved, revered, or renowned as the rose. It is older than the human hands that first cared for it, drew pictures of it, and celebrated it in lore. Forty million years ago, a rose left its imprint on a slate deposit at the Florissant Fossil Beds in Colorado. Fossils of roses from Oregon and Montana date back 35 million years, long before humans existed. Fossils have also been found in Germany and the Balkans.

Roses grow wild as far north as Norway and Alaska and as far south as Mexico and North Africa, but no wild roses have ever been found to grow below the equator.

Early development of roses

The rose apparently originated in central Asia about 60 million to 70 million years ago during the Eocene epoch and then spread over the entire Northern Hemisphere. Early civilizations, including the Egyptians, Chinese, Phoenicians, Greeks, and Romans, appreciated roses and grew them widely as long as 5,000 years ago.

Researchers discovered paintings of roses on a tomb wall of Thutmose IV, who died in the 14th century B.C.E. References to the rose have been deciphered from hieroglyphics.

In 1888, while excavating tombs in Upper Egypt, English archaeologist Sir Flinders Petrie, found the remains of rose garlands that had been used in a funeral wreath in the second century C.E. He identified the rose as *Rosa richardii*, a cross between *Rosa gallica* and *Rosa phoenicia*—the holy rose of Abyssinia, or St. John's Rose. The petals, although shriveled, had retained their pink color and, when soaked in water, were restored to a nearly lifelike state.

About 500 B.C.E. Confucius wrote about roses growing in the Imperial Gardens and noted that the library of the Chinese emperor contained hundreds of books on the subject. It is said that the rose gardeners of the Han dynasty (207 B.C.E.–220 C.E.) were so obsessed with this flower that their parks threatened to engulf land needed for producing food until the emperor ordered some rose gardens plowed under. Few records of the rose's evolution in Asia survive, although references do occur in Asian literature and art.

The world's oldest rose

The oldest rose identified today is *Rosa gallica*, also known as the French rose, which once bloomed wild throughout central and southern Europe and western Asia and still survives there. Although the exact origin of *Rosa gallica* is unknown, traces of it appear as early as the 12th century B.C.E., when the Persians considered it a symbol of love.

A generous bed
of 'Louise Odier'
(a Bourbon rose
dating from 1851)
graces a garden
of old roses with
beauty and
luscious fragrance.

Roses in the Ancient World

The White Rose of York (Rosa × alba), probably a hybrid of Rosa gallica and Rosa canina, developed as early as 100 C.E., produces abundant flowers only once in early summer.

Descending from *Rosa gallica* is *Rosa damascena*, the damask rose, whose well-known fragrance has been part of rose history since the rose first appeared about 900 B.C.E. About 50 B.C.E. a North African variant called *Rosa damascena semperflorens*, the 'Autumn Damask', thrilled the Romans because it bloomed twice a year—a trait previously unknown to them. The 'Autumn Damask', which has been traced back to at least the fifth century B.C.E., is believed to be a cross between *Rosa gallica* and *Rosa moschata*, the musk rose. Until European merchants discovered tea and China roses in Asia many centuries later, this rose would be the only repeat bloomer known to the Western world.

Rosa × alba—the famous white rose

Another important early rose was *Rosa × alba,* the 'White Rose of York'. Made famous as the emblem of the House of York during the 15th-century Wars of the Roses, this five-petaled rose is actually far older, dating before the second century C.E. It probably originated in the Caucasus and traveled west by way of Greece and Rome. *Rosa × alba* and its relatives, known as *albas*, are believed to have descended from some combination of *Rosa gallica, Rosa damascena, Rosa canina*, and *Rosa corymbifera*.

Beauty across the Mediterranean

The Phoenicians, Greeks, and Romans all grew and traded roses. As a result of these societies' travels and conquests, roses spread throughout the Mediterranean and the Middle East.

The Greek scientist and writer Theophrastus, cataloging roses known about 300 B.C.E., described their flowers as having anywhere from five to a hundred petals. His was the first known

Rosa Mundi *(Rosa gallica versicolor)* is the oldest striped rose, dating to before 1581.

detailed botanical description of a rose. Alexander the Great, king of Macedonia about this time, grew roses in his garden and is credited for introducing cultivated roses into Europe. He may have influenced their cultivation in Egypt as well.

Romans and their public rose gardens

Roman patricians tended rose gardens at their homes, and public rose gardens were a favorite place to pass a summer afternoon. Records show that there were 2,000 public gardens in Rome before its fall in 476 C.E.. The poet and satirist Horace complained about the shortsightedness of the Roman government for allowing rose gardens to be planted where the land should have been used for wheat fields and orchards. However, he was not opposed to taking advantage of their abundance. He observed that mixing rose petals in wine offered relief from hangovers.

From the Dark Ages to the 18th Century

After the fall of the Roman Empire, Europe fell into the Dark Ages, a period of violence and diminished learning. Rose gardening became impossible for all but a few. Charlemagne (742–814 C.E.) grew roses on the palace grounds at Aix-la-Chapelle. It was primarily the monks, however, who kept roses alive, using them and other plants for medicinal uses. Monasteries of the Benedictine order in particular became centers of botanical research, and preserved the legacy of roses.

Trade revives a passion for roses

As social conditions stabilized about 1000 C.E., roses reappeared in private gardens. During the 12th and 13th centuries, soldiers returning from the Crusades in the Middle East brought back tales of extravagant rose gardens, as well as sample plants. As travel and trade increased, merchants, diplomats, and scholars began to exchange roses and other botanicals. Interest in the rose rekindled.

Roses documented by herbalists

Early herbalists give testimony to the burgeoning knowledge of roses. John Gerard, an English herbalist, wrote in his *Herball* in 1597 that 14 kinds of roses were known. By 1629, John Parkinson, the apothecary to James I, had reported 24 different roses in his herbal *Paradisus*. At the end of the 1700s, English artist Mary Lawrance illustrated some 90 different roses in a book titled *A Collection of Roses from Nature*.

In late Medieval Europe the rose became a symbol of courtly love and the subject of numerous songs of the troubadours. Reflecting this courtly tradition was the French *Roman de la Rose*, (Romance of the Rose), one of the most famous poems of the Middle Ages. In this elaborate allegory, a lover wandering in a rose garden tries to pluck a rosebud but is warned by Cupid that he must first prove his devotion by surmounting a series of trials. The illumination at left from a 1498 edition shows the climactic moment when the Lover is led by *Bel Acueil* (Fair Welcome) to the rose at the center of the garden.

Roses in North America

Rosa setigera,
the prairie rose

'Rose de Meaux' (*R. centifolia*)

'Crested Moss' (*R. centifolia cristata*)

Across the Atlantic many separate strains of roses developed in the wilds of North America. Of some 200 rose species now known worldwide, 35 are indigenous to the United States, making the rose as native to North America as the bald eagle. These roses include *Rosa virginiana*, the first American species mentioned in European literature; *Rosa carolina*, the pasture rose; *Rosa setigera*, the prairie rose; *Rosa californica*; *Rosa woodsii*; and *Rosa palustris*, the swamp rose, named for the environment in which it grows best.

Embellishing the early colonies

Captain John Smith wrote that Native Americans of the James River valley planted wild roses to beautify their villages, thus making roses one of the first North American native plants to be cultivated as an ornamental. Edward Winslow, a founder of the Plymouth Colony, reported that in 1621 the Pilgrims also appreciated the flowers, despite the hardship of settling a new world. They planted "an abundance of roses, white, red, and damask, single but very sweete indeed."

When William Penn, the founder of Pennsylvania, lived in Europe in the late 1600s, he observed that roses enjoyed high favor in gardens as well as in the arts and sciences. Returning to America in 1699, he brought 18 rosebushes with him. A well-educated man, Penn later discussed their beauty and medicinal virtue in *A Book of Physic*, a text intended for the medical care of Pennsylvania settlers.

The many-petaled cabbage rose

One marvel that Penn had undoubtedly beheld in Europe (if he had not already seen it in the colonies) was *Rosa × centifolia*, the cabbage rose. True to its botanical name, this rose has an astounding 100 petals, so densely arrayed that the flowers resemble small cabbages. Once thought to be ancient—perhaps the 100-petaled rose described by Pliny the Elder in the first century C.E.—the cabbage rose is now considered by many to be a product of late 17th-century Dutch rose growers. Others believe that it was imported from Asia in 1596. Whatever its history, the cabbage rose is probably a complex hybrid of many ancient roses, including the gallicas, damasks, and albas.

A famous sport (mutation) of the cabbage rose is *Rosa centifolia muscosa*, the moss rose, which appeared about 1700 and is still grown and used in hybridizing. It has tiny, highly fragrant, mosslike hairs along its stems and flower buds.

The limits of early hybridizing

Although European hybridizers were busy during this period, they based their introductions on a limited gene pool, which made novelty hard to achieve. Moreover, the laws of heredity were poorly understood—a handicap that persisted until well after Gregor Mendel conducted his research in the mid-1800s. In addition, early breeders jealously guarded their methods, worried that competitors would put them out of business. Today's breeders are far more communicative, having learned that sharing knowledge benefits all who love roses.

Roses From Asia

A revolution in rose breeding and growing took place in Europe in the 18th and 19th centuries, when increased trade with Asia brought *Rosa chinensis*, the China rose, to the attention of Europeans. 'Old Blush', the first variety of China rose to reach the West, was introduced into Sweden in 1752. It reached the rest of Europe by 1793. *Rosa odorata*, the tea rose, made its European debut in 1808 or 1809. The flower earned this name because of the tealike scent of its foliage.

The China rose thrills Europeans

Although the Chinese had grown the China rose, the tea rose, and other roses for centuries, their impact in Europe was truly phenomenal. Their most remarkable quality—continual repeat blooming—was completely unknown in Europe at the time and made them an instant sensation. In contrast to the repeat-blooming 'Autumn Damask', which blooms briefly twice a year, continual repeat bloomers produce flowers over an extended period during the growing season.

In addition to their flowering capabilities, the China rose possesses a foliage that is almost evergreen; and the tea rose, a foliage that is resistant to mildew.

European rose breeders were eager to marry these traits into existing rose lines. Indeed, the China and tea roses laid the genetic foundation for almost all modern roses. Unfortunately, they also passed on a lack of cold hardiness to many of their descendants.

British traders import the China rose

The China rose had also been called the Bengal rose because it was imported to the West from Calcutta, the region's capital. In the 18th century a large botanical garden flourished there, containing roses brought from China by merchants of the British East India Company. In 1789 a British sea captain took a plant home to England. Beginning in 1793, more specimens were shipped from Calcutta to many parts of Europe by Dr. William Roxburgh, the director of the company.

Roses in America's first nursery

In the British colonies in America, rose commerce thrived during the 18th century. In 1737 Robert Prince opened the first American nursery in Flushing, Long Island, and started to import a mounting assortment of new plants. By 1746 he advertised 1,600 varieties of roses—no doubt one of the largest collections in the world at that time. Prince's records show that in 1791, Thomas Jefferson ordered two centifolias, a Common Moss, a *'Rosa Mundi'*, an unidentified yellow, a musk rose, and, quite interestingly, a China rose. Because China roses did not reach most of Europe until 1793, it is possible that the rose traveled directly from Asia on a clipper ship that crossed the Pacific by way of Cape Horn.

Jefferson was not the only president interested in growing roses. George

'Old Blush' (China)

'Mrs. B.R. Cant' (tea)

'Rose de Rescht' (Portland)

Washington cultivated roses at Mount Vernon.

A famous East-West hybrid

The Portlands were a class of rose that came into being about 1800, probably derived from a cross of the 'Autumn Damask' with the China rose and *Rosa gallica*. Named for the duchess of Portland, the Portlands were one of the first good garden hybrids to meld East and West, possessing the repeat-blooming ability of their China rose parent. Also called damask perpetuals, the Portlands were grown until the hybrid perpetual was introduced almost 40 years later.

Empress Josephine and Malmaison

No one did more to popularize the rose at the beginning of the 1800s than Empress Josephine, wife of Napoleon I. An ardent lover of the rose (one of her middle names was Rose), she started a "rose renaissance" by attempting to grow every known variety in her garden at Malmaison, her retreat near Paris.

Specimens from Napoleon's empire

Between 1798, when she first started the garden, and 1814, when she died a month before her 51st birthday, she collected 250 rose specimens. To support her hobby, Napoleon ordered his captains to bring home any new rose they found blooming on foreign shores.

Even the British, who were at war with the French, allowed plants for Josephine to cross blockades and permitted her head gardener to travel freely across the English Channel.

Josephine's lasting horticultural legacy

The reputation of Josephine's garden spread across Europe,

'Fantin-Latour', one of the many centifolia hybrids in Empress Josephine's garden

'La Belle Sultane' (1795) blooms in the present-day gardens of Malmaison, now a museum.

igniting an interest in rose growing and hybridizing that would eventually lead to the birth of modern roses.

More than half of Josephine's roses were gallicas. The rest consisted of 27 centifolias, 22 Chinas, 9 damasks, 3 mosses, 11 species, 4 spinosissimas, 8 albas, 3 foetidas, and 1 musk. (Each of these rose classes is described in the next chapter.) The empress's roses are a fair representation of those that were popular among all classes of Europeans during the Napoleonic era.

France exports thousands of roses

Because of the prestigious gardens at Malmaison, France became a leading grower and exporter of roses. In 1815 some 2,000 varieties of roses were available from French growers. That figure jumped to 5,000 varieties in only 10 years. French growers also exported roses to New Orleans and cities up the Mississippi River before the Civil War. Southern gardeners found the tender China and tea roses especially suited to their warm climate.

The Beginning of Modern Roses

The Bourbon rose, *Rosa × borboniana*, was brought to France in 1817 from the island of Réunion (then called Ile de Bourbon) near Madagascar in the Indian Ocean. Its background is unknown, but it is probably a natural hybrid of *Rosa chinensis* and 'Autumn Damask', because both roses were grown as hedges on the island. The Bourbon rose quickly became one of the most popular roses of the early 19th century due to its recurrent bloom. Like the Portlands, it was one of the first to combine the best of the European and Oriental roses. The original Bourbon was bright pink, although it is now lost. However, among the many remaining Bourbon hybrids is one that served as a primary source of red in today's roses.

Another product of a cross between European and Oriental roses was the hybrid China class. These tall and somewhat unattractive plants did not repeat bloom well, and never became popular on their own. They were, however, among the ancestors of the hybrid perpetuals, polyanthas, floribundas, and hybrid teas.

The British search Asia for new roses

In quest of roses and other plants, The Royal Horticultural Society of Great Britain sent a young Scot, Robert Fortune, to the Orient with 50 pounds sterling, a brace of shotguns, and instructions to bring back new plants of any kind.

From 1843 to 1845, Fortune traveled to the major ports of China, which had recently been forced open to foreign trade. He returned to England with 190 rose varieties, 120 of which were new to Europe. Fortune made three more botanical forays to Asia, during the last of which he gathered roses in Japan.

America's first hybridized rose

An American contribution to the history of the 19th-century rose was the noisette rose, *Rosa × noisettiana*, the first rose known to be hybridized in America. (Although tradition has it that the American hybrid 'Mary Washington' had appeared years before in George Washington's garden, it is not known whether this rose was created deliberately or

'Mme Alfred Carrière' (Noisette, 1879)

'Irene Watts' (China, 1896)

'Zéphirine Drouhin' (Bourbon, 1868)

'Harison's Yellow' (hybrid foetida, 1830)

'Champneys' Pink Cluster' (Noisette, 1811)

apple-scented foliage, mark the westward movement.

Rosa rugosa arrives from Japan

In the mid-1800s *Rosa rugosa*, well known as the rose of the seashore, came to the Western world from Japan. It does not hybridize well and therefore has not contributed much to the aesthetic history of roses. But for more than 1,000 years, *Rosa rugosa* has been valued for its crinkled foliage, single flowers, and copious production of hips—an excellent source of vitamin C.

'Therese Bugnet' (hybrid rugosa, 1950)

Rosa rugosa alba

accidentally.) The noisette rose was a cross between *Rosa moschata*, the musk rose, and *Rosa chinensis*, the China rose. It was hybridized in 1812 by a South Carolina rice grower named John Champneys, who called his creation 'Champneys' Pink Cluster'. But he lacked interest in marketing the rose, so he gave a cutting to his neighbor Philippe Noisette. Philippe, in turn, sent it to his brother Louis, a nurseryman in Paris. By crossing this low-growing rose with other taller roses, Louis developed a tall new rose that he dubbed 'Blush Noisette'—snubbing the original hybridizer.

Roses move west with pioneers

In the 1840s explorer Captain John Charles Fremont wrote of the roses growing in virgin prairies 500 miles west of St. Louis: "Everywhere the rose is met with, and reminds us of cultivated gardens and civilization. It is scattered over the prairies in small bouquets, and, when glistening in the dew and swaying in the pleasant breeze of the early morning, is the most beautiful of the prairie flowers." When Fremont arrived in California, native roses awaited him there as well.

As pioneers crossed the United States, especially during the gold rush, they took with them frivolous things of beauty, including roses, as well as supplies essential to survival. A hybrid of *Rosa foetida* called 'Harison's Yellow', now established in thickets across the country, and *Rosa eglanteria*, with its unique

The Beginning of Modern Roses
(continued)

**'Baronne Prevost'
(hybrid perpetual,
1842)**

The introduction of the hybrid perpetual

The creation of modern roses was well under way by 1837, when most of the Chinese roses had traveled to Europe. That year saw the introduction of the hybrid perpetual, a complex French hybrid whose ancestors included the Bourbon, damask, China, Portland, cabbage, tea, and noisette roses. The hybrid perpetual was extremely hardy; its flowers were large and fragrant. Early varieties of hybrid perpetuals were pink; however, when they were crossed with Bourbon roses, the Bourbons' red coloring entered the line. The hybrid perpetual was not a true perpetual bloomer, but it did bloom more frequently than many other roses that were widely grown at the time.

The hybrid perpetuals remained popular until the turn of the 20th century, when they were eclipsed by the superior hybrid tea. Unfortunately, most hybrid perpetuals have been lost. Of the more than 3,000 varieties hybridized during this golden age of roses—from the time of Josephine's garden at Malmaison through the assimilation of roses from Asia—only about 50 varieties can be purchased today.

The rise of the hybrid tea

The result of a cross between a hybrid perpetual and a tea rose, the hybrid tea had a more compact growing habit and more dependable everblooming qualities than its hybrid perpetual parent. The first hybrid tea, 'La France', was introduced in 1867. The National Rose Society of Great Britain formally recognized the hybrid tea class in 1893. Since then it has been improved and remains the most popular rose today.

The creation of the hybrid tea marked the start of a new era in rose breeding. All classes of roses in existence before 1867 were deemed old garden roses, whereas all new classes were to be called modern roses. These designations, subsequently endorsed by the American Rose Society, are still used.

The color range of roses brightens

By the end of the 19th century, many of the attributes of modern roses were in place except for one—the yellow to orange color range. Though appearing at times through genetic happenstance, the yellow color had hitherto been a recessive trait that would disappear under the dominant influence of pink.

In 1900, after 13 years of trying, French hybridizer Joseph Pernet-Ducher introduced 'Soleil d'Or', a cross between a red hybrid perpetual and 'Persian Yellow' (*Rosa foetida* Persiana), which had been brought from Persia to England by Sir Henry Willcock in 1837. This cross created a yellow color that survived interbreeding.

'La France' (the first hybrid tea, 1867)

Pernet-Ducher's 'Rayon d'Or', a golden yellow, soon followed. Thanks to these introductions, a range of colors never seen before in modern roses came into being: gold, copper, salmon, and apricot. Pernet-Ducher soon became known as the Wizard of Lyons, the town where he did his work. For the first 30 years of their existence, these roses formed a separate group, Pernetianas. Later, for the sake of simplicity, they were merged with the hybrid tea class.

Unfortunately, 'Persian Yellow' and its fellow descendants of the Austrian rose, *Rosa foetida*, contributed not only their yellow color but also a susceptibility to black spot, a serious rose disease. Many of these roses were also not hardy in winter, which is why most yellow roses today still do not survive cold winters without a great deal of care.

One that did perform well in the cold winters of colonial America was 'Austrian Copper' (*Rosa foetida* 'bicolor'), which had found its way from Asia Minor to Vienna before 1590.

Bicolored flowers

Following soon after the yellow hybrid teas came modern roses with bicolored flowers. Several older roses (including 'Austrian Copper') possessed this distinctive coloring, in which the inside and the outside of the petals have different hues, but there were none with the advantages of the hybrid tea. Combinations of red and yellow were the most prominent at first. In time, however, many other combinations emerged.

Grafting strengthens hybrid tea roses

Hybrid tea roses resisted cold weather but were not vigorous growers, having spindly roots. In the late 19th century, nursery workers learned that these roses could be made to grow better if grafted onto the roots of *Rosa multiflora*, a vigorous plant with nondescript flowers.

This practice continues in the 21st century. Other roses onto whose roots modern roses are grafted include 'Dr. Huey', *Rosa × odorata*, and *Rosa manettii*.

The American Rose Society and its roots

On May 21, 1892, a dozen leading greenhouse rose growers in the United States signed a document creating the National Rose Society. Its goals were to stimulate and encourage the raising of new rose varieties in America, to establish rose exhibitions, and to classify roses rigorously. Membership was limited to professional rose growers; amateurs were not admitted. This rule was gradually relaxed. Today its successor, the American Rose Society (ARS), boasts apoximately 20,000 members, most of whom are amateurs.

20th-Century Roses

'Else Poulsen' (floribunda, 1924)

At the beginning of the 1900s, Danish rose breeder Svend Poulsen hybridized many polyanthas. The polyantha was a new class of rose developed in the late 19th century by French nurseryman Jean Sisley, who crossed *Rosa multiflora* with a dwarf China rose. Polyanthas were low-growing bushes smothered in clusters of small flowers that bloomed repeatedly all summer. In much of his work, Poulsen used the East Asian species *Rosa wichuraiana*, which endowed its progeny with winter hardiness.

Floribundas are created

In the 1920s Poulsen crossed the polyantha with the hybrid tea to produce the first floribundas: the pink 'Else Poulsen' and the red 'Kirsten Poulsen'. As its name implies, the floribunda has an abundance of flowers, a legacy of its polyantha parent. From its hybrid tea parent, the floribunda inherited plant height and long stems.

Climbers and shrub roses come of age

While the development of bush roses was unfolding, climbers were coming into being. Climbers have complex histories and lineages that are often difficult to trace. Many evolved from ramblers, the first of which was 'Crimson Rambler', an import from Japan in 1893. 'Crimson Rambler' was descended from *Rosa wichuraiana* and *Rosa multiflora*.

Other climbing hybrids of *Rosa wichuraiana* are 'American Pillar', 'Blaze', 'Dr. W. Van Fleet', 'Dorothy Perkins', and 'New Dawn'. The large Bourbon roses also influenced climbers, as did the tall noisettes.

Other climbers are sports of bush roses that produced long, pliable canes; still others are descendants of large shrub roses. In recent years many have evolved from *Rosa × kordesii*, a tall, semiclimbing shrub rose that resulted from a cross between *Rosa rugosa* and *Rosa wichuraiana* in 1952. The hybrid musks, which are large shrubs or small climbers, were created in the 1920s from crosses between noisettes and *Rosa multiflora* ramblers.

Reimer Kordes, the 20th-century German hybridizer who created *Rosa × kordesii*, did a great deal of breeding using *Rosa spinosissima*, a rose that had existed since the Middle Ages or before. He crossed it with hybrid teas to develop a fine group of modern shrub roses called kordesii shrubs. These plants include 'Frulingsgold' and 'Frulingsmorgen', winter-hardy, low-maintenance plants that are commonly found in public areas and along roadsides in Europe.

American cultivars find prominence

In 1930 an event took place that revolutionized the American plant world: the extension of U.S. patent law to include plants. Until that time, Americans had looked to Europe for most of their new rose varieties. Now that American cultivars could be protected by a 17-year patent, commercial hybridizers were

Rosa wichuraiana poteriifolia

freed from the fear of piracy, which had dampened their efforts in the past. The first plant of any type to receive a U.S. patent was a climbing rose called, appropriately, 'New Dawn'.

Since 1930 thousands of American rose cultivars have received patents, placing the United States alongside Europe at the forefront of rose development.

All-America Rose Selections is formed

The surge of innovation unleashed by the extended patent law presented a new dilemma for gardeners: how to choose from the many new varieties that now appeared each year. Determined to solve this problem, a group of U.S. rose producers and marketers formed the All-America Rose Selections (AARS) in 1938.

The AARS, a nonprofit industry association, is not related to the American Rose Society. Its mission is to test and promote new varieties and to honor the most worthy with awards. Today, in more than two dozen test gardens around the country, new varieties undergo a two-year evaluation before the winners are decided. The AARS stamp of approval has become an important marketing tool for rose growers and is the gardener's assurance that a rose will perform well in a range of soils and climates.

'Buff Beauty' (hybrid musk, 1939)

'New Dawn' (large-flowered climber, 1930)

'Dortmund' (hybrid kordesii, 1955)

20th-Century Roses
(continued)

Rainbow's End
(miniature, 1984)

'Tropicana' (hybrid tea, 1960)

A new color: orange-red

With the coming of World War II, the rose-hybridizing boom slowed down, especially in Europe. It resumed once the war ended. Despite the proliferation of forms and colors, one long-sought-after color range—pure orange to orange-red—was still lacking in modern roses.

'Queen Elizabeth' (the first grandiflora, 1954)

In 1951 'Independence', a floribunda, was introduced as the first modern rose in this orange-red range. The key to its unique coloration was the pigment pelargonidin, which also gives geraniums their scarlet coloring. An orange-red hybrid tea resulted in 1960, when the German hybridizing firm Rosen Tantau introduced 'Tropicana'.

A new class: grandiflora

In 1954 a new class of rose was created to accommodate the rose 'Queen Elizabeth'. Called grandiflora, this class resulted from crossing a hybrid tea with a floribunda. Its flowers resemble those of the hybrid tea. However, they bloom in clusters like those of the floribunda.

Varieties of miniature roses abound

Today, activity is high among growers of miniature roses, who are introducing many new varieties each year.

The earliest known miniature was *Rosa chinensis minima*. Probably of Chinese origin, this rose inexplicably made its way to a botanical garden on the island of Mauritius in the Indian Ocean. An Englishman found it growing there and brought it home with him around 1815. For an unknown reason, it disappeared sometime afterward and was thought to be lost forever—until Dr. Roulet, an officer in the Swiss reserves, found it growing in a window box in Switzerland around 1920. It was renamed *Rosa chinensis* 'Rouletii'.

California nurseryman Ralph Moore dedicated his life to breeding miniatures and deserves much credit for their popularity. Instead of *Rosa* 'Rouletii', he used 'Oakington Ruby', a 1933 miniature, to introduce dwarfness into his breeding line. Many other breeders, chief among them Harmon Saville of Rowley, Massachusetts, have also introduced large numbers of miniatures.

The rise of the modern shrub rose

"Shrub" is the most recent class of roses created by the American Rose Society, originally intended to encompass hybrid rugosa, hybrid moyesii, hybrid musk, and hybrid kordesii roses, as

Constance Spry (the first shrub rose named by David Austin)

well as a few bushy roses that didn't quite fit into any other class (see page 34). Through the latter half of the 20th century and now into the 21st, intensive breeding has expanded this once-small class into a large and diverse group of roses especially appropriate for the landscape.

In the 1960s and 1970s Dr. Griffin Buck of Iowa State University began introducing a series of ultra-hardy, repeat-blooming floribunda and shrub roses, exemplified best by his award-winning shrub rose, 'Carefree Beauty' (1977). At about the same time, two series of extremely hardy, repeat-blooming shrub roses began appearing out of the Morden Research Station of Agriculture Canada: the Explorer series (each rose named after a famous Canadian explorer) and the Parkland series. Major international breeders quickly took note of the excitement engendered by these new hardy landscape roses, and by the early 1980s Meilland of France was introducing a new line of roses it called the Meidiland series of roses. The turning point in this breeding development occurred with the introduction in 1984 of Bonica, a famously popular shrub rose. Its abundance of flowers, disease resistance, and hardiness (it could be grown on its own roots without grafting) earned it many awards, including the AARS and, most recently, in 2003, the coveted Hall of Fame of the World Federation of Rose Societies. Since Bonica was introduced, a host of shrub roses have followed suit, bred specifically for landscape use—with a free-flowering habit, mounding or

spreading shrub form (many useful as groundcovers), disease resistance, hardiness, and low maintenance needs.

Around the same time that Dr. Buck and the Morden Research Station were developing their hardy landscape roses, the English rose breeder, David Austin, was following a different breeding agenda with the shrub class. In 1961 Austin introduced Constance Spry, the first of what has become an extensive line of shrub roses (Austin calls them "English Roses") bred to combine the romantic flower form, fragrance, hardiness, and graceful bushy habit of many old garden roses, with modern colors (such as yellows and salmons) and, most important of all, a true repeat-blooming habit. The result has revolutionized the development of shrub roses over the past thirty years. A number of the world's great rose breeders have moved to capitalize on the English Rose success—Meilland with its Romantica series, Guillot with the Generosa series of roses, Harkness with its Country rose series, and Poulsen with its Renaissance rose series, among others.

Kaleidoscope is an award-winning 1999 shrub rose that has caused a lot of excitement due to its unusual color combination of mauve, tan, and orange.

So prolific and diverse have been the breeding developments in the shrub class that the American Rose Society is moving toward breaking it into two subclasses: classic shrub roses (including hybrid rugosa, hybrid moyesii, hybrid musk, and hybrid kordesii roses), and modern shrub roses.

White Meidiland (a ground cover rose bred from *Rosa wichuraiana*)

Rose Breeding Today: Who's Who?

Country Music, a shrub rose developed by Harkness in 1998

Tamora, developed by David Austin in 1983

The world's leading hybridizers

The rose that catches your eye in a catalog or at a nursery may well be the product of a lifelong quest by a particular hybridizer. Indeed, several family dynasties have continued this work over a span of generations. Each breeder tends to have an area of special interest. Some concentrate on landscape appeal, whereas others make great effort to develop hardy roses. Some specialize in hybrid teas; others focus on floribundas or grandifloras.

Singin' in the Rain, a floribunda developed by Sam McGredy IV in 1994

Iceberg, an award-winning floribunda from Kordes

'Peace', perhaps the most famous hybrid tea in the world, developed by the House of Meilland in 1945

Right: Bill Warriner, a floribunda developed by Keith Zary in 1997 and named after his predecessor at Jackson & Perkins

Left: Magic Carrousel, an award-winning miniature rose (AOE in 1975, Miniature Rose Hall of Fame in 1999), developed by Ralph Moore in 1972

ROSE HYBRIDIZING TODAY

Here are some of the hybridizers who are currently instrumental in advancing the breeding of roses.

Hybridizer	Country	Purpose in Breeding	Variety	Year	Class
Austin, David (David Austin Roses)	Great Britain	Restore essential qualities of old roses in modern roses	Graham Thomas	1983	Shrub
			Gertrude Jekyll	1986	Shrub
			Abraham Darby	1990	Shrub
Carruth, Tom (Weeks Roses)	United States	Unique color and stripes; combine attributes of old roses with prolific blooms of modern varieties	Scentimental	1997	Miniature
			Fourth of July	1999	Climber
			Hot Cocoa	2001	Floribunda
Dickson, Pat and Colin (Dickson Roses)	Northern Ireland	Experimenting with improving classes of roses by using species and shrub roses; roses for groundcovers, hedging, patios	Elina	1984	Hybrid tea
			Dicky	1984	Floribunda
			Whisper	2003	Hybrid tea
Fryer, Gareth (Fryer's Roses)	Great Britain		Sunset Celebration	1999	Hybrid tea
			Day Breaker	2003	Floribunda
Harkness, Philip and Robert (Harkness Roses)	Great Britain	Better roses for groundcover; and colors in the amber, bronze, and orange range; improving species and shrub roses; new roses to fit the old garden rose class	Amber Queen	1983	Floribunda
			Livin' Easy	1992	Floribunda
			Easy Going	1999	Floribunda
			Gift of Life	1999	Hybrid tea
Kordes, Wilhelm (Kordes Rosen)	Germany	Hardiness, disease resistance, color, form, and fragrance	Caribbean	1992	Grandiflora
			Crimson Bouquet	1999	Grandiflora
			Red Ribbons	1998	Shrub
			Nicole	1985	Floribunda
			Summer Wine	1985	Climber
Lim, Ping (Bailey Nurseries)	United States	Disease resistance, easy care, hardiness, fragrance, form, and repeat blooming	Love & Peace	2002	Hybrid tea
McGredy, Sam	New Zealand	Unusual colors; roses that can be used in the landscape, especially groundcovers	Singin' in the Rain	1994	Floribunda
			New Zealand	1989	Hybrid tea
Meilland, Alain, and Jacques Mouchat (Meilland International)	France	Roses with wide appeal that can be used in massed plantings	Bonica	1985	Hybrid tea
			Carefree Wonder	1990	Shrub
			Carefree Delight	1994	Shrub
			Marmalade Skies	1999	Floribunda
			Glowing Peace	1999	Hybrid tea
			Cherry Parfait	2003	Grandiflora
Moore, Ralph	United States	Popularized miniature roses; first remontant yellow hybrid rugosa; hardy shrub roses reminiscent of old garden roses	Magic Carrousel	1972	Miniature
			Sequoia Gold	1986	Miniature
			Playgirl	1986	Floribunda
			Topaz Jewel	1987	Hybrid rugosa
			Playgold	1997	Miniature
			Out of Yesteryear	1999	Shrub
Noack, Werner (Noack Rosen)	Germany	Hardy, disease-resistant shrub roses and robust, easy-care garden roses	Flower Carpet	1989	Shrub
			Red Flower Carpet	2001	Shrub
Olesen, Mogens Poulsen Roser Aps	Denmark	Exceptionally hardy roses; everblooming shrub roses and climbers, as well as new colors and groundcover roses for the landscape	Cliffs of Dover	1995	Shrub
			Cape Cod	1995	Shrub
			Central Park	1995	Shrub
			Queen Margrethe	1995	Shrub
Orard, Pierre	France	Hardiness, disease-resistance, long bloom	Starry Night	2002	Shrub
Radler, William	United States	Breed the maintenance out of roses by developing disease-resistant, hardy, beautiful, long-blooming plants with attractive shrublike habit	Knock Out	2000	Shrub
			Blushing Knock Out	2002	Shrub
			Carefree Sunshine	2002	Shrub
			Pink Knock Out	2004	Shrub
Warner, Chris (Warner Roses)	Great Britain	Disease-resistant roses and climbing miniature roses	What a Peach	2002	Shrub
Zary, Keith (Jackson & Perkins)	United States	Strong, high quality, cold-hardy plants that are easy to grow and maintain	Bill Warriner	1997	Floribunda
			Candelabra	1998	Grandiflora
			Veteran's Honor	1999	Hybrid tea
			Artistry	1998	Hybrid tea
			Gemini	1999	Hybrid tea
			Honey Perfume	2003	Floribunda

Selecting the Right Rose

Roses come in an astounding variety of colors, scents, flower forms, and growth habits— a selection so vast that the beginning gardener may rightly feel overwhelmed. Roses also range in their tolerance of climate extremes and their resistance to diseases. To help you choose wisely, this chapter describes the major classes of roses and their characteristics.

Enjoy choosing your roses

Selecting the right roses for your garden may seem like a daunting task because there are so many kinds. But just as avid travelers believe that half the fun is getting there, so do rose growers enjoy poring over books, leafing through catalogs, and visiting shows and gardens in quest of unfamiliar varieties. Although these activities are pleasurable in themselves, dedicated gardeners know that extra effort spent in making the right choice is the key to a long and happy relationship with plants.

Consider landscape needs, site, and uses

Many of your decisions about which roses to plant will depend on your landscaping needs. Fences and trellises call for climbers, whereas cutting gardens need hybrid teas and grandifloras. Shrub borders incorporate floribundas and shrub roses, while small gardens rely on miniatures. If you prefer a low-maintenance garden, old garden roses will serve your site well. ("Using Roses in the Landscape," pages 46–63, addresses these types of landscaping considerations.)

In addition to choosing roses for their landscape value, you want to select those that grow well in your area because many varieties have trouble in very cold or hot regions, or are susceptible to locally bothersome diseases such as black spot.

You should also consider the uses to which your roses will be put—for example, exhibiting or flower arranging. Certain rose varieties far surpass others in flower form, length of bloom, and other pertinent traits. ("The Pleasure of Roses," pages 132–151, discusses these traits and lists some of the roses best suited for cutting and exhibiting.)

Above all, plant what you love. If you love fragrant roses, or roses of a certain color, blooming pattern, or growth habit, be sure to include them in your garden.

Signature
High-centered
Hybrid tea

'Playboy'
Single
Floribunda

Golden Celebration
Cupped
Shrub

Blueberry Hill
Semidouble
Floribunda

Evelyn
Flat Open
Shrub

'Salet'
Quartered pompon
Old garden rose

'Madame Hardy'
Quartered with central pip
Old garden rose

'Aunt Gerry'
Fully opened
Hybrid tea

Above right: Climbing First Prize, a climbing form of the popular hybrid tea, arches gracefully against a fence.

At left: An arrangement with a wide variety of rose cultivars, classes, and flower forms.

WHAT'S IN A NAME: ROSE NOMENCLATURE

BOTANICAL NAMES: Some roses are botanical species—a group of plants with similar inherited characteristics found growing naturally in the wild. An example is *Rosa rugosa,* a hardy species native to the Far East. Botanical species are always expressed scientifically with at least two parts to their name, always in italicized Latin.

The first indicates the genus. All roses are members of the genus *Rosa.* The second indicates the species. *Rosa rugosa* is a group, or species, of roses that share unique characteristics passed on from generation to generation that set that group apart from all other groups of roses.

Sometimes there is a subsidiary group that naturally occurs within a species (a botanical variety) expressed as a third italicized Latin name. For example, *Rosa rugosa alba* is a naturally-occurring white-flowered variety of the cerise-flowered species *Rosa rugosa.*

Common names are names developed from common usage with no rules. The same rose may have several common names that differ according to the place and the user. *Rosa rugosa,* for example, is called by some the Turkestan rose, by others the Japanese rose. On the other hand, different roses may share the same common name. Botanical names, however, because they are governed by an international authority, are unique to each kind of plant and are the same throughout the world.

HORTICULTURAL AND COMMERCIAL NAMES: Most roses in cultivation are the product of careful breeding and selection. When rose breeders are ready to introduce a new cultivated variety (called a *cultivar),* they must register the new plant's official name with the International Registration Authority for Roses. A cultivar name is capitalized, printed in regular typeface (never italic), and enclosed by single quotation marks. It must be unique to that cultivar. Once registered, it is the official name of that cultivar worldwide. A cultivar name must be universally available and can never be trademarked.

Around 1958 rose breeders began using a coding for cultivar names in which the first three letters were taken from their names or their company's name, written in capital letters, and followed by additional lowercase letters. In 1978 this coding became official practice. The fancy name previously used for the cultivar name was now often trademarked as a commercial name. For example, in 1961 David Austin introduced his first English rose, trademarked its fancy name Constance Spry, and registered its cultivar name as 'AUSfirst'.

In this book, capitalized names not enclosed in single quotation marks are the fancy names used commercially. Most are trademarked or registered. Only registered cultivar names appear in single quotation marks.

Anatomy of a Rose

Roses are classified by the form and color of their flowers, seed structures, leaves, and stems. It's useful to be familiar with this anatomy because plant descriptions reference them.

Flowers

This structure is technically known as the corolla. The corolla is made up of petals, with the number determining whether the rose is classified as single, semidouble, double, or very double. A single flower has just one row of petals—usually 5 petals but as many as 12. A rose with 13 to about 25 petals in two or three rows is said to be semidouble. A rose with more than 25 petals, in three or more rows, is called double. A very full flower having more than 45 to 50 petals in numerous rows is known as very double.

A quartered flower is one whose petals open in such a way that, when viewed from above, the rose appears to be divided into quadrants.

With some roses a solitary bloom appears at the top of the flower stem; these are usually referred to as one-to-a-stem roses. When multiple flowers appear on a stem, the grouping is known as a spray or a cluster.

Flowers open from flower buds, which are initially covered by leaflike green sheaths known as sepals. Collectively, the sepals and the bulbous structure below them—the calyx tube—are known as the calyx. As a flower opens, the sepals turn down and may eventually be hidden by the flower. Some sepals are small and plain; others are large and frilled.

When a flower has fully opened, thin filaments called stamens become visible in the center of the flower, which is called the disc. Stamens, the male reproductive portion of the flower, release pollen from parts at their tips called anthers. The stamens of roses are usually yellow, although sometimes they are red or maroon. The female portion of the flower, the pistil, is located at the center of the stamens. Only its topmost portion, the stigma, can be seen; hidden below it is the style, a slender tube that leads to the ovary, where seeds form if fertilization takes place. Seeds develop from ovules, egglike objects that are borne on structures called carpels within the ovary.

Once a rose has been pollinated—either by its own pollen or by pollen from another rose—the ovary swells and a seed-bearing fruit called the hip forms after the flowers fade. The hips of some roses are bright red or orange, with a characteristic pear, oval, or urn shape. Experts can often identify the variety of a rose by its distinctive hips alone.

Canes and stems

The main branches of rosebushes are known as canes. These arise from the crown, the point where the branches are joined to the root shank. (On roses that have been budded [grafted] to more vigorous root systems, the point where the canes are grafted to the roots is called the bud union; the bud union functions as the crown.) A new cane that arises from the crown or the bud union is often called a basal break.

Stems are growths emanating from the canes and terminating in flowers. Roses produce stems of differing lengths, depending on their class. For example, most hybrid teas have longer-than-average stems, making them good cut flowers.

Both canes and stems are usually covered by red or green thorns (also known as prickles), although some roses are thornless. Thorns vary in size, shape, and number. They can be so distinctive that they alone can be used to identify certain roses.

Leaves

Roses have compound leaves, which are made up of several leaflets. Most modern roses have five-leaflet leaves except in the area near the flower, where three-leaflet leaves usually appear instead. Old garden roses may have seven, nine, or even more leaflets. The top leaflet, called the terminal leaflet, is attached to the rest by a small stem known as a petiole; the other leaflets have stalks known as petiolules. The leaf's base has a winglike appendage known as the stipule; the tip of the stipule is called the auricle.

New stem growth emanates from a bud eye in the leaf axil, the point at which a leaf joins the stem. The part of the stem between the highest leaf and the flower is known as the peduncle, also referred to as the neck. Peduncles are generally thornless and soft wooded, and vary in length and thickness depending upon the variety. Often, a small leaflike structure known as a bract appears partway down the peduncle.

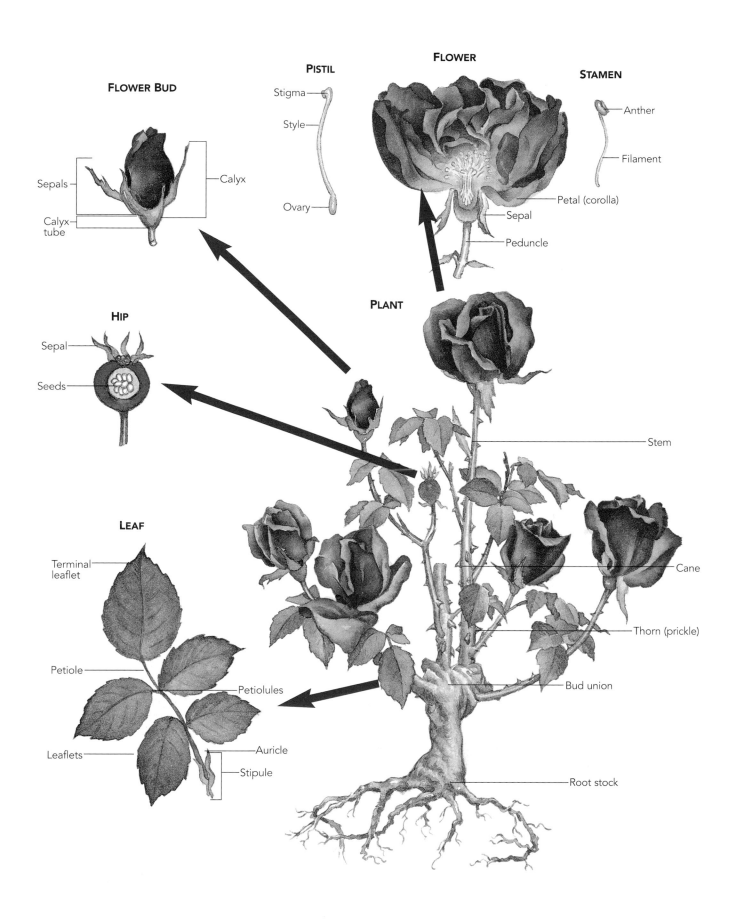

FLOWER BUD

Sepals

Calyx

Calyx tube

PISTIL

Stigma

Style

Ovary

FLOWER

STAMEN

Anther

Filament

Petal (corolla)

Sepal

Peduncle

HIP

Sepal

Seeds

PLANT

Stem

Cane

Thorn (prickle)

Bud union

Root stock

LEAF

Terminal leaflet

Petiole

Petiolules

Leaflets

Auricle

Stipule

Forms of Roses

Roses fit many landscaping needs with a variety of shapes and sizes, from tiny miniatures only 12 inches high and wide to giant climbers that can sprawl over a house and leap from treetop to treetop. From low, wide groundcovers 18 inches high and 6 or even 8 feet across, to rounded 5-foot mounds; from arching sprays to narrow vertical pillars and lollipop standards whimsically called "trees"—there is a rose for nearly every purpose and function in your landscape. Grow them as flowering shrubs, in mixed beds and borders, among herbs in containers, underplanted with annuals, surrounding a mailbox or lightpost, screening a fence, scrambling up trees, trailing over arches or arbors, and cascading down a bank or over a stone wall. The key is to ensure that the variety or varieties you choose are suitable for the use you have in mind.

If you intend to train the rose up a wall or along a fence, for example, then climbing roses or ramblers are best. For a mass planting, hybrid teas

and grandifloras may be dramatic, but they don't work well by themselves as single specimens. The flowers are quite spectacular, but their sometimes leggy form can be unattractive. A shrubbier rose might be a better choice as a single plant in the existing landscape. Shrub roses have a rounded form that works as a blooming hedge as well.

Use the helpful illustrations and descriptions on these pages to explore the variety of rose forms that will thrive in your own backyard.

A. PATIO TREE:
This is a wonderful way to grow floribundas and miniatures about 4 feet off the ground and is excellent for containers. Unprotected plants may suffer winter damage.

B. MINIATURE:
These dense, low-growing roses cover themselves with tiny blooms, usually in clusters. Use for edging, growing in pots or rockeries, or as a pot plant indoors. They reach 18 to 24 inches high.

C. FLORIBUNDA:
Known for its large clusters of medium-sized blooms that cover the bush all season long, it is generally hardy and easy to care for and usually grows to about 3 feet high.

D. HYBRID TEA:
The cut flower *par excellence* is easily recognized for the single, sculptural, high-centered bloom per long stem, which is usually large and symmetrical. Plants reach about 5 feet high.

E. CLIMBER:
Actually a shrub with long, arching stems, these roses grow 6 to 20 feet high when trained on walls, trellises, and fences. Train the long canes in a horizontal position to promote bloom production.

F. PILLAR:
A smaller category of climbing roses, this type is often trained around a tall vertical support, covering itself with flowers at each lateral. It can reach heights between 6 to 10 feet tall.

G. OLD GARDEN ROSES: (Types that existed before 1867.) Available in a wide range of sizes, shapes, and flower forms, they can grow 6 to 8 feet high or more. Many bloom only once. They are often fragrant.

H. GRANDIFLORA: Similar to hybrid teas, they are identified by their unique ability to send up clusters of large hybrid tea-type blossoms on strong straight stems. Plants are normally 6 to 8 feet tall.

I. GROUNDCOVER: This is a landscaping category of vigorous, disease-resistant, low-growing plants that spread up to 8 feet wide for bedding and massing. Varieties are usually hardy.

J. MODERN SHRUB: Recent hybridizing breakthroughs combine old garden rose flower form and fragrance with modern colors and recurrent blooms. Plants are 6 to 7 feet high.

K. STANDARD TREE ROSE: This is an excellent choice to grow hybrid teas and floribundas about 6 feet off the ground, often for formal effects. It is subject to winter damage in northern areas if left unprotected.

L. RAMBLER: Given adequate space, these roses can grow 30 feet in every direction to cover trees or even houses. They are usually winter hardy and often have only one bloom cycle each year in spring.

SELECTING THE RIGHT ROSE 29

Classification Of Roses

Complex hybridizing over thousands of years, in addition to the poor record keeping and once-secretive practices of hybridizers, has made it difficult to establish the lineage of many roses. As a result, their classification sometimes stymies even the experts.

To help simplify matters, the American Rose Society has arranged all roses under three broad categories: species, old garden roses, and modern roses. Old garden roses belong to classes that existed before 1867, the year the first hybrid tea was introduced. Modern roses consist of hybrid teas and other classes that were created after 1867.

A class of roses is a grouping of species or hybrid varieties with similar characteristics and sometimes a common heritage. For example, hybrid teas are typically bushy plants with large, showy, solitary flowers; all descended from a 19th-century crossing of a tea rose with a hybrid perpetual. New classes of roses are continually emerging; any distinctive breakthrough in plant form, flower form, or blooming characteristic can serve as the basis for a new class.

The following pages present general descriptions of the rose classes that are commercially available. For details on individual plants, consult the Gallery of Roses, starting on page 168.

Old garden roses

A variety discovered or hybridized after 1867 is still considered an old garden rose if it belongs to a class that predates the hybrid tea. Old garden roses have other characteristics that make them appealing. Most are long-lived, low-maintenance plants with good disease resistance; many are very winter hardy. They exhibit a wide range of plant sizes, flower forms, and flower colors. The following are the most common categories:

'Königin von Danemark' (Alba)
ALBA: Albas are tall, dense, cold-hardy plants that resist many pests and diseases. They date to before the second century C.E. Blooms are either single or double, borne in clusters only once a year, and usually fragrant.

'Sombreuil' (Tea)
TEA: Brought from China in the 19th century, tea roses are immediate ancestors of the modern hybrid tea. They are similar to the China roses but have larger, fuller flowers up to 4 inches across in pastel pinks and yellows, with a fresh, tealike fragrance. They repeat all season. Tea roses are tender plants and were one of the first to have the long, pointed bud that has been passed on to modern hybrids.

'Archduke Charles' (China)
CHINA: China roses (*R. chinensis* and its hybrids) have small, delicate, semidouble or double flowers and glossy, almost evergreen foliage on small- to medium-size plants. They played an important role in the development of today's hybrid roses because they exhibited continual repeat bloom all season, something unknown when they were brought to Europe by way of China through India in the 18th century. They are extremely frost tender.

'Louise Odier' (Bourbon)
BOURBON: Bourbon roses are vigorous, shrubby plants about 6 feet high that bear clusters of fragrant flowers. They are moderately hardy and good repeat bloomers.

'Petite Lisette' (Centifolia)
CENTIFOLIA: "Cabbage" roses bear globular, sweetly fragrant, small- to medium-size flowers in clusters once a year on slender, arching branches with crinkled leaves. Blossoms are packed with more than a hundred overlapping petals. The small- to medium-size plants are quite hardy.

'Madame Hardy' (Damask)
DAMASK: These very hardy roses bear richly fragrant, medium-size flowers in large clusters only once a year, except for the 'Autumn Damask', *(R. damascena semperflorens)*, which blooms twice a year. Damask roses are descendants of *R. gallica* and have been known since 900 B.C.E.

'Harison's Yellow' (H. foetida)
HYBRID FOETIDA: Most of the hybrids of the species *R. foetida* are pleasingly fragrant, unlike the parent species, which has an unpleasant, fetid odor. Hybrid foetidas are tall, vigorous plants that bloom only once a year. Because of these roses, we have the color yellow in today's hybrids. Unfortunately, hybrid foetidas and their descendants are vulnerable to black spot disease.

'Stanwell Perpetual' (H. spinosissima)
HYBRID SPINOSISSMA: The hybrids of *R. spinosissima* (the Scotch rose, which dates to before 1600 C.E.) are mostly 20th-century additions. They are large, vigorous plants and among the thorniest roses. Some bloom only once a year; others repeat throughout the summer.

'Marchesa Boccella' (Portland)
PORTLAND: The first Portland appeared about 1800. Only a few varieties are still available. They are descendants of a China rose, the 'Autumn Damask' and *R. gallica*. They resemble Bourbon roses, to which they are closely related, but they have smaller (3-inch) flowers. Double, very fragrant flowers bloom all summer on upright plants.

'Tuscany Superb' (Gallica)
GALLICA: The gallica, or French rose, is the class that contains the oldest identified rose. Gallicas bloom once a year with flowers of red, pink, or purple. Plants are hardy and compact with dark green, rough-textured foliage; they often spread rapidly by underground runners. Some varieties are richly fragrant; others have no scent.

'Henri Martin' (Moss)
MOSS: Moss roses are sports, or mutations, of centifolia roses. Their robust fragrance emanates from small, hairy, sticky red or green glands that appear on the sepals and sometimes on the stem and leaves. Plants are hardy with large globular flowers. Most bloom only once a season, with the blooms appearing later than those of other roses. Some produce a second, light bloom season in fall.

'Baronne Prevost' (Hybrid perpetual)
HYBRID PERPETUAL: An immediate ancestor of the hybrid tea, the hybrid perpetual is a tall, vigorous, hardy plant that blooms repeatedly all summer, although less prolifically than the hybrid tea. Its large double flowers are pleasantly fragrant.

'Blush Noisette' (Noisette)
NOISETTE: The first hybrid group to originate in the United States, noisettes are a cross between the musk rose (*R. moschata*) and the China rose (*R. chinensis*), made in South Carolina in 1812. Noisettes are tall, bushy, tender plants that make good climbers, bearing fragrant clusters of flowers throughout the season.

Rosa rugosa alba (Species)
SPECIES: The species roses are the wild and original roses. Most species roses have 5-petaled single flowers, although some have double flowers, with 25 petals or more. Most are large, low-care plants; many can tolerate cold winters. Most species roses bloom only once in summer, although a few repeat their bloom. Species roses are referred to by their botanical names—for example, *Rosa multiflora.*

Classification of Roses
(continued)

Modern roses

Since the modern classification of roses began in 1867, hybridizers have created many new classes and varieties of modern roses, expanding the color palette to bright colors, blends, and bicolors, and introducing more and more continually blooming varieties. Although some old garden roses showed repeat bloom (such as 'Autumn Damask', which blooms twice a season), it was not until the China and tea roses were brought to Europe from the Orient that rose growers knew continual repeat bloom. This capacity for summerlong blooming has been passed on to modern roses. Modern roses include (in approximate order of popularity) the hybrid tea, floribunda, grandiflora, climber, miniature, polyantha, rambler, shrub classes, and tree roses.

**'Gift of Life'
(Hybrid tea)**

HYBRID TEA: The classic high-centered beauty of the rose flower is epitomized by the hybrid tea, which eclipses all other classes in popularity. As with other modern roses, varieties are available in every color except true blue and black, for which roses lack the necessary pigment. Many hybrid teas are fragrant, and almost all bloom repeatedly through summer. Most produce one flower to a stem although some bloom in sprays. Typically a double or semidouble flower (with the single, five-petaled 'Dainty Bess' a notable exception), their large, long-lasting blooms and long, strong stems make hybrid teas excellent for cutting and a mainstay of the cut-flower trade.

A cross between the hybrid perpetual and the tea rose, the hybrid tea surpasses both parents in hardiness and repeat blooming, a decisive breakthrough that marked the beginning of modern roses. The first hybrid tea, 'La France', was introduced in 1867. The first yellow hybrid tea, 'Soleil d'Or', introduced in 1900, opened up a new world of color, since yellow was unknown in modern roses until that time. Six decades later, orange hybrid teas followed, and today an exceptionally wide color range is available.

GRANDIFLORA: The grandiflora class began with the rose 'Queen Elizabeth', and grand it is. A cross between a hybrid tea and a floribunda, the grandiflora inherits the best characteristics of both parents. The hybrid tea side of the cross contributes high-centered flowers and long cutting stems. The floribunda side provides hardiness, continual flowering, and clustered blooms. Grandifloras are generally the tallest of the modern roses (except for climbers). Their height makes them most useful at the back of a border or as a screen.

'Crimson Bouquet' (Grandiflora)

FLORIBUNDA: As its name suggests, the floribunda has an abundance of flowers. It was crossed from a hybrid tea and a polyantha, and often has hybrid tea-type flowers, although not always. Some floribundas have single or semidouble flowers that are cup-shaped or flat. Plants tend to be hardy and low growing, and produce flowers of varying size and color in sprays all summer. The low, bushy form of floribundas makes them excellent plants for landscaping, especially as hedges, edgings, or mass plantings.

Kristin (Miniature)

'China Doll' (Polyantha)

POLYANTHA: The forerunners of floribundas, polyanthas are low-growing, compact, hardy plants that flower continually. The origin of the class is clouded, but it is believed that the first polyantha descended from *R. multiflora* and *R. chinensis* in the late 19th century. Their flowers are small and decorative, opening flat, but are abundantly produced in clusters. They are available in white, pink, red, yellow, or orange. Foliage is fine and narrow. Although many polyanthas have been eclipsed in popularity by floribundas, which have more attractive flowers and a wider color range, several are still popular and make excellent plants for hedges and edging.

MINIATURE: Miniature roses are miniature in every sense of the word, with stems, leaves, and flowers all petite versions of full-size plant structures. Miniature roses have become a special focus of hybridizers in the last few decades because their small size makes them easy to grow in any garden, indoors or out.

The miniature is descended from *R. chinensis* Minima and reached Europe in 1815 from the island of Mauritius in the Indian Ocean. It was thought to be lost but was rediscovered growing in Switzerland in the 1920s. Plants range in height from 3 inches to 2 feet or more, and have flowers that range from less than an inch to several inches across, in a wide range of colors. Although many miniatures resemble tiny hybrid teas or floribundas, they are a class unto themselves.

Classification of Roses
(continued)

Golden Celebration (Shrub from David Austin's English Rose collection)

'Henry Hudson' (Hybrid rugosa from the Explorer series)

'Belinda' (Hybrid musk)

Shrub roses

This class of hardy, easy-care plants was created by the American Rose Society to encompass bushy roses that did not fit any other category. Some make good groundcovers; others work well as hedges and screens. Some bloom only once a year; others bloom repeatedly, with single or double flowers in all colors.

The shrub class is divided into several major subclasses: hybrid moyesii, hybrid musks, hybrid rugosas, kordesii, and a catchall category whose members are known as shrubs.

HYBRID MUSKS are partial descendants of *R. moschata*, the musk rose, and will tolerate less sun than other classes of rose. These hardy, disease-resistant, fairly tall plants bloom all season in large, heavily fragrant clusters; most have single flowers, although some have semidouble or double blooms.

HYBRID RUGOSAS are disease-resistant, dense, low-growing plants with wrinkled foliage and are descendants of

'August Renoir' (Shrub from the Romantica collection of the House of Meilland)

'All That Jazz' (Shrub)

R. rugosa. They can have single or double flowers, and their hips are a valued source of vitamin C. Among roses, hybrid rugosas are the most tolerant of wind and sea spray, and therefore make excellent beach plantings.

KORDESII ROSES are 20th-century hybrids of *R. kordesii*, a new species that arose in 1952 when the German hybridizer Reimer Kordes crossed *R. rugosa* and *R. wichuraiana*. Boasting glossy, disease-resistant foliage and exceptional hardiness, these shrubs or low-growing climbers come in a variety of flower forms and colors.

The remaining shrub roses, known simply as shrubs, are generally vigorous, hardy, and disease-resistant. Some

are tall, upright plants excellent for hedges or inclusion in a mixed shrub border; others are low-growing, trailing plants useful as ground covers. Flowers can be single or double and of varying sizes and colors.

Alba Meidiland (Shrub used as groundcover)

'John Cabot' (H. kordesii)

'Paul's Himalayan Musk' (Rambler)

Climber

It is difficult to trace the exact background of today's climbing roses. Many derive from species and old garden roses with long, arching canes—most important, the species rose *R. wichuraiana*. Some descend from shrub roses; others, from ramblers. The climbers of today are technically called large-flowered climbers although in common practice they are referred to simply as climbers. Many are sports, or mutations, of bush roses; thus in books and catalogs you will see reference to climbing hybrid teas, climbing grandifloras, climbing floribundas, climbing miniatures, and others. One exception is 'Climbing Summer Snow'; in this case, the original plant was a climber, which sported to produce the lower-growing 'Summer Snow', a floribunda. Curiously, climbers that are sports of bush roses often have larger flowers.

Climbers are not vines; unlike climbing plants such as clematis and ivy, they lack tendrils to help them cling to

walls or trellises and must be tied to their supports. Their long canes are sometimes pliable enough to be trained horizontally along a fence, a practice that forces them to produce more of the lateral branches on which flowers appear. Stiffer-caned climbers are excellent roses to train upright on a pillar or trellis, and thus are sometimes called pillar roses. Most climbers produce flowers in clusters. Some bloom only once, in spring; others bloom on and off all summer.

RAMBLER: Ramblers were one of the forerunners of today's climbers, which have largely succeeded ramblers because of their more compact shape and larger flowers. Ramblers descended primarily from *R. multiflora* and *R. wichuraiana*. They are very large, rampant, hardy plants with pliable canes that generally bloom only once, in early summer. Although many varieties still survive in old cemeteries and around old cottage-style houses, most have disappeared from the marketplace.

Tree roses

These roses are not a product of interbreeding but rather a plant form produced mechanically by grafting. A tree rose is usually a composite of three separate rose plants—one providing sturdy roots; another supplying a long, straight stem; and a third grafted to the top to produce flowers and foliage. Any rose variety that might look pleasing atop a trunk can be grafted onto a stem to make a tree rose. The length of the stem depends on the variety to be grafted to

Climbing First Prize (Climbing hybrid tea)

it and the role the plant is destined to play in the garden. Some tree roses are stiff and stately; others have a graceful, weeping form created by grafting a pliable-caned variety to the top of the stem. Tree roses are the crowning glory of a formal rose garden, lending it an aristocratic air. Unfortunately, they are all very tender even though the component plants may be hardy.

Bonica tree rose

Choosing Roses for Color

The pale pink of 'Mlle Cécile Brünner' and the bright pink of 'Zéphirine Drouhin' on the arch and the cerise single blooms of the hybrid *rugosa* 'Frau Dagmar Hartopp' create a lovely monochromatic blend.

Warm colors

Flower color is an important factor in selecting roses for your garden, for the colors you choose project your personality and that of your home. A warm color scheme, made up of red, orange, gold, and yellow tones, is exciting, happy, and cheerful. It draws the eye to the garden and makes it look smaller than it is. However, such a color scheme also makes the garden seem hotter, so it would not be a good choice where temperatures scale high in the summer, especially if the roses are planted near outdoor living areas.

Cool colors

A cool color scheme, composed of violet, mauve, and purple, is soothing and refreshing. It is the best choice for a quiet garden meant for relaxing. It also makes a small garden look larger and is a good color scheme to use when you want to hide an eyesore because it does not draw attention to itself. Although they are technically not cool colors, whites, pastel yellows, and light pinks also have this same low-key effect.

Modern hybridizers have enlarged the palette of rose colors to an extent that would amaze the gardener of a hundred years ago. Whereas old garden roses were restricted mainly to stripes and solids in the white, pink, lavender, and red color range, today's modern hybrids come in vivid admixtures of every color except true blue and black—although genetic engineers may well achieve these colors in the future. (There is indeed a green rose, *R. chinensis* 'Viridiflora'.) Flowers may be solid-colored, bicolored (different colors on the insides and the outside of the petals), or blends (two or more colors intermingled on each petal).

Creating harmony with confidence

When planning a garden, work within a limited color scheme to avoid a busy, distracting look. Start by choosing one color as the dominant hue, and add one or two other colors as subordinates. As you gain experience, you will learn how to add more colors safely without creating discord.

To help select color harmonies, use a color wheel (you can buy one at an art supply store). Colors opposite each other on the wheel, such as purple and yellow, or blue and orange, are called complementary. They make a strong and attractive harmony, yet may be too overpowering for a small garden. A useful compromise is split complementary harmony, in which one color is complemented by a color adjacent to its opposite on the wheel. An example of this type of harmony is yellow with red-violet or blue-violet.

Analagous harmony uses two or three colors that are adjacent on the color wheel such as, yellow, yellow-orange, and orange. Putting two strongly colored roses with analogous harmony together, such as the pure orange 'Orangeade' with the red-orange 'Sarabande', creates drama.

Monochromatic harmony is a color scheme that uses shades and tones of a single hue. An example would be a garden using a variety of pinks, perhaps mixing light pink, medium pink, and deep pink roses.

Working with pastel colors

Pink and white do not appear on the color wheel, yet are important colors in the garden. Pink, a tint of red, is used like red to complement colors such as yellow or mauve. Paler pinks tend to have a more cooling influence than darker, more saturated pinks or reds. White, the absence of pigment, can be used on its own as the dominant color or as a buffer

between bright colors. When used as an edging, white can have a unifying effect on a bed or border of multicolored roses behind it because its brightness stands out as a vivid common denominator. Using white-flowered plants only here and there can make for a spotty look, so use white flowers only in contiguous masses or borders.

White, pink, and other light pastels are excellent tones for a garden that will be viewed at night since dark colors fade into the background after sunset. Like cool colors, light colors are also good for camouflaging eyesores such as work sheds, gas tanks, and trash bins, as the eye is less drawn to them than it is to warm or dark colors.

Working with strong color

Roses with strong colors such as red or orange are good for accenting focal points, such as the end of a garden path, or a garden ornament, like a bench, a statue, or a birdbath. Repeating the accent color in a nearby bed carries the eye along through the garden.

Using single-color plantings

In very large gardens, plantings have a more dramatic effect if masses of the same variety—or at least of the same color—are together. These masses give an impression of abundance. If you grow mass plantings of a single color, keep an extra plant or two growing in pots in case disease or winterkill makes replacement necessary.

Bear in mind that solid-color roses can be more difficult to

mix together than blends or bicolors because they have no secondary tones to be picked up by a neighboring rose. However, placing too many blends together can cause the subtleties of their coloration to be lost. A good rule is to place solid colors next to blends, which makes the better qualities of each stand out.

Considering the effect of climate

The local climate may moderate your choice of colors, and even the colors themselves. For example, the heat and bright sunlight of warm climates can cause yellow roses to fade and deep pink and red roses to develop darkened edges. In damp climates many yellow roses are exceptionally prone to black spot. Many white roses are prone to water spotting, so you may wish to avoid planting them in rainy climates or placing them where water will drip on them from eaves and trees.

Matching color to structure

Before making a final color selection, study the color of the house, fence, or wall against which your roses will be seen. Be sure that the juxtaposition is harmonious. A red or brick-colored structure looks best with yellow or white roses; a blue one with red, pink, white, or yellow. Against a white house, bright red and orange are dramatic. The weathered gray surface of an unpainted barn or a split-rail fence is complemented well by roses with soft pink, yellow, or apricot tones.

Choosing Roses for Fragrance

'Mme Isaac Pereire' is thought by some experts to be the most fragrant of all roses.

What's the first thing most people do when they are handed a rose? They smell it. The fragrance of roses has been cherished for ages and is one of the main motivations for growing them. Fragrant rosebushes, placed under windows, along walkways, or near outdoor seating areas, fill the air with a wonderful scent that complements the beauty of the flower. If a fragrant garden is your goal or if you want fragrant roses to use in potpourris or recipes, you need to choose from the most fragrant varieties available.

Understanding fragrance

Like other sensory stimuli, fragrance is subjective. A scent that appeals to one person may repel another and be barely perceptible to a third. And a rose itself may have different degrees and types of fragrance at different times.

A rose is most fragrant when it is one-quarter to two-thirds open and has been slightly warmed by morning sun. This heating causes the rose to release droplets of fragrant oil from tiny scent emitters on its petals and, in some types of roses, from the leaves. Too much sun or wind, however, can quickly carry these oils away and leave the rose with a faint or disagreeable odor. On a sunny day, fragrance declines by as much as 40 percent. On a cool or damp day, by contrast, a rose releases little or no fragrance, and what fragrance is released may be masked by mildew.

Basic fragrances

Not all roses are fragrant, and the classic "rose" scent is just one of a variety of rose fragrances. Roses have seven basic fragrances: rose,

GOOD ROSES FOR FRAGRANCE

'Angel Face'
'Autumn Sunset'
Constance Spry ('AUSfirst')
'Crimson Glory'
'Chrysler Imperial'
Evelyn ('AUSsaucer')
Fair Bianca ('AUSca')
Fragrant Apricot ('JACgrant')
Fragrant Cloud ('TANellis')
Fragrant Plum ('AROplumi')
Gertrude Jekyll ('AUSbord')
Golden Celebration
    ('AUSgold')
'Henry Hudson'
Iceberg ('KORbin')
Intrigue ('JACum')
'Ispahan'
'Jens Munk'
Johann Strauss ('MEIoffic')
'Konigin von Danemark'
Leonardo da Vinci
    ('MEIdeauri')
'Louise Odier'
'Mme Alfred Carriere'
'Mme Isaac Pereire'
New Zealand ('MACgenev')
Papa Meilland ('MEIsar')
Peter Mayle ('MEIzincaro')
'Roseraie de l'Hay'
Rouge Royal ('MEIkarouz')
'Royal Highness'
'Royal Sunset'
Scentsational ('SAVamor')
Sheila's Perfume
    ('HARsherry')
'Stanwell Perpetual'
Summer Wine ('KORizont')
Sweet Chariot ('MORchari')
The Prince ('AUSvelvet')
Toulouse Lautrec
    ('MEIrevolt')
Valencia ('KOReklia')
Y2K ('SAVyk')

'Chrysler Imperial' is a classic hybrid tea famous for its stunning fragrance.

nasturtium, violet, apple, lemon, clove, and tea. The traditional rose scent occurs only in red or pink roses—possibly for genetic reasons—although many red and pink roses are scentless. White and yellow roses tend to have tea, nasturtium, violet, or lemon scents. Orange roses usually smell of tea, nasturtium, violet, or clove. Eglanteria roses have an apple scent, which comes primarily from the leaves.

Rose breeders do not yet understand the genetics of rose fragrance, but they are aware that there are fewer fragrant modern roses than old garden roses. This may be because the primary goals of modern breeders are flower form, color, and disease resistance, with fragrance a lesser priority.

If fragrant roses are your goal, choose from the varieties in the list at left. These roses are among the most fragrant available today. Some have been awarded the James Alexander Gamble Fragrance Award of the American Rose Society, one of the most prestigious awards for fragrance in the horticultural community.

In addition, almost all alba, Bourbon, centifolia, damask, gallica, hybrid musk, hybrid perpetual, moss, noisette, Portland, and tea roses have fragrant flowers.

Choosing Roses for the Climate

Rosa rugosa, native to Asia, has naturalized in many harsh areas of northeastern North America. Many of its hybrid cultivars display a similar tolerance of sandy, infertile soil, strong wind, and harsh salt spray—in addition to winter hardiness as far north as Zone 2.

Kordesii hybrids in the Canadian Explorer series were developed for extreme winter hardiness. Shown here is 'John Cabot', which makes an outstanding climber hardy to Zone 2.

Although most roses will grow in a range of climates, many are susceptible to drought, dampness, heat, cold, and other extremes. If your climate is less than ideal, you can guard many sensitive roses by planting them in protected spots or by giving them extra care. But it is far better to choose varieties that can stand up to the worst your climate can inflict. Here are some guidelines for selecting the right ones.

Drought and dampness

Although no rose will thrive under drought conditions, *R. rugosa* and its hybrids do better than most, surviving without water for several weeks at a time once the plants are established. They will also tolerate the salt air and sandy soil that are found in beach zones.

At the other extreme, many roses are susceptible to the fungal diseases that prevail in damp climates. Yellow roses in particular are susceptible to black spot. If you live in a humid or rainy area, you need to pay strict attention to a program of preventive spraying (see Protecting Roses, pages 116–131). In these circumstances, choose a disease-resistant variety (see page 43). In damp, cloudy regions, avoid roses with very double flowers, which may not open properly if they are constantly moist or if they lack the heat of sunshine to open them before they start to fade.

Hot climates

Rose gardens in warmer climates, be they in subtropical, tropical, or desert areas, can be very successful if you select the right roses. Most modern roses will not live long in these climates as they quickly exhaust themselves when denied winter dormancy. Two notable exceptions are the floribunda Iceberg and the grandiflora 'Queen Elizabeth', which rose growers in subtropical Bermuda have found to be quite long-lived. In general, however, the best choices for hot climates are the old garden roses, especially Chinas, teas, hybrid

TOP ROSES FOR HOT CLIMATES

Bonica ('MEIdomonac')
Brandy ('AROcad')
Crystalline ('ARObipy')
French Lace ('JAClace')
Intrigue ('JACum')
'Mister Lincoln'
Moonstone ('WEKcryland')
'Oklahoma'
'Royal Highness'
Showbiz ('TANweieke')
Sun Flare ('JACjam')
Sunset Celebration ('FRYxotic')
St. Patrick ('WEKamanda')
'Uncle Joe'

perpetuals, and shrub roses. Yellow roses fade in the heat, so you may want to avoid this color in such climates.

You may be able to coax a wider range of roses to grow in hot climates by taking some extra precautions. Keep the soil from drying out too quickly by working in extra organic matter and covering the surface with a mulch (see pages 90–91). Keep the plants from drying out by sheltering them from the wind. Protect your roses against burning by placing them where they will be shielded from the glare of the afternoon sun.

Cold-winter climates

Gardeners who live in cold northern regions must face the fact that their climate is less than hospitable to some types of roses that cannot adapt to cold weather. Although burying or covering the canes of these varieties will help many of them to survive the rigors of winter (see pages 128–131), choosing roses with built-in hardiness can enable you to avoid this drudgery. This is a special boon to people whose time for gardening is limited.

Unfortunately, no one has ever tested each rose variety for winter hardiness in all of the 11 climate zones designated by the U.S. Department of Agriculture (see the map on page 244). This is despite the fact that nearly every other garden plant has been assigned a hardiness rating. However, most roses can be expected to be hardy to Zone 6 (where average minimum temperatures range between -10° and 0°F) without winter protection. Some can

withstand the colder winters of Zone 5 (between -20° and -10°F) and Zone 4 (between -30° and -20°F). See page 129 for a list of hardy roses. In addition to the plants listed, most ramblers are hardy to at least Zone 6, and many are hardy to Zone 5. Most shrub roses are hardy to at least Zone 6. Old garden roses, except for tender China, noisette, and tea roses, are hardy to Zone 6, and centifolias and damasks are hardy to Zone 5. (See the "Gallery of Roses" starting on page 168 for detailed descriptions of each variety.)

Shade

Most roses need full sun in order to grow and bloom successfully. However, a few can do with less sunlight than others. The roses that are most tolerant of shade are the hybrid teas 'Blue Moon', 'Christian Dior', 'Fred Edmunds', 'Garden Party', and 'Swarthmore'; the shrub rose 'Alchymist'; the rambler 'Etain'; and all of the hybrid

musks. In addition, many climbers and miniatures can grow in less sun than other kinds of roses.

However, no rose will thrive with fewer than four hours of bright sunshine per day. If your garden does not provide this, there are ways to compensate for the lack of light.

The Lady Banks rose is a large, once-blooming rambler excellent for Zones 8–11.

ROSES TOLERANT OF PARTIAL SHADE

Abraham Darby ('AUScot')
Amber Queen ('HARroony')
'Angel Face'
'Ballerina'
'Blush Noisette'
'Buff Beauty'
Carefree Delight ('MEIpotal')
'Cornelia'
English Garden ('AUSbuff')
Golden Celebration ('AUSgold')
'Gruss an Aachen'
'Mlle Cécile Brünner, Climbing'
'New Dawn'
'Playboy'
'Sally Holmes'
The Prince ('AUSvelvet')

The hybrid musks and some of the more disease-resistant shrub roses (such as Carefree Delight, shown above) are good choices for partial shade.

Choosing Roses for Disease Resistance

Roses have a lot to offer as terrific landscape plants with a wide diversity of habit, form, and shape and a long color season. Among some home gardeners, however, roses have acquired a reputation as garden prima donnas—delicate and temperamental but beautiful stars that are susceptible to attack by a number of diseases. Although good hygiene and preventive spraying can go a long way toward keeping diseases in check, you may find it preferable to plant tougher, more durable varieties that have built-in resistance.

Weather is one factor affecting the susceptibility of roses to disease. Cool temperatures and high humidity promote fungal problems, while hot, dry climates keep them at bay.

For example, if your climate is cool, humid, or rainy, you may find fungal diseases such as mildew especially difficult to control. Black spot, another fungal disease, is a significant problem in all regions of the United States except the arid West. If you live in one of these areas and lack the time to spray as often as recommended, disease-resistant plants are almost a necessity.

The list on page 43 identifies some rose varieties that are the most resistant to rose diseases. (Note, however, that no rose is completely invincible.) In addition to these, virtually all members of the shrub rose classification resist rose diseases, as do most alba and damask roses, and species roses except those with yellow flowers.

Plant genetics also plays a role in a rose variety's ability to ward off disease. A rose's immune system consists of phenolic compounds that resist infection. Lack of

Knock Out is a relatively new floribunda developed for virtually complete resistance to black spot.

Blushing Knock Out is one of the many new disease-resistant offspring from Knock Out.

GOOD ROSES FOR DISEASE RESISTANCE

Blueberry Hill
 ('WEKcryplag')
Blushing Knock Out
 ('RADyod')
Carefree Sunshine
 ('RADsun')
Gemini ('JACnepal')
Gizmo ('WEKcatlard')
Gourmet Popcorn
 ('WEOpop')
Iceberg ('KORbin')
Ingrid Bergman ('POUlman')
Knock Out ('RADrazz')
'Loving Touch'
Moonstone ('WEKcryland')
Napa Valley ('POUlino')
New Zealand ('MACgenev')
Pillow Fight ('WEKpipogop')
Pink Knock Out ('RADcon')
'Playboy'
'Sea Foam'
Showbiz ('TANweieke')
'The Fairy'

'The Fairy' is a polyantha rose that revolutionized gardening and landscaping with roses when it was introduced in 1932. It is highly resistant to disease and perfectly hardy to Zone 4.

moisture or nutrients can cause these protective chemicals to weaken, letting infection take hold.

In recent years, breeding efforts have resulted in the further development of varieties that are nearly impervious to disease. While the degree of disease resistance and shade tolerance will vary among classes, such as between a hybrid tea and a shrub rose, these newer rose introductions offer a wide variety of choices.

Knock Out, a shrub rose bred by William Radler and introduced by Conard-Pyle in 2000, is the epitome of these roses. It has shown nearly complete resistance to black spot and excellent resistance to other fungal diseases and some pests.

Now its relatives are making a splash. Blushing Knock Out, a lighter pink sport of the deeper cerise Knock Out, is a compact shrub hardy in Zones 5–9. Carefree Sunshine, introduced in 2001, is one of the most disease-resistant yellow roses and is hardy in Zones 4–10. And the newest family member, Pink Knock Out, carries the same black spot resistance and is hardy in Zones 4–9.

Most yellow roses are genetically highly susceptible to blackspot. Carefree Sunshine is the rare exception.

Buying a Rose

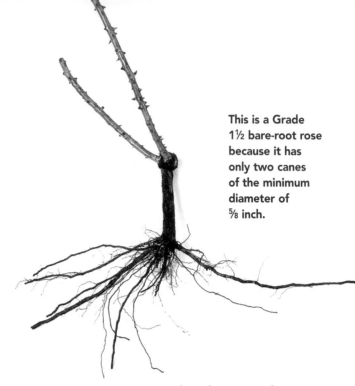

American gardeners purchase some 60 million rosebushes each year from garden centers and mail-order nurseries across the country. The vast majority of these are sold in one of two forms: bare root or in containers.

Bare-root plants

Bare-root roses are dormant plants whose soil has been removed from the roots to reduce the weight for shipping;

This is a Grade 1½ bare-root rose because it has only two canes of the minimum diameter of ⅝ inch.

The rose above and the rose below are both Grade 1 because they have at least three canes ⅝ inches in diameter.

they are sold by mail order and at some garden centers. Container roses are dormant or growing plants sold in small pots; garden centers and houseware stores offer them from early spring until the end of the planting season, or until the available stock sells out. If you buy your roses from a mail-order nursery, you will almost certainly receive bare-root roses. Miniature roses are the one exception; being lightweight, they are usually shipped in pots.

Buying bare-root roses by mail

Many rose growers prefer to buy their roses by mail because the selection is greater and they can choose the varieties they want, rather than settle for those that are locally available. Rarer varieties of modern roses, as well as most varieties of old garden and shrub roses, are available only by mail. The biggest drawback to buying by mail is that you cannot inspect your purchases in advance. To avoid disappointment, deal only with reputable sources. Ask fellow rose gardeners for their recommendations, or refer to the list on page 243. Reputable firms usually guarantee the safe arrival and successful growth of everything they ship and will replace any plants that are not satisfactory. Beware of advertisements touting low-price specials; if something sounds too good to be true, it probably is.

Even if you are buying locally, you may prefer to purchase bare-root plants rather than potted ones. The roots of bare-root plants are typically larger than those of potted plants because they have not been cut to fit into a container. Stripped of soil, they are also easier to inspect for general vigor and signs of damage or disease. (To keep their roots moist, some bare-root roses are wrapped in damp sphagnum peat moss and placed inside a plastic bag. Although this prevents you from seeing the root system, you can usually feel it through the bag.) Where available, bare-root plants are sold only in early spring because they must be planted before they start to grow. (For instructions on planting bare-root roses, see page 76.)

Buying quality plants

To ensure uniform quality in rose stock, the American Association of Nurserymen, a nonprofit trade organization, has established a set of standards for bare-root and potted roses. If you buy only roses that conform to these standards, you'll be assured of receiving healthy plants that will grow and bloom satisfactorily.

To conform to the standards, bare-root roses should have three or more strong canes. (An exception is polyanthas, which should have at least four canes.) The standards also specify that nurseries must allow at least two of the canes to reach a length of 18 inches and the remaining cane or canes 13 inches before pruning them in preparation for sale. There is no way you can know for sure that the canes actually reached these lengths, but if they extend at least 6 to 8 inches above the bud union and are about ½ inch thick, you can assume that the plant is probably a good one.

If these standards have been met, bare-root plants are known as Grade 1. This is sometimes marked on the plant's container or label and is often listed in mail-order catalogs. Slightly smaller plants are known as Grade 1½. Although not as large or robust as Grade 1 plants, they can usually be grown quite successfully with a little extra care. Still smaller plants are sold as Grade 2; these are rarely satisfying to rose growers.

For potted roses, the standards permit the canes of Grade 1 plants to be cut to 4 inches above the bud union before the plant is placed in its container; this shorter length is allowed to provide for easier shipping. The container should be at least the 2-gallon size, measuring a minimum of 7 inches across the top and 7½ inches high. When buying potted roses that have already leafed out, look for three or more canes with strong, healthy leaves and additional growth buds in the area of the bud union.

With all roses, bare-root or potted, the standards state that the canes should branch no more than 3 inches above the bud union. Plants should have a well-developed root system. and although the standards do not specify root size, you should choose a plant whose roots are in at least equal proportion to the above-ground portion of the plant.

The standards do not address the issue of insects and diseases, but obviously you should avoid plants that show signs of these.

With the exception of some mild areas such as Southern California, most roses sold in nurseries and garden centers today are container-grown.

Using Roses in the Landscape

Roses tend to be the focal points of a garden, so their selection and placement deserve special care. Although they are most often planted in beds, their many forms lend them to a variety of other applications— from barrier hedges and groundcovers to cultivation in containers as accents for a deck or patio. By thoughtfully combining the forms and colors of your roses, you can create a spectrum of moods and effects.

Any garden spot that is bathed in at least six hours of sunlight each day can be a home for roses, even if only for one or two plants. Stationed by themselves or combined with other flowers, roses can be a rewarding part of any garden.

Fitting roses into your landscape is easier if you think in terms of the problems to be solved and the tone and feeling you want to achieve. Do you need to create a boundary? Brighten a dull expanse? Screen an eyesore? Accent an architectural feature? Enhance an outdoor living space? Grow flowers for cutting?

Roses can do it all, evoking moods that can range from serenely majestic and passionately romantic to charming and demure. Perhaps more than any other type of garden, rose gardens are the stuff of dreams. Whether adding to an existing landscape or planning a new one, use roses to create almost any garden fantasy.

Royal Bonica is one of the most dependable roses you can grow for a 3-foot carpet of color all summer.

Mary Rose grows along the sidewalk as New Dawn and America climb over fences and gates in this Midwestern suburban landscape.

Formal and Informal Gardens

A monochromatic pink color scheme and rigid bilateral symmetry imbue this formal rose garden with an elegant simplicity understandable at a glance.

One of the greatest virtues of roses is that they are equally at home in formal and informal settings. Whether arrayed in dignified beds on a country estate or allowed to ramble over the eaves of a bungalow, they add an enchantment that no other flower can match.

If you are creating a new rose garden, you must first decide whether you want a formal or an informal design. Although to some extent this is a matter of taste, the design also depends on the style of your house and the size of your garden.

Controlled beauty

Formal gardens, with their symmetrically shaped beds filled with rigid rows of plants, best complement classical styles of architecture, such as French provincial, Georgian, and federal. In keeping with their stately tone, formal gardens usually demand ample space. They also require meticulous grooming because overgrown edgings and unkempt beds can easily spoil the effect.

The shape of a formal garden is up to you; it may be round, oval, square, rectangular, or even triangular. A small formal garden can be limited to a single bed; a large one can encompass several beds that carry out a grand geometric scheme. The simpler you keep each bed, the more dramatic it will be. Edge it with tidy plants such as germander, boxwood, begonias, or miniature roses. Use a statue, pottery, garden pool, fountain, sundial, or tree rose as a focal point at the center. Formal rose gardens may also be bordered with fences or evergreens to set them apart from the rest of the plants in the garden.

Imaginative informality

Informal gardens strive for a look that is free-flowing and spontaneous even though they are often carefully planned. Today's smaller gardens and modern styles of architecture are best enhanced by an informal design. In an informal garden, roses and other plants are arranged in asymmetrical groupings, with wavy or indistinct edges, rather than planted in regimental rows. These groupings may line a walkway, hug a wall or a fence, or stand alone in the middle of a lawn. They may feature roses alone or may include roses and other plants. Their shape is limited only by your taste and ingenuity, and the space available to you.

The freedom of an informal style is in appearance only. In reality each player in this studied chaos is carefully chosen and placed for coordination of color, form, and timing of bloom— a process rather like orchestrating a complex symphony.

Below, an informal entryway casually beckons with flowers allowed to billow over edges for a soft, natural look.

Above, a formal entryway flanked with hybrid tea roses channels the visitor quickly and commandingly toward the front porch.

Borders and Beds

Because they often have a leggy, upright form with flowers at the top on long stems, hybrid tea roses may be thought of as plants for formal gardens. Below, however, an informal bed of them presents a spectacular show.

Most formal gardens, and many informal ones, group plants within beds and borders. These groupings may contain plants of a single type or may feature a wide variety. A bed is a planting area that is accessible from all sides and is usually surrounded by lawn. If formal, it will have a geometric shape; if informal, its perimeter will have more graceful, flowing lines.

Fronted with an edging of agapanthus to hide their leggy form, the hybrid tea roses in this informal border blend well with perennials such as bearded iris.

Border basics

A border is the narrow area along a path, wall, fence, or other structure, accessible from three sides at most. Although some rose borders are only one plant deep (such as along a path or a foundation), they look fuller and more pleasing if they are two or three plants deep. Rose borders deeper than three plants are usually difficult to tend because you may have trouble reaching the plants at the back.

In a formal design, the rose border might be fitting for a straight pathway to the front door, perhaps accented by tree roses; in an informal design, the border could line a curved walkway and be interplanted with annuals or other garden flowers.

Ideal selections for mass plantings

Large beds and borders composed of only one rose variety are known as mass plantings. Mass plantings of roses can be dramatic in both formal and informal settings. When selecting roses for a mass planting, choose from floriferous classes such as floribundas and miniatures to enhance the visual effect.

Plan space wisely

If you are laying out a network of beds or borders, be sure to leave enough space for paths, and make the paths wide enough so that garden equipment such as a lawn mower or a wheelbarrow can pass through easily. To allow for comfortable strolling, paths should be at least 2 feet wide; if you want two people to be able to walk side by side, construct the path 4 feet wide. Paths can be paved with brick, slate, gravel, or other construction material, or can be lined with grass.

An informal border incorporates several large shrub and old garden roses for masses of color over a long season.

Place plants appropriately

Set the roses far enough back from the path (about 2 feet back for most rosebushes) so that they do not entangle visitors in their thorns.

Plant height is an important consideration. In beds, the taller plants are usually grouped in the center and are framed by lower plants. In borders, the tallest plants are typically placed at the back.

Containing beds of hybrid tea roses with a wall serves double duty—effective facing to hide the shrub's leggy form, and a raised bed for better soil conditions. Shown here is a bed of the hybrid tea rose, Gemini.

Landscaping Roles for Roses

The Simplicity series of roses have been bred specifically for hedging. Shown here are Pink and Red Simplicity.

Thanks to their remarkable range of sizes and growth habits, roses lend themselves to a variety of applications outside traditional beds and borders. The following are some other landscaping roles for roses.

Defining a boundary

Living barriers can be beautiful when they are composed of rosebushes. Instead of erecting a fence, plant a hedge of shrub roses. One of the thornier varieties, such as the hybrid *rugosa* 'F. J. Grootendorst', will also deter pets and intruders. Unlike constructed fences, living fences look equally pleasing from both sides. When using roses in this way, stay with a single variety for uniformity and visual appeal.

Low-growing floribundas or miniature roses can lend a finishing touch as an edging for a perennial or shrub border. They can also be used to line a path to a front door, to parallel a driveway, or to separate a patio from a lawn without creating an obstacle. For an informal look, plant roses in beds or borders with scalloped or gently curved edges. If the edging is two plants deep, choose a taller variety for the back and a lower-growing variety for the front. Roses for hedges and edgings should be planted up to 6 inches closer together than normal to ensure dense, floriferous growth.

GOOD ROSES FOR HEDGES

'Betty Prior'
Betty Boop ('WEKplapic')
Bonica ('MEIdomonac')
Confetti ('AROjechs')
'F. J. Grootendorst'
Gizmo ('WEKcatlart')
Iceberg('KORbin')
Knock Out ('RADrazz')
Livin' easy ('HARwelcome')
Purple Simplicity
    ('JACpursh')
Red Simplicity ('JACsimpl')
Simplicity ('JACink')
Sunsprite ('KORresia')
White Simplicity ('JACsnow')

Covering the ground

A barren expanse or a bare slope becomes a bank of color when roses are used as groundcovers. Spreading, low-growing varieties also prevent erosion and smother weeds. The best roses to use as ground covers are the hybrid *rugosa* 'Max Graf', the shrub rose 'Sea Foam', the miniature 'Red Cascade', or one of the several low-growing Meidiland shrub roses. Ramblers also make good groundcovers if allowed to grow along the ground instead of on supports. Many of these roses will take root along their canes as they sprawl, making them seem more like vines.

Screening an area

Almost every home has an eyesore, such as a gas tank,

GOOD ROSES FOR GROUNDCOVER

Aspen ('POUlurt')
Cape Cod ('POUlfan')
Central Park ('POUlpyg')
Cliffs of Dover ('POUlemb')
Electric Blanket
   ('KORpancom')
First Light ('DEVrudi')
Flower Carpet ('NOAtraum')
Gourmet Popcorn
   ('WEOpop')
Napa Valley ('POUlino')
Natchez ('POUllen')
Newport ('POUlma')
Pillow Fight ('WEKpipogop')
Red Ribbons ('KORtemma')
Royal Bonica ('MEImodac')
Starry Night ('ORAwichkay')
White Meidiland
   ('MEIcoublan')

a storage shed, or a trash receptacle that is in need of tasteful concealment. A rosy solution is to place a trellis in front of the area and let climbers do the screening. One or two large shrub or old garden roses substitute nicely for climbers and are just as appealing.

Tall privacy screens of roses can block out distracting street traffic, neighbors, or nearby buildings, and are more attractive than high fences.

Evergreen shrubs are usually the plants of choice to hide the unsightly foundations of houses because their foliage makes a year-round screen. But conifers do not flower, and broad-leaved evergreens flower mainly in spring. Mixing roses among these plants or planting them in front of the evergreens adds summer color without detracting too much from the winter beauty of the evergreens.

'Beauty Secret' is an award-winning miniature rose that grows 12 to 15 inches tall. Like many miniatures, it makes an outstanding low groundcover with summer-long color. When planting miniature roses for mass effect, space them 15 inches apart.

In mild climates the Lady Banks rose provides massive color once in early spring. Provided you give it sturdy support, this large, heavy, and densely-foliaged rambler can make an effective privacy screen.

Landscaping Roles for Roses

(continued)

Roses are the cut flower *par excellence*. Cutting properly actually stimulates plants to produce more blooms.

Providing cut flowers

No cut flower is more esteemed than the rose. You can grow long-stemmed beauties for the home or office by dedicating a few plants as cutting material.

If you plant a few rosebushes near the back door, it will be easy to reach out and snip a few blooms for the dining-room table.

Rose beds devoted to cutting can also be laid out; such gardens are usually situated in an out-of-the-way place, with the roses aligned in functional rows. With their long stems and long-lasting, classically shaped flowers, hybrid teas and grandifloras are the best roses for cutting gardens. Some floribundas also make good cut flowers.

Adding fragrance

Think of fragrance when planning locations for roses. Fragrant varieties are especially effective when planted near windows, alongside a patio or a porch, or flanking a garden bench. If you have a fence with a gate, plant fragrant rosebushes at both sides of the gate to create a scented welcome for visitors. Many rose gardeners plant fragrant varieties exclusively because they want to use the roses in potpourri or cooking. (A lists of fragrant roses appears on page 39.)

Enhancing the view from indoors

Roses can enhance not only the beauty of their outdoor setting but also the view from inside the house. If you place them within sight of a window, you can watch the buds unfold into exquisite flowers that glisten with morning dew, or enjoy your roses at day's end as they reflect the brilliance of the sunset. A many-windowed sunroom or conservatory can make a brilliant vantage point for viewing your roses. Roses in containers, placed near the windows, can make the room and its plants seem an extension of the garden.

Fragrance is reason enough to incorporate roses into the landscape. Shown above is Heritage, a shrub rose prized for its delicious fragrance and elegant, blush pink, old-fashioned flowers.

Climbing roses are the perfect complement to architectural features you want to accent. Here, Blaze Improved calls attention to an attractive garden gate.

Landscaping Roles for Roses
(continued)

Filling small spaces

You don't need much room to grow roses; they can be effective even in small spaces. Look for pockets in the garden where roses will work—around the base of a flagpole or beside a rustic mailbox. Use roses to disguise an outdoor light. Rock gardens are ideal spots for small polyanthas, floribundas, and especially miniatures. Rock gardens are traditionally designed with more spring-blooming plants than summer-blooming ones, so using roses prolongs the attractiveness of the rock garden by several months.

A spot near where the driveway swings into the street is ideal for a welcoming burst of roses. Plant it with white or pastel roses, and it will stand out at night. A small brick wall in front of or behind the planting and a spotlight to illuminate it will complete the effect.

Miniature roses can play an important role in a garden where space is especially limited. Plant them in accent spots or in drifts; use them in mass plantings instead of annuals. They are excellent for edging a bed or border, or in containers. If there are young children in your family, give them a few miniature roses to tend and watch them thrill at the appearance of tiny flowers, which they can present to friends, teachers, or grandmothers.

Adding height

A traditional rose arbor is a perfect addition to a sunny garden. Breezy and romantic, an arbor made of lath provides dappled shade if left unadorned or becomes a focal point when embellished with climbers or ramblers. The top can be covered with coarsely woven shade cloth or a nonwoven material known as landscape fabric; both are available at hardware stores and garden centers. This will offer additional shade and protect the blooms growing under it from wind and hail while letting rain drizzle through.

The uses of climbers and ramblers extend far beyond the rose arbor. Train them

Baby Grand is a delightful miniature rose excellent for small spaces.

GOOD ROSES FOR EDGING

Autumn Splendor
  ('MICautumn')
Baby Love ('SCRivluv')
Behold ('SAVahold')
Figurine ('BDNfig')
Gizmo ('WEKcatlart')
Goldmarie ('KORfalt')
Gourmet Popcorn
  ('WEOpop')
Hot Tamale ('JACpoy')
Kristin ('BENmagic')
Old Glory ('BENday')
Pillow Fight ('WEKpipogop')
Ralph Moore ('SAVaralph')
Scentsational ('SAVamor')
Sun Sprinkles ('JAChal')
Y2K ('SAVyk')

'Mlle Cécile Brünner' is a polyantha that produces sprays of small, pale pink flowers. It is a favorite climber for a delicate, old-fashioned effect.

along split-rail or picket fences to brighten up the wood and add curving grace to the straight lines. A portico at the entrance to a house can be accented with climbing roses that are trained to grow up the sides and over the roof. If you have a porch, you can tie the garden and the house together by planting low-growing roses along the base of the porch or at the sides of its steps and by letting climbers sprawl from the ground to the porch roof or overhang.

Climbers can be espaliered (pruned and trained in two-dimensional patterns) against a stockade fence or the wall of a house. They can also cover eaves or outline windows and doors, adding graceful color to the outside of the home and softening hard edges. Climbing roses can ramble up posts, cover old tree stumps, grow high into trees, or spill over from the tops of stone walls. Darkly colored wooden retaining walls can be brightened by planting climbing roses atop them and letting the canes

hang over the walls. Keep the canes in place by pegging them to the wall with hooks or clips; for summerlong color, be sure to select an everblooming variety of climber.

Some climbers, such as 'Don Juan' and 'Golden Showers', grow tall and erect because they have stiffer canes. They're perfect for trellises, arches, and pergolas. Large beds of roses or perennials can incorporate a freestanding pillar of climbing roses in the center to add height and break up the monotony. In large beds or borders, you can also install two posts or pillars and connect them with a chain. Plant a pliable-caned climber or rambler at each post or pillar, and train them to grow along the chain until they meet.

Tree roses, too, bring needed height and accent to the garden. They may be used as solitary specimens in a formal rose garden or planted amid low-growing floribundas

or annuals for a more informal look. If you plant them against a wall or fence of a contrasting color, the beauty and form of the tree rose will stand out even more. Tree roses are also effective in lining a walk. Standing straight and tall, they give direction to the path. To tone down their stiffness, surround them with mounds of lower-growing roses, annuals, perennials, or a mixture of all three.

GOOD CLIMBERS FOR SMALL SPACES

Cal Poly, Climbing ('MORclpoly')
'Candy Cane'
Chick-a-dee, Climbing ('MORclchick')
Cliffs of Dover ('POUlemb')
Earthquake, Climbing ('MORshook')
'Jeanne LaJoie'
'Lavender Lace, Climbing'
'Lavender Lassie'
Work of Art ('MORart')

This tall, elegant pergola creates a secluded passageway while 'Joseph's Coat' and 'Sally Holmes' make brilliant foils for each other.

Combining Roses with Other Plants

Because they bloom at the same time, combining wisteria and the Lady Banks rose is popular in mild-climate gardens in the west and south.

Roses do not need a special place for themselves but can be mixed with other plants throughout the landscape. Any plant—be it an annual, a bulb, a perennial, a shrub, or a small tree—can be combined with roses as long as it enjoys the same growing conditions. Roses and companion plants can complement one another in many ways, providing color harmony, filling in color between the other's blooming periods, providing greenery during the winter, and enriching the garden with a variety of heights and textures.

Set off low-growing plants

Roses are especially effective in border plantings because of the height and the color continuity they provide. Use shrub roses or floribundas as a backdrop for lower-growing plants in a border instead of other more commonly used deciduous shrubs. You'll be pleased with their especially long season of bloom.

Combine with shrubs in spring and summer

Roses can also be combined with other shrubs in a mixed border. Planted with spring-flowering azalea, forsythia, lilac, spirea, viburnum, and similar shrubs, they will extend the blooming period of the border substantially.

When used with summer-flowering shrubs such as abelia, hydrangea, or rose-of-Sharon, they provide a colorful complement. The roses can be placed either in an alternating pattern with other shrubs or in rows in front of or behind them.

Canna 'Tropicanna', Fuchsia, and Rosa glauca with its showy fall hips make a stunning show of foliage, fruit, and flower.

Large-flowered clematis and old garden roses are a classic combination. Here, *Clematis* 'The President' grows through *Rosa* 'The Prince'.

Mix with bulbs and perennials

Colorful flowering bulbs add life to rose borders and beds that are bare in early spring. Try snowdrops, crocus, squill, glory-of-the-snow, or early-blooming species of tulips. Between rose plants grow clumps of daffodils to glisten in the sunshine just as the rose leaves start to unfurl. By the time the bulbs have finished blooming and their foliage begins to fade, the roses will be ready to take over the limelight. As a bonus, you will find that the fertilizer you apply to your roses will make the bulb plants larger and more free flowering.

Many spring-flowering perennials, such as basket-of-gold, mountain pink, candytuft, primrose, and forget-me-not, bloom before the roses are ready, adding color to bare spots in the same way that bulbs can. Because their blooming period ends before the roses come into flower, you can use them without worrying about clashes with the color scheme of the roses. During their brief flowering seasons, perennials can also add exciting dashes of color to roses that are already in bloom.

Perpetuate color with annuals

For longer-lasting color harmony, mingle roses with low-growing annuals that bloom throughout the summer. Whether used as underplantings or planted in adjacent beds, annuals will not compete seriously with roses for food or water.

Lend verticality with ornamental trees

Small, ornamental flowering trees, such as flowering cherry, dogwood, or magnolia, can be planted near roses as vertical accents, bringing color to the rose garden before it is in bloom. Miniature roses can be planted under the canopy of ornamental trees. However, take care that trees do not shade the roses and that their roots are not so close that they contend with the roses for water and fertilizer.

Bicolored dianthus and creeping thyme bloom in harmony under the grandiflora 'Earth Song'.

The shrub Golden Celebration and annual forget-me-nots produce an electric contrast.

Choosing Color for Companion Plantings

Of all the qualities that companion plants impart to a garden, color has the greatest impact. In choosing color companions for your roses, you should try to complement them without overwhelming them, taking into account the hues of your roses and the color scheme you have established. Different companion colors have different roles to play.

The well-crafted symphony of color in this California garden relies heavily on a palette of pinks, with occasional accents of blue (see photos on facing page). Warm whites blend and hold the composition together.

Cheerful orange and yellow

Orange flowers bring warmth to a rose garden, blending best with dark red, yellow, or white roses. Good sources of orange are orange varieties of annual marigold, calendula, gazania, and portulaca; as well as perennial black-eyed Susan and daylily. Yellow flowers, ranging from cream-colored annual zinnias to bright gold perennial coreopsis, add gaiety and a light touch. Use them with yellow roses of different tones and shades or with almost any other rose.

Red accents

Red is best used as an accent color because too much of it is overpowering, especially in small gardens. Red-flowered plants, such as annual petunia, salvia, geranium, verbena, phlox, begonia, and impatiens, look good either bordering or accenting white, soft yellow, or clear pink roses.

Pale and deep pink shades

Pink companions go best with pink roses and are most effective if they provide a contrast. With pale pink roses, use deep pink annual geraniums; with deep pink roses, choose light pink annual vinca. Pink annual petunias, snapdragons, begonias, phlox, impatiens, and zinnias blend well with red or yellow roses; select a tone and shade of pink that will best complement the color of the roses. Pink can also be used with mauve; put light colors next to dark colors for best effect. Next to white roses, pink companion plants look even pinker.

Blue flowers for contrast or harmony

Blue is a popular companion color because there are no blue roses. Deep blue annual cornflowers or perennial anchusa blend well with soft yellow or red roses, whereas sky blue perennial delphiniums harmonize successfully with white, orange, or pale pink roses. Perennial bellflower and veronica, and annual ageratum, petunia, and verbena are also good sources of blue. Avoid planting blue-flowered companion plants alongside pale mauve roses because they will make these roses look washed out.

Effective use of violet and purple

Violet and purple—found in perennial asters, heliotrope, and annual petunias, sweet alyssum, nierembergia, and lobelia—blend best with pink, yellow, or white roses. However, they can clash with some oranges and orange-reds. But when orange and purple do work well together, the effect can be quite dramatic.

Versatility of white flowers

White is sometimes used in the garden as a buffer between strong colors or as a unifying border. Plant white flowers in large groups, as too few scattered about can create a spotty effect. White companions can be used with almost any rose. White has a softening effect alongside brightly colored roses; it strengthens the color of pale roses. Rely on other plants for color. Plants with silver or gray leaves, such as artemisia or dusty miller, can be planted in place of white-flowered annuals or perennials.

When choosing a companion for blended or bicolored roses, select a plant whose flowers will complement or enhance either the main color of the rose or one of the colors in its shading. With these multicolored roses it is simplest and best to use solid-colored companions.

In two other views of the garden shown on the facing page, the bright blues of bearded iris and delphiniums provide startling contrast to the pinks and whites of the roses and foxgloves. At the same time, the spiky form of the delphiniums and foxgloves make a necessary complement to the more rounded masses of the roses.

Using Containers in the Landscape

Containers of miniature, floribunda, and hybrid tea roses enliven a small urban patio. Behind is a raised bed of miniatures.

'Easy Going' is a floribunda ideal for a patio container.

Roses growing in portable planters can make a lively addition to the landscape, either out among the garden plants or on a deck or a patio. They are a perfect way to enhance small spaces, accent colorless expanses, or quickly change the look and mood of the garden.

Wide paths and walkways can be highlighted with tubs of roses placed along them at intervals. Steps leading to a doorway can be animated by a pot of roses on each tread.

Dress up window boxes with miniature roses. Rather than planting them directly into the box, fill the box with individual flower pots. That way, the roses can easily be moved indoors in winter or replaced if something goes wrong.

Patios, decks, and terraces are favorite spots for relaxing and entertaining on warm summer evenings. Pots or planters of roses, teeming with color and fragrance, can add to the pleasure of these moments.

Wherever you have a spot to hang a basket, fill it with miniature roses for summerlong color. Suspend baskets from lampposts, tree limbs, gutters, overhangs, the porch roof, or brackets attached to fences or the house. In winter the baskets can be moved indoors. 'Red Cascade', with its long, graceful flowing canes, is one of the best miniature roses to use in baskets.

If you have room in an out-

Anne Boleyn, an English rose from David Austin, is more compact than most other shrub roses, making it good for container culture.

of-the-way place, you can grow extra containers of roses to hold in reserve as replacements. That way, when a container rose on display goes out of bloom, you can quickly replace it with another one.

Container gardening makes it possible to grow roses without a garden—on balconies, terraces, and rooftops high above city streets. The limited gardening space of many townhouses and condominiums can be augmented with planters.

When selecting roses for containers, limit your choice to floribundas, polyanthas, miniatures, and the shorter hybrid teas. When planted in pots, these roses look better than taller hybrid teas or grandifloras. Container-grown roses are best enjoyed when plants are low-growing, enabling you to look down on an abundance of flowers as you walk by.

GOOD ROSES FOR CONTAINERS

Behold ('SAVahold')
French Lace ('JAClace')
Glowing Amber
  ('MANglow')
Hot Tamale ('JACpoy')
Ingrid Bergman ('POUlman')
Knock Out ('RADrazz')
Little Flame ('JACnuye')
Minnie Pearl ('SAVahowdy')
Outta the Blue
  ('WEKstiphitsu')
'Party Girl'
Petite Perfection ('JACrybi')
Sexy Rexy ('MACrexy')
Stainless Steel ('WEKblusi')
Sun Flare ('JACjam')
World War II Memorial Rose
  ('WEZgrey')

Tree roses, whether full size or the smaller type known as patio tree roses, are perfect for formal containers because of their manicured look. These roses are always tender, so growing them in containers makes it easy to move them indoors for the winter.

Containers for outdoor roses can be rounded or rectangular, but they should be at least 18 inches across and deep (approximately 13 gallons) for good root growth of full-size roses. Smaller 5- or 7-gallon pots (5-gallon pots are approximately 12 inches across and 15 inches deep; 7-gallon pots are approximately 15 inches across and 15 inches deep) can be used to grow excellent roses if watered properly and regularly, but the larger container is better. Miniatures can be grown satisfactorily in pots 6 to 8 inches across and deep. Containers can be made of plastic, clay, concrete, or wood. Metal containers should be avoided because they can get too hot, damaging the roots and hindering growth. Very heavy containers should be equipped with casters or set on a dolly so that they can be easily moved or rotated.

Longer planter boxes—either freestanding ones for a deck or smaller ones designed as window boxes—can also be good niches for roses. For best results with large plants, use a container that is 18 inches wide and deep (although with proper care, you can use a container as small as 12 inches wide and 15 inches deep). Miniatures will do nicely in containers measuring only 6 to 8 inches deep and wide. The length of the container should be a multiple of 2 feet for large

plants or 1 foot for miniatures, depending on the number of plants you wish to grow in the container.

Instead of planting roses in containers to add interest to flower and shrub beds, try the opposite. Portable planters of annual marigolds, zinnias, geraniums, petunias, or phlox can add a contrast in color and texture to rose beds when placed alongside them.

Miniature roses are favorite subjects for containers because of their compact growth. Shown here is 'Sabel Hit'.

The miniature rose Pink Symphony, (sometimes called Pretty Polly) is underplanted with lobelia, in a bright blue glazed ceramic pot.

Planting Roses

Roses need a place where they can receive adequate sunshine, water, nutrition, and protection from chilling weather. Some roses are more demanding in these matters than others, but all thrive best if provided with optimum conditions. The roses you plant in your garden today may be with you for decades, so preparing for them properly is well worth the effort.

Enjoying roses

Once you have decided what roses to grow and how they fit into your landscaping plan, the next step is to acquire and plant them. The advice that preparation is the key to success is nowhere more important than with rose planting. No matter how much you pamper your roses, they will never reach their potential unless they get a good start.

In this chapter you will learn the four steps to establishing successful roses: finding a suitable site, preparing the ground properly, improving the soil, and planting roses in it correctly.

When to plant

The proper time for planting roses depends on your climate and whether you purchase bare-root or container roses. Bare-root roses are planted when they are still dormant and the ground is workable. In mild-winter climates where temperatures stay above freezing, bare-root roses

are usually planted in late winter. In regions where winter temperatures do not fall below 0°F, roses can be set into the garden in early spring or late fall. Where winter temperatures drop below 0°F, it is wisest to plant only in the spring, as roses planted in fall may not have time to become well established before winter.

Container-grown roses can be planted anytime from early spring through midfall.

When it is time to plant any type of rose, whether in spring, summer, fall, or winter, choose a day that is not windy—for your own comfort and for the plant's sake. Strong winds can dessicate rose canes and the exposed roots of bare-root plants. If possible, plant late in the afternoon or on a cloudy day, especially when planting bare-root roses that have been shipped. When plants are shipped in a dark box, sudden exposure to bright sun can scald or dehydrate the canes. Planting late in the afternoon or on a cloudy day also lessens transplanting shock, as planting in full sun can cause foliage to wilt. This is especially true with plants already in leaf.

Instructions for planting bare-root roses roses are on pages 76-77; for container-grown roses on pages 78–79.

'Cornelia' (shown blooming in inset, above) is a hybrid musk that is ideal for a partially shady spot next to a picket fence.

Selecting a Site

Like most roses, Bonica—a hardy, tough, and disease-resistant shrub rose—performs best in a location with plenty of sun (at least six to eight hours a day) and good air circulation.

The success of your roses depends a great deal on the conditions in which they are grown. Most roses need plenty of direct sunlight each day. They also need rich, fertile, moist but well-drained soil along with good air circulation, ample growing room, and protection from harsh elements. In addition, your caretaking tasks will be easier if you can locate the plants within easy reach of your water source and the place where you store tools and supplies.

Sunshine

Most roses need at least six hours of direct sun a day to grow and flower their best. It is better that the sunny hours occur in the morning than in the afternoon because morning sun dries off the foliage early, reducing the chance of disease. Morning sun is also less likely than stronger afternoon sun to burn leaves and flowers, especially in hot climates.

Roses that are not receiving enough sunlight will show spindly growth and have thin, weak canes. Leaves will be farther apart than normal and flower production will be poor. If these symptoms appear in your garden, you may be able to correct them by moving the plants to a sunnier area, trimming nearby tree limbs that block the light, painting an adjacent wall or fence white to reflect available light, or using a light-colored mulch.

Some roses can grow in partial shade if you take extra precautions. Locate your roses where they will not compete with other plants for food and water. Even though shaded roses do not grow as large as those grown in full sun, the spacing of plants should be the same. This ensures good air circulation—a necessity in shady areas, where disease organisms such as mildew can thrive. Before planting, work in extra compost or other organic matter to hold moisture and nutrients.

Some roses will tolerate more shade than others. Hybrid musks, for example, can grow and bloom in only about four hours of direct sun a day. Miniature roses, too, tolerate a little more shade than some of their larger cousins and are happy in four hours of direct sun or the daylong dappled shadow of an ornamental tree. Many climbers also grow happily in the filtered shade of a tree. A list of roses that tolerate some shade appears on page 41.

Water

Although roses will survive with less than optimal watering, they will not fulfill their potential for lush growth and large, richly colored flowers with thick, firm petals unless they receive adequate moisture. A complete discussion of watering needs for roses begins on page 86. Be sure to locate your rose plants within reach of a garden hose or irrigation system, especially if you live where rainfall is unreliable.

If you are planting roses on a hillside, terrace the slope with railroad ties, landscape timbers, bricks, or stones to retard runoff and to ensure that each plant receives enough water. Roses usually do not grow well in low areas where water collects and keeps the soil soggy. If you cannot avoid this type of planting site, take the steps that are described on pages 70 and 71.

Humidity

When the air around roses is extremely humid, the incidence of disease rises because the fungal spores that attack roses thrive in high-moisture conditions. For this reason you should select a site where air can move freely. But avoid a windy location because rapid airflow can dry out roses and tear the flowers and foliage. In humid climates particularly, choose a spot where roses will not be closely surrounded by hedges, large plants, or walls that can constrict air movement.

Spacing between other plants

Because roses are demanding of sun, water, and nutrients, they should be placed where they will not be crowded by other plants. Keep roses at least 3 feet away from the bases of other large shrubs. If possible, avoid positioning

them at the bases of trees or where their roots will compete with those of other vegetation. If you must plant near a tree, locate your roses no closer than halfway between the trunk and the farthest spread of the tree limbs. Better still, place your rose completely outside the canopy of the tree. When planting roses near trees, prune away the lower tree limbs to improve air circulation and let in more light.

Roses can be interplanted with small shrubs, perennials, annuals, bulbs, and some groundcovers, such as ajuga and periwinkle. Be aware that roses stationed among other plants need a little more fertilizer and water.

When planting roses near a building or a solid fence, set the plants at least 18 inches from the structure to allow room for growth and air movement. In hot climates, avoid planting roses in front of a white wall or fence that can reflect burning light and heat. However, in cool climates or where light is low, planting near a reflective wall or fence can increase growth.

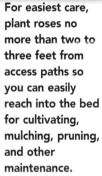

For easiest care, plant roses no more than two to three feet from access paths so you can easily reach into the bed for cultivating, mulching, pruning, and other maintenance.

Roses need regular moisture, so plan for a water source within easy reach.

Selecting a Site
(continued)

Spacing between roses

This bed of the floribunda Amber Queen is planted on 30-inch centers, a generous spacing between plants that allows for easy access and plenty of air circulation.

In an ideally laid-out rose garden, plants are spaced closely enough that they fill out the beds attractively yet far enough apart that they will not crowd one another's growth or foster disease. Optimum spacing between plants depends on your climate, the type of roses you are growing, and the visual effect you are trying to achieve.

In frigid or temperate regions, you should plant hybrid teas, floribundas, and grandifloras 24 inches apart (if floribundas have a spreading habit, plant them 30 inches apart). Plant polyanthas about 18 inches apart (larger polyanthas such as 'The Fairy' require wider spacing). In warmer climates with little or no frost, add about 6 more inches between plants to allow room for more profuse growth. For a dense hedge or "living fence" effect, plant roses a little closer together.

Shrub and old garden roses vary widely in size, and their ideal spacing ranges accordingly. A good rule to follow is to plant them as far apart as they will ultimately grow in height. In most cases, this will be about 4 to 6 feet apart. In warmer climates, add another 6 to 12 inches between plants.

Climbers to be trained horizontally on a fence in any climate should be planted 8 to 10 feet apart. Climbers to be trained vertically up and over an arbor, or on a trellis or a wall, can be planted as close as 3 feet to create a more solid cover.

Miniature roses, too, should be spaced in proportion to their ultimate size. Tiny minis that grow only 6 inches high should be planted about 6 inches apart. Tall minis that grow to 24 inches are best spaced 12 to 18 inches apart, as their growth is more vertical than horizontal. In warm climates add about another 3 inches to these spacing guidelines.

Protection from wind and cold

Although some roses can tolerate brisk conditions, most are warm-weather plants that thrive best when sheltered from wind and cold. Just as water can accumulate in low spots where drainage is poor, cold air, too, can collect in low areas. Denser and heavier than warm air, cold air flows downhill and pools at the bottom of the depression if it has no outlet. Roses planted

In this bed, the floribunda Showbiz is planted on 18-inch centers—a minimum spacing between plants that is enough to allow adequate circulation while achieving maximum density of color effect.

in such a site will be subject to colder, more stationary air and thus more winter damage than roses planted on a hillside. If this is your situation, try to locate the plants in a part of the garden at a higher elevation. (But avoid hilltops, which are often exposed to chilling and drying winds.) If this is not possible, choose hardier roses, apply extra winter protection, or build a raised bed.

Easy access

An important consideration when planting roses is choosing a spot you can easily get to and work in. If you are planting your roses against a wall or a fence, be sure you can reach the plants in the back row easily in order to spray, prune, or deadhead flowers because walking on the bed will compact the soil. If you're planting on a hill, plan so that you can get yourself and your equipment up and down easily. You may need to install steps and landings to make maintenance easier.

The fences in this small garden create a favorable rose microclimate by providing protection from harsh drying winds while storing and radiating heat in spring and fall.

Providing Drainage

When paired with underground tiling, even a slightly elevated bed can improve drainage.

Good soil drainage is essential for roses. If drainage is too slow, water will replace air in the soil, taking the place of oxygen vital for root growth and leaving roots no room to develop. Ideally, the space between the particles in the soil should be one-half water and one-half air.

To test your drainage, dig a hole about a foot deep and wide. Fill it to the top with water and measure how long it takes for the water to drain. If the hole empties in an hour or less, the drainage is fine. But if water remains there longer, you need to take steps to improve the drainage. In many cases, mixing organic matter, gypsum, or another soil amendment into the soil as described on page 72 will be sufficient to correct a drainage problem. After working this material into the soil, repeat the test. If your soil fails again, you need to take more serious steps.

One solution is to add several inches of coarse gravel to the bottom of each planting hole. Alternatively, you can dig a large trench beneath the planting bed and install drainage pipe or tile at the bottom. The gravel, pipe, or tile should be slightly pitched to take the water to a lower spot where it can drain off or into a ditch, sewer, or dry well.

MODIFYING SOIL DRAINAGE

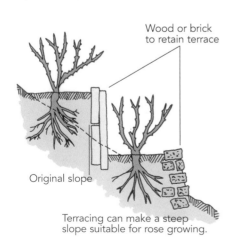

Wood or brick to retain terrace

Original slope

Terracing can make a steep slope suitable for rose growing.

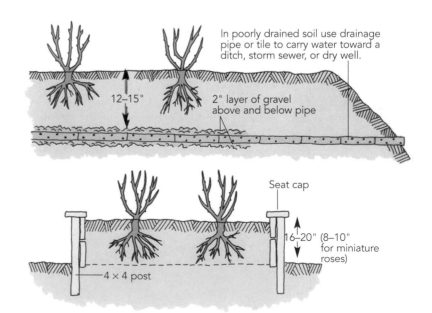

In poorly drained soil use drainage pipe or tile to carry water toward a ditch, storm sewer, or dry well.

12–15"

2" layer of gravel above and below pipe

Seat cap

16–20" (8–10" for miniature roses)

4 × 4 post

Growing Roses in Raised Beds

Another attractive solution to poor drainage is a raised bed. This elevates your roses above the surrounding soil and allows extra water to drain out along the bottom or sides of the bed. Using wood, brick, or stone, construct a planting bed about 18 to 24 inches above ground level. Add improved soil or purchase a high-quality topsoil or soilless mix and work it in with the soil below grade to a depth of 18 to 24 inches, adding other amendments as necessary to achieve proper soil structure and pH.

Advantages of raised beds

Raised beds are a landscaping feature often used to compensate for poor soil, bad drainage, or high pH. By elevating plants above the soil line and surrounding their roots with improved growing medium, raised beds enable roses to grow where they might otherwise not survive.

Raised beds are also attractive, drawing the eye to their contents. If the walls of the beds are made wide enough and are topped with wood or paving material, the edges of the beds can double as seating areas.

There are other, more practical advantages to raised beds. Rosebushes raised off the ground are easier to reach for pruning, watering, spraying, and other gardening chores. Should you choose to install an automatic watering system, you'll find it easy to do with raised beds. Moreover, in spring the beds warm up faster than the surrounding soil, speeding growth. However, in regions where the soil freezes quickly, roses should be planted at least 2 feet in from the walls of the beds to insulate their roots from the cold.

Raised beds are usually made with wooden sides (redwood, cedar, pressure-treated pine, railroad ties, or landscape timbers), but they can also be constructed of durable brick or stone. Regardless of the material used, a well-constructed bed will leak water from the sides or the bottom, making it impossible to overwater.

Where to place a raised bed

When deciding on a location for a raised bed, weigh all the factors you would when selecting a site for any rose garden. The foremost of these are sunlight and access to water. Another element to consider is the presence of any underground utility lines, such as electrical conduits, telephone cables, and water or sewage pipes. Although you can build over these, it is wiser not to, as you may some day have to dig them up for repair. Most utility companies will come to your house and mark the location of the lines for you without charge.

In finding a place for raised beds, you should take into account the natural flow of drainage on your property. Position the beds where water will flow away from them— not where water will collect along their outer walls.

Designing the bed

The size and shape of the raised beds are largely up to you, but consider a few practical points. Be sure to design the beds so that you can easily walk around them or pass by with a lawn mower or other large garden tool. Make the beds narrow enough so that all the plants are within easy reach of the sides, as walking on the soil of a raised bed compacts it too much. A good rule is to plant only two rows of large roses and never more than three. Raised beds of miniature roses can have three to four rows of plants.

To allow proper depth for root growth, the bed should be tall enough to hold 10 to 15 inches of soil for miniature roses or 18 to 24 inches for full-size plants. Good drainage is important for roses. In a large bed, you may need to improve this by burying drainage pipe or tile in coarse gravel in trenches beneath the bed.

Raised beds can solve several problems at once. They compensate for poor soil or bad drainage, and the walls that contain them can be designed to provide seating.

Preparing the Soil

Roses thrive in good loam high in organic matter. Usually this "dream" soil doesn't happen by accident but is the product of careful soil stewardship.

Although roses can grow in any reasonably good soil, they will thrive so much better in improved soil that it is worth making the effort to fine-tune it. The best growing medium for roses is soil that is fertile, moisture retentive, rich in organic matter, and loose enough in texture to allow penetration by air and water.

Soil texture and soil structure

Soil is composed of particles of sand, silt, and clay. Sand particles are largest (0.2 to 0.05 millimeters), clay particles are smallest (0.002 millimeters or less), and silt falls in between (0.05 to 0.002 millimeters). The size of the soil particles determines the soil texture. The arrangement of the particles is referred to as soil structure.

A soil that is too sandy cannot hold onto the water and fertilizer you give it, so plants growing in sandy soil must be fed and watered frequently. On the positive side, the coarse texture of sandy soil provides aeration for good root growth, and its fast-draining qualities help keep it relatively free of soilborne diseases.

Heavier clay soil holds water and nutrients well, but it usually has poor drainage because the tiny spaces between its small particles do not let water through easily. Because of the compact nature of clay, aeration is also poor.

Silt, ranking between sand and clay in fineness, has both the good drainage of sand and the nutrient-holding capacity of clay. Silty soil is also extremely friable, or easy to work. It is almost as good as loam for growing roses, but like loam it rarely occurs naturally. It is usually mixed with sand and clay.

The best soil of all, called loam, is a mixture of 30 to 50 percent sand, 30 to 40 percent silt, and 8 to 28 percent clay (the total must naturally equal 100 percent). Like silt, loam drains well yet retains enough water to promote growth. It has good aeration, allowing roots to absorb oxygen and have room to grow, and it has

HOW TO CHANGE SOIL ACIDITY (PH) WITH LIME OR SULFUR

SOIL TEST: Test the pH of your soil or have it tested before you start. Then decide on the amount of change you need to make in your soil pH. Next, identify which category best describes your soil: sand, sandy loam, loam, silt loam, or clay loam.
RAISING SOIL PH: To make your soil less acidic, find your soil type on the chart above. In this case, the factors to the right of each soil type simply represent the pounds of ground limestone needed per 1,000 square feet to raise the pH one-half unit (0.5). If you want to raise the pH more than half a unit, multiply the factor to the right of your soil type by the number of times you wish to raise the pH by one-half unit.

FACTORS FOR MAKING A PH CHANGE OF ONE-HALF UNIT (0.5) FOR DIFFERENT SOIL TYPES	
Sand	8
Sandy loam	16
Loam	24
Silt loam	32
Clay loam	40

EXAMPLE: In a 1,000-square-foot bed, to raise the pH of clay loam from pH 5.0 to 6.5 (three one-half units), add 120 pounds of ground limestone ($40 \times 3 = 120$).
LOWERING SOIL PH: To make soil more acidic, figure the pounds of aluminum sulfate or iron sulfate needed per 1,000 square feet to lower the pH by half a unit, as follows: First, multiply the factor listed in the column for your soil type by 60 percent. (If you use fine-powder flowers of sulfur to lower the soil pH, multiply the factor shown in the table by only 10 percent.) Next, multiply the resulting number by the number of times you wish to lower the pH one-half unit.
EXAMPLE: In a 1,000-square-foot bed, to lower the pH of silt loam from pH 6.5 to pH 5.0 (three one-half units), add 57.6 pounds of iron sulfate or aluminum sulfate ($32 \times .6 \times 3 = 57.6$), or 9.6 pounds of powdered sulfur ($32 \times .1 \times 3 = 9.6$).
SOIL TEST: After four to six weeks test the soil pH again to make sure it is reasonably close to your target.

excellent nutrient-retaining properties. Loose and friable, good loam is composed of 50 percent solid matter, 25 percent air, and 25 percent water.

Soil testing

Because there is no way to be sure what kind of soil you have by looking at it, it's a good idea to have your soil tested. This can be done by a private soil-testing laboratory (check the Yellow Pages or advertisements in gardening magazines) or with an inexpensive soil-test kit available at garden centers and agricultural supply stores. Some county agricultural extension services will also perform soil tests.

Soil-test kits usually measure only pH (see below) and thus may not reveal other, potentially serious defects of your soil. The tests done by laboratories are more complete, indicating not only pH but also the soil texture, the amount of organic matter, the major and minor nutrients present, the level of plant toxins present, and often the corrective measures you need to take.

Soil pH

The pH of a soil is the measure of its acidity or alkalinity—a characteristic that is independent of soil texture and structure but is just as essential to good plant growth.

The pH of soil is expressed on a scale of 0 to 14, with lower numbers indicating acid soil and higher numbers indicating alkaline (basic) soil. A pH of 7.0 is neutral.

In a soil that is too acidic or too alkaline, plant nutrients become insoluble and cannot be absorbed by the roots of the plant. At the same time, toxic elements are more soluble, potentially killing the plants or severely damaging their roots. Moreover, beneficial soil bacteria will not grow in highly acid or alkaline soil.

Roses, along with many other plants, grow best at a pH of 6.0 to 6.5. In this slightly acid range, most of the nutrients that roses need are readily available. Roses will tolerate a pH as low as 5.5 or as high as 7.8, but they will not grow as well as they could at the ideal pH.

If a soil test indicates that the pH of your soil is too low, you can raise it by adding limestone (calcium carbonate). Ground dolomitic limestone (calcium magnesium carbonate) is the best type. Do not use hydrated lime (calcium hydroxide), which can burn plant roots. Use the chart in the sidebar on page 72 to determine how much limestone to apply. Spread it on the surface of the soil with a trowel, mix it with the top few inches of soil, and water it in. The pH should be corrected before roses are

planted. Repeat treatments will undoubtedly be needed every few years, as confirmed by soil testing.

If your soil is too alkaline, you can lower its pH by adding agricultural sulfur. It is sold in powder form in bags, boxes, or cans at garden centers and agricultural supply stores. Spread agricultural sulfur over the soil, dig it into the top several inches, then water it in. Use the chart in the sidebar on page 72 to determine how much agricultural sulfur to apply. If a second or third application is needed, wait a month between applications.

You can roughly judge the proportion of sand, silt, and clay in your soil (soil texture) by performing a simple siltation test. Take a sample of soil from your yard, pulverize it, add about three cups to a quart jar of water, shake until the soil is well distributed in the water, and then set the jar in a place where it won't be disturbed for a few weeks. The soil will settle into layers of sand (on the bottom), silt (in the middle), and clay (on the top). Be aware that clay particles settle very slowly, if at all. Even after weeks the smallest particles will not have settled out.

To take a soil sample for testing by a laboratory, dig trowel-size samples from several places and thoroughly mix in a clean container of neutral reaction that can be closed tightly. Fresh, new plastic bags are convenient and easy to handle.

Preparing the Soil
(continued)

An array of soil amendments are assembled prior to spading them in. They include composted leaf mold (in the garden cart), sphagnum peat moss, and packaged garden soil for adding organic matter; gypsum to help water penetrate in soil that is heavy for clay; bone meal and superphosphate for incorporating long-lasting phosphorus into the root zone, and lime for raising the pH of soil that is too acidic.

Soil amendments

Because good loam rarely occurs naturally, your soil will probably need improvement with one or more soil amendments. These are organic or inorganic materials you can mix with the soil to improve its drainage, aeration, and nutrient and water retention. Many soil amendments also enhance soil structure, supply nutrients, and neutralize acidity or alkalinity.

ORGANIC MATTER: Organic matter in the form of humus (decomposed animal or plant material) is the most valuable and versatile amendment you can apply to your soil. Added to clay soil, it makes the soil coarser and thus more airy and fast draining. Added to sandy soil, it helps retain moisture and nutrients. There are many sources of organic

matter for the garden. Among the most popular are sphagnum peat moss, packaged garden soil, packaged potting mix, leaf mold (shredded and composted leaves), shredded bark, dehydrated manure, and composted kitchen or garden waste. Some are sold at garden centers; others can be made inexpensively in a backyard compost pile. The amount of organic matter to add to your soil depends on the condition it is in. Ideally, the solid portion of the soil should contain about 25 percent organic matter.

GYPSUM: Gypsum, or calcium sulfate, is an inorganic compound that is often used in soils with a high sodium content to improve the structure of heavy clay that does not drain well. Worked into the soil, it helps break up the sticky clay to allow air

and water to penetrate the soil more efficiently. In addition to improving the soil structure, it forces toxic sodium in these soils to leach out.

Gypsum is usually sold in 50-pound bags at garden centers and agricultural supply stores, in either granular or powdered form. Use 10 to 20 pounds per 100 square feet of garden, spreading it over the soil each spring and watering it in. When gypsum is added to individual holes as roses are planted, mix one-third to one-half pound of gypsum with the improved soil per hole.

SAND, PERLITE, VERMICULITE, AND PUMICE: Other amendments used to improve the structure of soil are coarse builder's sand, perlite, and pumice. They are helpful in clay soils with poor drainage and aeration. If their use is called for, they should be mixed with the soil when it is being improved for planting. Unlike gypsum, which reacts chemically with the soil, these amendments are mechanical in action—they add bulk and texture. The material to use will depend on the type of soil you have; check with your county agricultural extension or garden center to find the best solution for your region. Any of these amendments may be mixed into the soil so that up to 20 percent by volume of the final soil consists of one of the amendments.

Improving the soil

Once an inspection and a soil test have determined the deficiencies of your soil, the next task is to begin improving it. First decide whether to improve an entire planting bed or just the soil in individual planting holes. Preparing an entire bed is more work, but in poor soil it is almost a necessity. If you don't prepare the entire bed, the roots of your roses will be trapped in pockets of ideal soil and surrounded by poor soil, which will damage them or retard their growth. If your soil is relatively good, however, you can normally get away with improving only the soil in each of the planting holes.

Whether you are improving a large bed or just the soil in individual holes, the procedure is similar. For individual holes, dig out the soil to a depth of 24 inches. For large beds, cultivate as deep as possible, up to a depth of 16 inches. Use a hoe to break up clods of earth. For both individual holes and large beds, add 25 percent by volume of organic matter such as peat moss, leaf mold, or compost. If you are preparing an entire bed, spread the organic matter over the area and work it in well, to the full depth you have dug. If you are digging individual holes, remove the soil from the hole and mix the organic matter with it. The final soil mixture will have a larger volume than it did previously. Do not add a complete granular fertilizer at this time unless you plan to leave the site unplanted for at least a month; this gives the fertilizer time to diffuse evenly through the soil so the plant roots will not be burned.

Do, however, add a source of phosphorus, such as bonemeal, rock phosphate, or superphosphate, at the rate of 3 to 4 pounds per 100 square feet, or about a half-cup per

If you add only one amendment, a premium packaged garden soil is excellent for rose beds. High in sphagnum peat moss and other ingredients that roses like it should be tilled at least 12 inches into the soil.

planting hole. Phosphorus, which is essential for good root growth, moves very slowly through the soil. If it is applied to the top of the soil, it may take several years to filter down to the root level where it is needed. The best way to get phosphorus to the root level is to put it there at the beginning.

Adjust the pH if necessary at this time. If there are any rocks, stones, root fragments, or other pieces of debris in the soil, remove them. Combine the soil, organic material, phosphorus source, fertilizer (if any), and any pH-adjusting materials, and mix them well; in large areas, a rotary tiller is helpful in breaking up large clods of soil and mixing in the soil-improving ingredients. If preparing a large bed rake the soil level before planting.

It is best, although not always practical, to improve

the soil one to six months before planting; this allows the soil to mellow and settle and the pH to become properly adjusted. It lessens the chance that fresh organic matter or fertilizers will burn the roots of new plants.

Soil should be improved only if it is in workable condition; that is, fairly dry and friable. Working with soil that is too wet will ruin its structure by binding its particles together. These will be difficult or impossible to break apart in the future. To test the workability of your soil, pick up a handful of it and squeeze it into a ball. If the soil sticks together, it is too wet. Wait several days and perform the test again. Soil is ready to be worked when, after you squeeze it into a ball and then gently prod it with your finger, it easily breaks apart.

Planting Bare-Root Roses

Check the planting hole to make sure it's the right depth. Remove most of the soil from the hole. Make a small pyramid at the bottom of the hole with the remaining soil.

Test the height of the pyramid by setting the bare-root bush on it, then laying a broom handle across the top to make sure the bud union is at the correct level. Gently spread the bare roots over the cone of soil.

Carefully add the remaining soil to cover the roots, leaving a 4-inch gap at the top of the hole.

Bare-root roses are dormant plants with the soil washed away from the roots to reduce the cost of shipping. Although they are most often sold by mail order, roses in this form can also be found at some home and garden centers and supermarkets. It is important to plant them as soon after purchase as possible so that they do not dry out or start to push new growth.

If for some reason you cannot plant your new bare-root roses immediately, keep them in a dark, cool (but frost-free) location. Wrap the roots in damp newspaper, sphagnum peat moss, sawdust, or burlap and wrap or cover them with plastic to prevent them from drying out.

Preparing bare-root roses for planting

Immediately before planting, soak the roots of bare-root roses in a bucket of water for 6 to 24 hours to restore lost moisture. Place the bucket where sunlight is good but not full.

Dig a planting hole about 18 to 24 inches across and deep. If you have not yet adjusted the pH or the texture of the soil, do so now, following the directions on pages 72 to 75. Place a cone-shaped mound of improved soil in the bottom of the hole, high enough so that the bud union or the crown will be in the proper position after planting.

Figuring the correct depth

Most experts believe that exposure to sunlight encourages the crown or bud union to produce new canes, so it is a good idea not to cover this part of the plant unless absolutely necessary. In moderate climates where winter temperatures do not drop below 20°F, the bud union should be positioned so that it rests just above the soil surface. In frost-free areas, it can sit 1 to 2 inches above the soil level. Where winter temperatures drop below 20°F, the bud union should be placed 1 to 2 inches below the soil level to protect it from freezing. In summer the soil should be moved away to expose it to the sun. When planting into containers, position the bud union so that it rests just above the surface of the planting medium.

Because most miniatures, species, and old garden roses have no bud union, plant them so that the crown is just at soil level.

Planting the rose

Before planting any type of bare-root rose, examine the roots for breaks or other damage. If you find any injured roots, cut them off with pruning shears. Also shorten any roots that are too long to fit easily into the planting hole without curling or twisting.

Set the plant on top of the cone of soil at the bottom of the planting hole, positioning the plant so that the bud union or the crown is at the proper level. You may need to add or remove soil to achieve this. Lay a broom or shovel handle or a wooden stake across the hole to serve as a reference. When the plant is at the proper level, spread out the roots so that they radiate evenly.

Holding the rose upright and in place with one hand, fill the planting hole with improved soil to within 4 inches of the top. Gently tap the soil around the roots with your hand and fill the hole with water to eliminate air pockets. After the water has drained, fill the hole to the top with improved soil. Make a catch basin for water by mounding a ring of soil in a circle around the perimeter of the plant. Water again.

Mound up soil around the bottom of the plant to cover the bud union and the lower 6 to 8 inches of the canes to prevent them from drying out in the sun or the wind.

Establishing bare-root roses

When new growth on the canes is 1 to 2 inches long, remove the soil or other protection. The best way to remove the soil mound is to wash it away with a gentle stream of water. Washing, rather than digging, soil away keeps new canes that have developed under the soil from being damaged.

Take a look at your newly planted roses at least once a week to make sure they are growing and healthy. A small amount of dieback—the blackening and dying of cane tips—is to be expected and should not be cause for alarm.

Bare-root tree roses are planted in essentially the same way as other bare-root roses but should be staked with a wooden, plastic, or bamboo pole to keep them upright and to support them against wind damage. The stake should be carefully set at planting time so that roots will not be damaged.

Water the plant slowly so the soil can begin to settle. Water carefully several more times to let the soil fill in completely. Add soil to the hole to bring it to the proper level and water again.

Mound soil or mulch over the exposed bud union or base of the plant to prevent moisture loss. Make a soil dam around the plant to collect water.

After a few weeks of careful watering and when the roots are established, buds and leaves will appear. It is now time to begin removing the protective mound of soil.

Each time you water the rose, gently wash away some of the soil mound until the bud union is at the proper level.

Planting Container-Grown Roses

While some roses are still sold as bare-root plants, especially through the mail and at some mild-climate nurseries in late winter, the majority of roses in North America are now sold as container-grown plants. Container-grown plants hold longer in the nursery and can be planted in the garden over a longer season. It's also easier to select and purchase roses when you can see the actual bloom.

Unlike bare-root roses, which can be planted only in the colder months when they are dormant, roses grown in containers can be transplanted anytime from spring through fall. This allows you to fill in a bare spot or add bits of color whenever you so fancy.

Especially during the hot months, planting early in the day and in overcast weather is best. Depending on the size of your rose, dig a hole about 2 feet wide and 2 feet deep, or at least 6 inches deeper and wider than the container. Fill the hole with enough improved soil to ensure that the bud union or crown will be at the proper level after planting. This level depends on the climate. (See page 76.)

The next step is to remove the container. Do this carefully to avoid disturbing the root ball. Even if instructions accompanying your plant state that the container may be planted, your rose will grow more freely if its container is removed because containers can take years to disintegrate.

To remove a container, first place the plant into the hole in order to adjust the depth of the hole until the bud union or the crown is at the

PLANTING CONTAINER-GROWN ROSES

1. Remove the bottom: Lay the container on its side. Cut off the base of the compressed fiber pot with a small saw, taking care not to damage any of the roots.

2. Place in hole: Place the root ball in the hole that has been dug out to about 2 feet wide and 2 feet deep. Make sure the bud union is at the proper level.

desired level. Next, use a knife to cut the bottom out of the container. Remove the bottom panel carefully so that you don't disturb the roots. Working from the bottom, slit the sides of the container three-quarters of the way to the top. Then place the plant back into the hole and backfill to slightly below the tops of the cuts.

With the soil now holding your plant in place, complete the cuts and gently pull the sides of the container up, bending them outward as you pull to avoid damaging the canes and foliage.

Finish backfilling around the root ball, water thoroughly, and allow the backfill to settle. Add more soil and water until the desired level is attained. Finally, make a catch basin for water by mounding soil in a circle around the perimeter of the plant; then water the plant once again.

Roses planted from containers, especially during midsummer heat, need frequent watering and misting with a fine spray from a garden hose until they are well established. Expect some wilting after planting, but it usually will not last more than five days to a week. If the wilting is prolonged, prune the plant back by about one-third and remove all flowers and flower buds to force the plant to direct its energy into developing strong roots.

Propping a shingle or a piece of wood next to the plant to shade it for about a week after transplanting also helps to reduce wilting, as does an antidesiccant spray. Antidesiccant sprays are waxy liquids available in garden centers either in aerosol cans or as concentrates to be mixed with water. Sprayed once on the canes and leaves, they help prevent plants from transpiring water and wilting.

Labeling

The final step in planting roses is labeling them. Whether you're a novice or an expert, you will want to keep track of the varieties in your garden for your own satisfaction and to share information with friends.

Metal labels are durable and widely available, and can be written on with waterproof ink or affixed with plastic labeling tape. Plastic labels can be used, but they break easily. Wooden labels are also available, but the writing fades from them quickly.

Most roses come with name tags wired to them. It is a good idea to remove these completely or reattach them with string, as the wire can cut into the cane.

It's also a good idea to keep a written record of the varieties that you have planted. Write down their names, where they were purchased, and when and where they were planted. Labels can get lost outdoors, but a garden schematic is safe inside. Such recordkeeping can also help when you want to add new varieties to your garden or share information with fellow rose growers.

3. Remove the container: Remove the rest of the compressed fiber pot as if you were peeling an orange. Don't worry if some roots show on the surface of the root ball.

4. Fill in with soil: Fill the remaining space with a good quality potting soil or amended soil. Water, allow to settle, and finish off with more potting soil.

Planting Roses in Containers

Roses in containers have even greater needs for water, nutrients, and good drainage than roses in the ground. Be sure to use a large enough container and a premium potting mix. Water and feed regularly. Shown here is the miniature rose Behold.

Growing roses in containers is a practical way to make the most of your garden space. You can display them when they are blooming and remove them when they are bare and severely pruned. Roses in containers can also add decorative touches around the garden or on the patio, porch, or deck.

Because roses grown in containers are showcase plants, choose varieties that are compact and free-flowering for maximum visual appeal. You can plant either bare-root or container-grown roses, but the latter seem to get a better start because their roots are already growing in a confined space.

Choosing a container

For all roses, too little root space leads to stunted growth and poor flower production. For full-sized rosebushes, the ideal container is in the 15- to 20-gallon range (about the size of a half a whiskey barrel) to provide roots with adequate growing space. A container 18 inches across and deep is a minimum size. Containers for miniature roses should be in the 5- to 7-gallon size (a minimum of 12 inches across and deep). Because their roots tend to spread out, miniature roses are best in containers that are wider than they are tall.

Containers can be made of a variety of materials, including wood, clay, cement, and plastic. Stay away from metal containers for outdoor growing because they absorb too much heat and can stifle growth. Whatever type of container you use, be sure it has adequate drainage as rose roots do not like to sit in water. Choose a container with drainage holes at the bottom or on the sides near the bottom.

If drainage holes are absent and cannot be drilled, plant the rose in a smaller container that has holes and set it inside the larger container. Place a layer of gravel at the bottom of the solid container to raise the inner container above the drainage water. Although you

Original root ball

Main root system

Fine feeder roots

Amended soil

Drainage hole

Saucer

Wine or whiskey barrel

Large terra-cotta pot

Plastic pot

can grow a large rose in a container that lacks drainage holes by placing a deep layer of gravel and charcoal in the bottom, it is not advisable because you must take great care not to overwater.

If you are reusing a container, it is essential to clean the vessel thoroughly so that disease organisms will not be transmitted to the new plants. Scrub the pots with warm soapy water, and rinse well with clear water. Then rinse the container in a 10 percent solution of household bleach to disinfect it, and rinse with water again.

Planting a rose in a container

Because root space is so limited in a container and roots cannot forage far and wide for water, nutrients, and oxygen, plants growing in containers have special needs for a growing medium. It is best to avoid native soil from your garden. No matter how well-amended and earthworm-laden your soil is, it is too heavy for roses in containers and will not provide optimal drainage and aeration. Native soil can also harbor harmful insects and diseases. Instead, use an all-purpose, premium soil mix available in bags and packages at garden centers.

Set the plant in the container in the same way that you would plant it in the ground, positioning the bud union or crown at soil level about 1 inch below the rim of the container. Water well.

Container culture

Place the container where it will receive at least six hours of sun each day. Avoid putting a container where it will become too hot, such as on an asphalt driveway or against a highly reflective wall. Feed regularly with a plant food formulated for roses, and keep roots evenly moist. In hot weather you may need to water daily.

When a rose outgrows its container, it needs to be repotted. Check the soil surface to see if it is too dense with roots. If the plant wilts even when you water frequently, then it is probably time to repot. To repot, simply remove the plant from its pot, clean some of the soil off the roots and prune them by one-third, then replant in a container that is a few inches larger than the old one. Be sure to use fresh new potting mix. Roses grow quickly and may need repotting every two or three months.

Plastic pots are light and inexpensive and often require less watering. Porous terra-cotta lets water pass through its walls, as does wood. The evaporation helps keep roots cool, but plants may need watering more frequently. Miniature roses need pots in the 5- to 7-gallon range; larger roses need more room—15 to 20 gallons, about the size of a whiskey barrel.

If your container doesn't have drainage holes, you will need to make some. Here, a power drill makes short work of improving drainage in a plastic foam pot.

Relocating Roses

The roses in both of these photographs are prime candidates for relocation. Above, the vigorous Sally Holmes has thorns destined to attack whoever goes in and out of the garage. At right, the climber Handel is growing too large for the space and covers the window.

You may need to relocate rosebushes to give them more light, provide them with more growing space, or improve color harmony. Do this when the plant is dormant and the ground is workable.

The day before you transplant a rose, water the soil around the rosebush well to ease digging and ensure that the plant is turgid, or filled with water. A turgid plant experiences less transplanting shock.

Carefully lift the dormant plant from the ground with a shovel, a spade, or a garden fork, taking care to damage as few roots as possible. Perform the rest of the transplanting as if planting a bare-root rose. Take a careful look at the roots before planting to be sure you have pruned away any damaged or broken ones. You'll undoubtedly lose some roots in the transplanting process, so cut the plant top back by up to one-half to compensate for the root loss.

Transplanting and moving large roses

If the rose is very large or has been growing in the same spot for many years, it is a good idea to prune the roots while the plant is still in the ground; do this at least one month (and no longer than six months) before moving it. With a straight-edged spade, cut a circle into the soil in an 18- to 24-inch radius from the base of the plant. Your cuts should sever the roots to the depth of the spade's blade. Cutting off the outer roots in this way encourages new roots to develop closer to the base of the plant, enabling you to dig the plant up more easily. The plant will also recover more quickly after transplanting because it will have a more compact root system and therefore less root breakage in relocating it.

Larger plants, particularly shrub roses and old garden roses, can be unwieldy to move. Dig a narrow trench around the root ball and undercut it with a spade. Tuck burlap underneath, wadding enough to pull through to the other side. Wrap and tie the burlap around the root ball to keep it intact, and lift the plant out of the hole.

Minimizing transplant shock

Sometimes it is impossible to avoid transplanting roses that have already started to leaf out in the spring. A transplanted rose will most likely wilt as soon as it has been moved. To help a leafed-out rose recover from the shock of transplanting, cut the canes back hard by one-half to two-thirds and keep the rose well watered and misted until it revives. An antidesiccant spray also helps prevent wilting.

It is possible to transplant a rose that has fully leafed out or is in bloom. Follow the directions above, taking extra care to treat the plant gently. In addition, remove all the flowers and buds to direct the energy of the plant into producing new roots.

Be on the lookout for any perennials and bulbs in the planting bed, and dig carefully so that you disturb their roots as little as possible. Mark the location of the perennials and bulbs from the previous season with small labels, stakes, or sticks.

1. One to six months before transplanting, cut roots on all sides with a sharp spade.

2. At transplanting time, use a spade to lift the rose from the ground. Move the plant to a new hole and backfill with soil.

3. Cut back the top of the rose by one-third to one-half to compensate for root loss.

Caring for Roses

The care you give your roses on a daily basis has long-term effects on their health and flowering. Although roses make more demands than the average garden plant, they are not especially difficult to grow. All that is required is a basic command of a few simple techniques. This chapter describes in detail watering, mulching, weeding, and feeding roses. On pages 100–103 is a complete month-by-month calendar of rose care for every climate Zone in North America. Later chapters discuss pruning (see pages 104 –115) and protecting roses (see pages 116–131), including instructions for preventing, identifying, and treating problems caused by insects and diseases, as well as protecting roses from damage in harsh cold-winter climates.

True, roses are harder to grow than marigolds or petunias, or even most other shrubs; but rose lovers agree that expending extra effort is more than repaid by the beauty it achieves. Also, some roses are easier to care for than others. For example, most old garden roses and shrubs require much less care than do hybrid teas and grandifloras, because they need less pruning and are not as prone to diseases. If you're concerned that you don't have time to tend a rose garden, start small; any garden can support even a few bushes. As you become experienced, you can add to your garden and increase your enjoyment of the Queen of Flowers.

Perfect, award-winning roses such as at David Austin's show gardens (below) are the product of lavish care. But you can still enjoy beautiful roses with considerably less effort.

Mulching helps make growing roses easier. See pages 90–91.

Watering

Roses need water to grow to their fullest and to produce large, long-lasting flowers with rich color and excellent substance (thick, sturdy petals). In areas with steady and sufficient rainfall, supplemental watering should not be needed. Even in these regions, however, extraordinary conditions may exist. Sometimes it does not rain deeply or frequently enough for roses to survive and prosper. Sometimes extreme heat or wind evaporates soil moisture and causes leaves to transpire excessively. When rainfall or other natural water sources are insufficient, watering is necessary.

Quantity and timing

Roses need to be watered throughout the period when they are growing or flowering. However, the question of how much and how often to water has no hard-and-fast answer. Under normal conditions, roses need 1 inch of water per week from rainfall or other sources. Watering more or less depends on the circumstances. The condition of the soil, the temperature, exposure to the elements, and the proximity of other plants all affect the watering requirements of your roses.

Sandy soil dries out more quickly than clay or loam and thus needs more frequent watering, perhaps every five days instead of once a week. Gardens in hot, dry, or windy surroundings also need more frequent watering than normal. In areas where the soil is heavy and retains moisture, less frequent watering is necessary. Overwatering heavy soil can keep rose roots overly moist, making them prone to root rot.

A rain gauge keeps track of precipitation so you know how much shortfall to make up for. Under normal conditions, roses need an inch of water a week.

A moisture sensor at the proper depth signals an irrigation system to water as needed.

Reaching roots

It is important to water deeply (12 to 18 inches) but as infrequently as possible to encourage deep roots. In temperate climates a weekly watering is usually sufficient. Roses with deep roots will be stronger, healthier, and more drought-resistant than those with shallow roots. Water early in the day so that the leaves do not stay wet through the night, as this fosters disease, especially if you are using an overhead watering system rather than a drip system (see the next section). If the soil is heavy, apply water slowly and evenly so that it is absorbed rather than lost through surface run-off.

No matter what type of watering system you use, make certain that the water is getting down to the roots where it is needed. Using a trowel or a pipe, probe the soil to a depth of 12 to 18 inches, and bring up a column of soil. Do this right after you have finished watering. If the soil is moist to the lower level, you know that you have applied the right amount of water. If it is partly dry, you will need to apply more water for a longer period until your soil can pass the test.

Testing to ensure proper watering

To ensure that you are watering often enough, take another soil probe one week after you have watered. If the soil at the bottom of the probe has completely dried out, you need to water more than once a week. Try watering every five days to see if the soil passes the test. If it does not pass, shorten time between watering until it does. If, however, the soil is still moist at the bottom of the probe when you first test it, an interval of 10 days might be better.

Adding organic matter such as compost or leaf mold to a sandy soil (see pages 74–75) can help it hold moisture so that watering is not needed as frequently. A mulch applied to the top of the soil (page 90) not only holds moisture but also deters weeds, which are notorious water thieves. If your roses are planted near a large tree or shrub, you may need to compensate by giving the roses extra water. Probe the soil around the roses as described above to determine whether more water is needed.

One exception to the watering rule is newly planted roses. They should be watered daily for about a week and then every few days until new growth is evident. At that time they can be watered in the same way as any other rose in the garden. If they show signs of wilting, you need to keep up the more frequent watering until they become established.

Roses in containers

Roses growing in containers require more frequent watering than the same plants growing in the ground. Water is quickly depleted from the limited growing space in a container and can evaporate from the sides of porous pots. In hot, windy locations, container plants may need watering once a day or more, with smaller pots needing more frequent replenishing.

To determine when it's time to water, check for moisture below the soil surface by digging with a trowel. Soil can appear dry on the surface while containing adequate moisture at the level of the roots.

Check the medium in the container every day, and water when the top becomes dry, applying water until it runs out of the drainage holes. Use a type of nozzle known as a bubbler or soaker head, which administers water in a soft flow, to keep holes from being created in the planting medium. A water wand, which is a long tube with a nozzle at the end, is useful for watering hanging baskets or out-of-reach containers. Roses can be watered with a watering can, but if you have many plants, this method consumes time.

To help roses survive the winter, make sure that the plants are watered before the soil freezes. If it has not rained in fall, apply a deep watering before draining the hoses and shutting down the watering system during cold weather.

Watering Methods

There are a number of ways to supply water to rosebushes. The most traditional is with hoses and sprinklers, available at garden centers and hardware stores. The equipment for overhead watering with sprinklers is less expensive than that for drip irrigation. However, overhead watering uses much more water and can promote fungal disease. Because of increasing concern about water conservation, many people are turning to drip irrigation, which is the most efficient way to water.

Drip irrigation

Drip irrigation uses less water than overhead watering because the water is applied only to the ground where it can be absorbed by the roots. Irrigation prevents foliage and flowers from getting wet, thus protecting them from diseases and water damage.

A water ring is a convenient way to provide roses in containers with a slow, steady supply of water. The soil is completely soaked in only five minutes.

A drip irrigation emitter releases water slowly for deep penetration in precise locations.

Emitter system

There are two major kinds of drip systems: emitters and soaker hoses. An emitter system consists of a rigid main tubing interspersed with small holes from which flexible, narrow tubes called emitters extend. The ends of the emitters are capped with small nozzles that emit water in a gentle drip or stream. These are placed wherever there is a plant to be watered; if there are no plants for a stretch of the main tubing, the holes can be plugged. Purchase components of an emitter system from garden centers or irrigation supply stores.

An emitter system can be laid on the ground, buried, or hidden beneath a layer of mulch. It is better to bury the system, as this keeps the ultraviolet rays of the sun from weakening the plastic hoses and insulates the system from winter freezing. It is also more attractive. In areas with cold winters, an aboveground system should be removed in autumn to prevent it from freezing and cracking. The holes in an emitter nozzle system are very small and can clog easily. To prevent clogging, install a filter at the water source and clean the filter once a month.

Soaker hoses

Like emitter systems, soaker hoses deliver water directly to the soil at the base of the plant. But unlike them, they exude water through pores or pinholes all along their length instead of at designated locations. The oldest kinds of soaker hoses are made of heavy canvas through which

Micropore soaker hoses have spongelike sides through which water seeps into the ground.

water seeps into the ground. Another type is made of flat plastic, punctured with pinprick-size holes every few inches. The newest types are the tubular micropore hoses, which have a spongelike network of tiny holes through which beads of water "sweat" over the surface of the hose. These hoses are made from white plastic or recycled black rubber tires.

Like emitter systems, soaker hoses can be laid on the ground, but it is best to conceal them under mulch or bury them underground to protect them from the elements and prolong their life. The hoses are twined through the garden so that each plant will receive water.

Sensors and timers

Any type of irrigation system can be set up to work automatically, using a moisture sensor or a watering timer to turn the water on and off. Moisture sensors, available at garden centers and irrigation supply stores, are probes placed in the ground to measure its moisture content. When the ground starts to dry out, they automatically turn on the water. Watering timers, available at the same places, are similar to the timers used to control household lights. They turn the water on and off on preset days at preset times. Moisture sensors are preferable to timers because they deliver water to the garden only as needed and not on an imposed schedule.

Roses can be watered with sprinklers or other overhead methods if watering is done in the morning so that the foliage has time to dry out.

Leaves and canes that stay wet overnight are vulnerable to disease. For this and other reasons, it is far better to water with a drip irrigation system or with soaker hoses. But even if you have a drip irrigation system, occasional overhead watering every several weeks can help rid leaves of dust and spray residue, and can discourage spider mites, which thrive on foliage that is hot and dry. Many types of sprinklers are available. The oscillating type is usually better than the rotating kind for large gardens, because its rectangular coverage results in less overlapping and thus less wasted water.

Whatever type of watering system you use, shut it off and drain the lines after the final watering in the autumn. This prevents the water in the lines from freezing, which can crack the hoses and tubes

Hoses

Hoses, like sprinklers, come in various sizes. You should buy a hose that is long enough to reach across your garden and that is ⅝ inch in diameter (rather than the less common ½ inch) so that it can deliver more water. There are also ¾-inch-diameter hoses, but these work well only with very large sprinklers and with very high water pressure. Hoses are made of plastic or rubber; those of rubber are less likely to kink, while those of plastic are more flexible. Plastic hoses do not work well in cold areas because they lose their flexibility and are likely to crack. Some hoses are reinforced with an internal mesh that protects them

against bursting and kinking.

You can reduce kinking by coiling hoses when not in use. A wall-mounted hose hanger or a mobile hose reel makes this job easier. To keep hoses from dragging over low-growing plants, place guide stakes at the corners of the beds or in other strategic positions. Should your hose spring a leak, you can fix it with a repair kit from your garden center or hardware store. Be sure that the kit you buy will fit the diameter of the hose you are using.

Several types of nozzles are also available. Handheld pistol nozzles can deliver water from a hard spray to a fine mist, as can nozzles with twist controls. The hard spray is for knocking aphids and other pests off plants, the intermediate spray is good for general watering, and the fine mist can be used to raise humidity. Fan-shaped nozzles give a wide, coarse spray that is useful for watering small rose beds. Soaker heads are good for watering containers or filling the catch basins of plants.

Adding water to the root area of a newly planted rose does not require a nozzle. Simply place the end of the hose into the catch basin around the plant and let the water run gently until the catch basin is full.

Roses have large root systems, and efficient watering must provide a relatively quick and even distribution of water to all the roots. A watering wand is a gentle yet thorough way to get a large quantity of water to penetrate to the root zone fairly quickly.

Mulching

A mulch is a layer of natural or synthetic material that is placed atop the soil to blanket it from the elements. Natural mulches include tree bark; leaf mold; compost; leaves such as pine needles; agricultural by-products such as buckwheat hulls, peanut hulls, and cocoa-bean hulls; gravel; and stones. Synthetic mulches include landscape fabric and black plastic.

The benefits of mulching are many. A good mulch keeps the soil evenly moist, insulates it from rapid temperature fluctuation, and reduces erosion by wind and water. Its protective covering keeps weeds down and helps prevent mud and disease organisms from splashing onto plants during watering. It also adds an attractive finish to the garden. Moreover, some mulches contribute organic matter and nutrients to the soil.

Natural mulches

Once applied, mulches can be left in place permanently, and more mulch can be added as

Mulching helps to prevent weeds or make them easier to remove, retain moisture in the soil, provide organic matter, and keep soil loose and friable. Reducing the need for cultivating soil is good for roses, as their feeder roots lie near the soil surface.

required. All mulches made of plant material can be worked into the soil once each season in spring or fall and then replaced, thereby doing extra duty as soil conditioners. The selection of natural mulches available for sale varies from region to region. In the eastern and midwestern United States, many garden centers offer wood chips, bark chips, shredded pine bark, and cocoa-bean hulls. On the West Coast and in the Southwest, cedar chips, fir-bark chunks, peat moss, and redwood-bark chips are more commonly available. In the South, shredded fir bark, pine chips, bagasse, and cottonseed hulls are common.

When shopping for a natural mulch, look for one that is permeable, attractive, and relatively slow to decompose. Your selection will also depend on price. Keep in mind that there is no panacea among mulches; each kind has trade-offs.

If you use buckwheat hulls, cocoa-bean hulls, or peanut hulls on your roses, pile the material to a depth of 2 to 4 inches. These mulches are moderately long lasting and do not need to be replaced for two to three years. Cocoa-bean hulls have the added advantage of supplying extra potassium whereas peanut hulls have more fertilizer value than most other mulches. But if you purchase peanut hulls, be sure that they have not been salted and that they have been fumigated for nematodes (microscopic worms that infest the soil and can damage plants). Fir and pine bark and pine needles also make excellent mulch materials because they decompose slowly and control weeds better than the others; apply them 2 to 3 inches thick. Bagasse, the chopped remains of processed sugarcane, is sold primarily in sugar-producing areas. It is slow to decompose and retains heavy amounts of water, which will assist in keeping the ground cool and moist. Apply it 1 to 2 inches thick.

Compost and leaf mold

Although compost and leaf mold are more often used as soil conditioners, they can also be applied as a mulch. Layer compost or leaf mold 2 to 3 inches thick. Their main disadvantages are that they decompose rapidly, within one year, and may not be readily available. On the plus side, if they are available or if you can make your own, they are economical and add nutrients to the soil.

Peat moss, sawdust, and wood chips

Sphagnum peat moss, though an excellent soil conditioner, makes a poor mulch because it actually pulls moisture from the soil. And as it dries out, it forms a thick crust that is difficult to moisten again. Avoid using sphagnum peat moss if possible. Sawdust can be used as mulch, but it will rob nutrition from your roses as it disintegrates if additional nitrogen is not added. If you use sawdust, apply a 1- to 2-inch layer and mix in 9 to 18 pounds of 5-10-5 fertilizer per 100 square feet to compensate. Wood chips must also be supplemented with nitrogen (use 5 pounds of 5-10-5 per 100 square feet), but they are superior to sawdust because they are slower to decompose. They are also heavier than most other mulches and are thus less likely to blow away. Apply wood chips 2 inches thick.

Limestone chips and gravel

Marble chips and gravel make excellent mulches where wind or water erosion is a problem. Their weight keeps them from blowing or washing away, and they last indefinitely. Their light color also makes them excellent reflectors of light and heat in shady gardens. Marble chips, actually a form of limestone, can raise the pH of the soil. Gravel is a generic term for hard, crushed rock. When gravel is made from granite, it is inert; when it is made from limestone, it can raise the pH of the soil the way marble chips do.

When to mulch

Timing is important when applying mulches. If you live where summers are hot, apply mulch in early spring to help moderate the buildup of heat in the soil and keep the soil cooler, which roots prefer. In areas with short, cool growing seasons, it's better to hold off on mulching until the ground has warmed up in late spring; mulch applied too early will delay soil warming. Once the ground is warm and the mulch has been applied, the mulch will keep the ground warm. Winter mulch refers to material used for winter protection. For more information on winter mulch and protecting roses during the winter, see pages 128–131.

Weeding

Weeds are simply plants out of place. Although they may not seem overtly harmful to your roses, they can thwart proper growth by robbing desirable plants of sunlight, nutrients, and water. They may also harbor destructive insects and diseases. If not properly controlled, aggressive weeds can completely overrun a rose garden.

A rank growth of weeds is often an indicator of poor and compacted soil, improper pH, poor drainage, incorrect fertilization or watering, or insufficient light. The appearance of weeds can be a sign that other corrective actions may have to be taken.

It is easiest to eliminate and control weeds when they are young and actively growing. If your rose garden is small or if weeds are few, simply pull them out by hand or with a hoe. Mulching helps reduce weed growth by smothering weeds and their seeds and by keeping the soil cool, which prevents the germination of crabgrass and other grassy seeds. The few weeds that may pop through can easily be removed.

Key to controlling weeds is to keep up with them. A five-minute walk through the gartden once each morning, removing a few weeds when they are small, can turn this onerous chore into a pleasure.

In larger gardens, eradicate weeds with a chemical herbicide. There are two classes of chemical herbicides: preemergent and postemergent.

A preemergent herbicide turns the soil surface into a barrier that kills germinating seedlings as they try to emerge into the light and air. Most usually last for the entire growing season, so early application is best.

PREEMERGENT HERBICIDES
prevent seeds in the ground
from germinating. Apply these
herbicides to the soil
beginning in early spring,
depending on the weeds
you want to control. See the
product label for information.
Some preemergent herbicides
contain ingredients that may
be harmful to roses, so read
the label carefully before
using one of these products.

POSTEMERGENT HERBICIDES
kill weeds that are actively
growing. While some are
labeled for use in rose
gardens, be sure to follow
label directions carefully and
avoid getting any spray on
rose leaves.

If you are preparing a new
rose bed, give your roses a
good start by eliminating all
weeds before planting either
by manually removing them
or by treating them with an
herbicide. If you are using a
postemergent herbicide, apply
it far enough in advance so
that it will have time to
decompose before you plant
your roses; otherwise they
may be harmed.

Preemergent herbicides that
are labeled safe for roses can
be applied either before or
after planting, depending on
the product. Some will not
work if they are disturbed
after they have been applied.
Check the product label to be
sure. Preemergent herbicides
will not control weeds that
have already sprouted.

A lawn that is allowed to
grow into your rose beds can
be troublesome. Metal, brick,
or stone edgings around the
rose beds will help keep the
lawn at bay.

Here's a useful tip: Use a vise grip to help you grab and pull stubborn tree seedlings.

Feeding

Fertilizer basics

Like other flowering plants, roses need food in order to grow and bloom successfully. Roses, however, have greater nutritional needs than many other plants. Although small quantities of nutrients are available naturally in the soil and air, supplemental fertilizing is essential if you want your roses to perform their best. Your fertilizer must not only be of the right formulation for roses but also be applied in the right amounts at the right times.

In this section you'll learn about the nutritional components of fertilizers, the different types, how and when to apply them, and how to recognize nutrient deficiencies.

Fertilizers contain three elements that are basic for plant growth: nitrogen, phosphorus, and potassium (abbreviated N, P, and K, respectively). Nitrogen promotes stem and leaf growth and deep green color and stimulates early spring growth. Phosphorus encourages root growth and

flower production and is necessary for photosynthesis. Potassium helps regulate the metabolism of the plant and contributes to hardiness, vigor, good flower color, and disease resistance. A fertilizer containing all three elements is said to be complete.

Because plants differ in their nutritional needs, fertilizers come with differing proportions of these three elements. A typical formulation is 5-10-5, containing 5 percent nitrogen, 10 percent phosphorus, and 5 percent potassium (the

READING A FERTILIZER LABEL

A Guaranteed Analysis statement must appear on all mixed fertilizer labels. The label must indicate the proportion of each element present, as well as its sources (in this example, ammonium phosphate, potassium chloride, etc.). The numbers 15-30-15 denote the percentages of nitrogen,

phosphorous, and potassium present in this mix. This example contains 15 percent nitrogen, 30 percent phosphorous, and 15 percent potassium. Some fertilizers also contain secondary and micro-nutrients. Look for fertilizers with micro-nutrients derived from EDTA complexes

as these chelating agents keep nutrients immediately available to the root system. Rose foods containing all three levels of nutrients (primary, secondary, and micro-) are the best choice. In some cases, a soil penetrant will be added to the fertilizer to assist in delivery of the nutrients in clay soils.

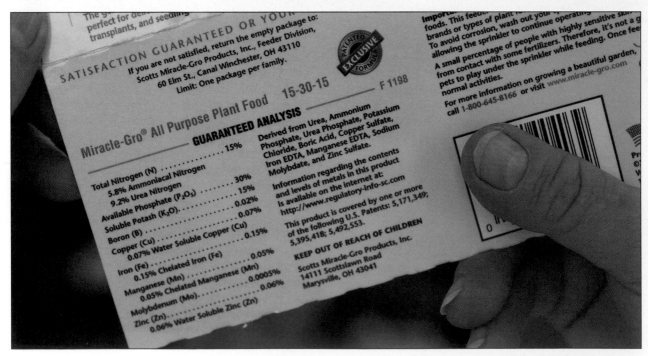

other 80 percent is inert material that helps distribute them evenly). These percentages always appear in the same order on product labels. Two other common formulations of rose fertilizers are 5-10-10 and 8-12-4.

Roses, like many other flowering shrubs, grow best when you use a fertilizer whose nitrogen, phosphorus, and potassium exist in approximately 1:2:1, 1:2:2, or 2:3:1 ratios. The relatively lower proportion of nitrogen keeps the plants from producing lush leaves at the expense of flowers.

Superphosphate (0-20-0) and triple superphosphate (0-45-0) are special fertilizers used at planting time to encourage root growth. They supply only phosphorus.

Fertilizers are often referred to as organic or inorganic. Organic fertilizers contain carbon and may be either natural or synthetic. Natural organic fertilizers, such as bonemeal, cottonseed meal, and fish emulsion, are minimally processed animal or vegetable by-products. Synthetic organic fertilizers, such as IBDU (isobutylidene diurea) and sulfur-coated urea, are manufactured from organic materials by more elaborate methods. Organic fertilizers of both types take the form of particles, granules, powders, or liquids.

Inorganic fertilizers are synthetic products containing no organic materials. They are manufactured from mineral salts, typically potassium nitrate, ammonium nitrate, ammonium phosphate, ammonium sulfate, calcium nitrate, potassium chloride, and potassium sulfate. These fertilizers are solids in their pure form but are often sold in solution.

Although both organic and inorganic fertilizers supply plants with the same nutrients, each has its particular advantages and disadvantages.

Choosing fertilizers

Some organic and inorganic fertilizers are known as slow-release fertilizers because they release their nutrients over a long period, usually three to nine months. They are more convenient than the regular type because you don't need to apply them as often. Some slow-release fertilizers, for example, are applied only once per year in late winter or early spring whereas regular fertilizers are applied more frequently (see the next section on page 96). The release is sometimes activated by soil moisture and sometimes by high soil temperature.

A good way to determine whether a fertilizer is the slow-release type is to look on the label for the percentage of water insoluble nitrogen (abbreviated WIN). If the WIN number is 30 percent or more, the fertilizer is considered slow release.

The labels of some products also indicate the number of months they will last. If you want to fertilize only once a year, choose a product that will remain active throughout your roses' growing cycle, whether it is four months, six months, or nine months. Note, however, that slow-release products lack the trace elements that are present in many other fertilizers, so supplemental applications of these elements may be needed. Another important choice you face is whether to apply fertilizers in dry or liquid form. Although there are some natural organic liquid fertilizers, such as fish emulsion, the term liquid fertilizer usually refers to dry or liquid concentrates of water-soluble inorganic fertilizers that are mixed with water before application. Typical formulations are 20-20-20 or 15-30-15. Because of their water solubility, they are fast acting, releasing their nutrients quickly. This is a special boon for container-grown roses, which must be watered frequently. Frequent watering can cause dry fertilizers to leach away before they can act.

Liquid fertilizers are less appropriate for roses growing in the ground because they must be applied as often as once every two weeks. They are therefore not as convenient as dry fertilizers and are usually used only as a supplement. Rose growers who exhibit at shows often apply liquid fertilizer about 10 days before a show to give the plants a "boost," promoting deeper green foliage and larger, more colorful flowers. Liquid fertilizers can, however, be combined with fungicide and insecticide sprays for convenience. See page 120 for a discussion on spraying.

When you are deciding on which fertilizer to use in the garden, choose a slow-release type if saving time is one of your goals. Otherwise the best fertilizer to choose is one that combines organic and inorganic fertilizers. Use liquid fertilizer as a supplement if desired. For container-grown roses, liquid fertilizers are the best choice.

Feeding
(continued)

Apply slow-release rose food the same way you would apply granular fertilizer: moisten the soil, spread the plant food over the root zone, and lightly cultivate it in.

How and when to fertilize

Proper timing is essential when applying fertilizer because nutrients must be present in the soil when the plants need them most—at their most active stage of growth and flowering. This time will vary with the climate, but it starts with the first signs of growth in late winter or early spring and lasts until cool fall weather slows growth. Fertilizer must also be applied in the proper amount, which depends on the type and size of the roses, the length of the growing season, possible competition from other plants, and the soil. A yearly soil test can tell you the nutrient content of your soil and what fertilizing regime is best for you.

Roses, being hungry plants, need to be fertilized often. Using a complete fertilizer or rose food whose N-P-K ratio is 1:2:1, 1:2:2, or 2:3:1, feed roses as soon as they are pruned, after the first flush of bloom, and about two months before the first fall frost. Gardeners who want to grow exhibition-size roses can feed them once a month from early spring to late summer or fall, depending on the length of the growing season. They can also use liquid fertilizers in advance of rose shows to produce better specimens.

If the soil pH needs to be adjusted, it should be done about a month before fertilizing to create the optimum pH for roses, which is 6.5. The more efficient nutrient absorption at this pH will make your fertilizer go further. (For information on adjusting pH, see pages 72–73.)

Slow-release fertilizers

Slow-release fertilizers need to be applied less often, at a frequency that depends on the formulation. For example, a six-month formulation is applied only once in early spring in Zone 7, where the growing season is six months long. If a three-month formulation is used instead, it would be applied twice, in early spring and again in early summer. When applying slow-release fertilizers, it is best to move the mulch aside, lightly scratch the fertilizer into the ground with a handheld cultivator, then put the mulch back. Unless the fertilizer is in contact with the soil, it will not work properly.

Liquid fertilizers

Liquid fertilizers must be applied as often as every two weeks. Pour them over the ground with a watering can or a sprayer, or spray them on foliage with the same equipment. Leaves as well as roots can absorb nutrients; in fact, fertilizer applied directly to the foliage will be put to use more quickly. Do not apply any liquid fertilizers to foliage when the air temperature is over 90° F, since rapid evaporation at these temperatures makes the fertilizers more concentrated and thus more likely to burn the plants.

Dormant feeding

Many experts recommend dormant feeding, which is the application of fertilizer during the late fall or winter when the plant tops are not growing. Because roots continue growing in fall and winter until the soil temperature falls below 40°F and start growing again in spring before top growth appears, they can absorb fertilizer supplied during the dormant period as soon as they are ready for it. If roses are dormant fed in fall or winter, an early spring application of fertilizer is not necessary. In warm areas, where roses grow all year, dormant feeding is not needed unless the plants are forced into dormancy to prolong their life, or unless their growth slows significantly.

Fertilizer amounts

Always follow the directions on the label regarding the amount of fertilizer to apply since this will vary with the formulation. It takes twice as much 5-10-5 fertilizer as 10-10-10 fertilizer to provide plants with the same amount of nitrogen and potassium. (The increased amount of phosphorus will not harm the plants since phosphorus moves slowly through the soil.)

Large shrub roses, old garden roses, and climbers need more fertilizer than hybrid teas—about twice as much per plant. Miniatures need much less than any other rose—about half as much. Adjust your applications accordingly.

Because fertilizers leach more rapidly from sandy soils than they do from other types of soil, they may need to receive fertilizer more often. If you see signs of reduced growth from nutrient deficiency, either correct the soil or shorten the interval between fertilizer applications by about one-third. When roses are growing near other plants, they may need about 20 percent more fertilizer if they show signs of reduced growth.

To keep from burning the roots, always apply any type of fertilizer to moist soil, spreading it over the entire area under which roots are growing. Generally this is the soil under the spread of the plant. Be careful not to spill fertilizer on the bud union. If you do so accidentally, wash the fertilizer off to avoid burning the plant. Work the fertilizer lightly into the surface of the soil with a trowel or a handheld cultivator and water again.

Stop fertilizing before cold weather

Fertilizing too late in the season can be detrimental to roses, as nitrogen encourages new growth that will not have time to adapt to the cold before winter chill can damage it. It is best to stop using complete fertilizers about two months before the first frost.

However, a fertilizer that contains little or no nitrogen but has phosphorus and potassium (such as bonemeal or superphosphate) can be applied in early fall. Phosphorus and potassium help the canes adapt to cold weather, lessening dieback and other winter injury.

Avoid overdoing

If rose foliage turns crisp and brown, it may be a sign of overfertilizing. Water the plants heavily to leach excess fertilizer out of the ground,

Spread granular fertilizer on moist soil above the root area, then lightly cultivate it in. Always follow package label directions.

Water-soluble plant foods can be sprayed directly onto leaves, which absorb nutrients quickly. Iron deficiencies are often remedied in this way.

and adjust the amount or concentration of future feedings to keep the problem from recurring. Fine-tune this by trial and error. Better yet, have your soil tested.

Feeding
(continued)

NUTRIENT DEFICIENCY SYMPTOMS AND TREATMENT

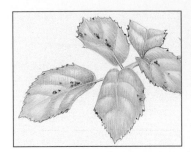

Nitrogen Deficiency:
Especially in the lower, more mature leaf sets, leaves are lighter green to yellow, with random leaf spots. If soil is too acidic (pH 5.8 or less), apply lime. If pH is ok, fertilize with high nitrogen fertilizer.

Phosphorous Deficiency:
Leaves are dark green developing dark red and purple colors, mainly within leaf (colors can spread to outer edges). If soil is too acidic, apply lime. If pH is ok, fertilize with high phosphorous fertilizer.

Potassium Deficiency:
Dead tissue is found, mainly at the edges of leaves. If soil is too acidic, apply lime. If soil pH is ok, feed with potassium nitrate.

Zinc Deficiency:
Large areas of dead tissue appear at tips and between veins. If pH is ok, then apply zinc chelate (1 teaspoon per bush).

Magnesium Deficiency:
Yellowing starts from center of leaf, with signs of dying tissue overlaying the affected parts. Apply Epsom salts, ½ cup sprinkled around the base of each bush.

Trace elements

In addition to nitrogen, phosphorus, and potassium, roses require small quantities of 10 other elements, called trace elements, for proper growth. These elements are boron, calcium, chlorine, copper, iron, magnesium, manganese, molybdenum, sulfur, and zinc. Most already exist in sufficient amounts in the soil, water, or air. But calcium, magnesium, sulfur, and iron may need to be supplemented occasionally because they are scarce in most environments. Sometimes they are present in fertilizer formulations; check the label to be sure. If not, you will have to purchase a supplemental source. Deficiencies of the other trace elements are possible but rare. Keep in mind that only a soil test can reliably confirm any deficiencies.

In addition to containing calcium, dolomitic limestone also contains magnesium, the basic element in chlorophyll that enables plants to utilize other nutrients, especially phosphorus. Magnesium is also essential for leaf production. If you are applying dolomitic limestone, follow the directions on the product label. If dolomitic limestone is not available, magnesium can be supplied with 1 to 2 ounces of Epsom salts (magnesium sulfate) per rosebush. Sprinkle Epsom salts over the ground and work it into the soil. You can purchase Epsom salt at a drugstore.

Sulfur promotes root and top growth and helps maintain a dark green color.

Sulfur, either pure or in some compounds, is also used to acidify the soil; see page 72 for more information. Sulfur is present in gypsum and Epsom salts, and in many inorganic fertilizers, including those containing iron sulfate or ammonium sulfate. It is also possible to buy powdered agricultural sulfur at garden centers or agricultural supply stores. Check the soil pH after adding pure sulfur to make sure that it hasn't lowered the pH too much.

Iron is needed for the production of chlorophyll; if iron is lacking, leaves turn completely yellow or stay green only along the veins. A solution of chelated iron, a powder or liquid sold at garden centers, can be sprayed onto plants if this yellowing, known as chlorosis, occurs. Also check the pH of the soil and correct it if necessary because iron in alkaline soils is chemically unavailable to plant roots. Applying chelated iron to roses in alkaline soil is only first aid; adjust the pH to correct the deficiency permanently.

In addition to the special supplements already mentioned, many general-purpose fertilizers also supply trace elements. These elements are listed on the label and will probably be sufficient to cure all but extreme deficiencies. It is also possible to buy mixtures containing some or all of the 10 trace elements. Garden centers and agricultural supply stores are sources of these. Follow the label for application rates and frequency of application.

NUTRIENT DEFICIENCY SYMPTOMS AND TREATMENT

Calcium Deficiency:
Terminal buds are dead, and young leaves are hooked. Apply calcium nitrate (1 to 2 tablespoons per bush per week) until corrected.

Boron Deficiency:
Terminal buds are dead, and young leaves are light green at base and twisted. Apply 1 teaspoon Borax per bush.

Copper Deficiency:
Terminal buds are dead, and young leaves are permanently wilted with no chlorosis (yellowing). Apply copper sulfate (¼ teaspoon per bush).

Sulfur Deficiency:
Leaves are light green with lighter-green veins. Apply soil sulfur (2 tablespoons per bush) or apply a fertilizer containing this element.

Iron Deficiency:
Leaves are yellow with principal veins light green. Use iron chelate (¼ teaspoon per bush) for immediate correction. Iron sulfate takes longer to act.

Care Calendar

ROSE CARE MONTH BY MONTH

Zone	1	2	3	4	5	6	7	8	9	10	11
January											
Study catalogs; order roses	■	■	■	■	■	■	■	■	■	■	■
Clean and sharpen tools	■	■	■	■	■	■	■	■	■	■	■
Test pH; adjust if necessary								■	■	■	■
Plant container roses									■	■	■
Plant bare-root roses									■	■	■
Transplant roses									■	■	■
Prune roses									■	■	■
Fertilize after pruning									■	■	■
Resume watering									■	■	■
Spray as needed									■	■	■
February											
Study catalogs; order roses	■	■	■	■	■	■	■	■	■	■	■
Clean and sharpen tools	■	■	■	■	■	■	■	■			
Test pH; adjust if necessary								■	■	■	■
Plant container roses								■	■	■	■
Plant bare-root roses								■	■	■	■
Transplant roses								■	■	■	■
Prune roses								■			
Fertilize after pruning								■			
Apply summer mulch									■	■	■
Water as needed									■	■	■
Spray as needed									■	■	■
March											
Study catalogs; order roses	■	■	■	■	■						
Clean and sharpen tools	■	■	■	■	■						
Test pH; adjust if necessary						■	■				
Plant container roses						■	■	■	■	■	■
Plant bare-root roses						■	■				
Transplant roses						■	■				
Remove winter protection							■				
Prune roses							■				
Fertilize after pruning							■				
Fertilize roses								■	■	■	■
Apply supplemental liquid fertilizer								■	■	■	■
Weed rose beds							■				
Weed rose beds; apply preemergent herbicide								■	■	■	■
Apply summer mulch								■			
Begin regular spraying								■			
Continue regular spraying									■	■	
Water as needed								■	■	■	■
Disbud for larger flowers								■	■	■	■
Deadhead faded flowers									■	■	■

ROSE CARE MONTH BY MONTH

Zone	1	2	3	4	5	6	7	8	9	10	11
April											
Test pH; adjust if necessary	■	■	■	■	■	■	■				
Plant container roses	■	■	■	■	■	■	■	■	■	■	■
Plant bare-root roses	■	■	■	■	■	■	■				
Transplant roses	■	■	■	■	■	■	■				
Remove winter protection	■	■	■	■	■	■					
Prune roses	■	■	■	■	■	■	■				
Fertilize after pruning	■	■	■	■	■	■	■				
Fertilize roses								■	■	■	■
Apply supplemental liquid fertilizer								■	■	■	■
Weed rose beds							■				
Weed rose beds; apply preemergent herbicide								■			
Apply summer mulch								■			
Continue regular spraying								■	■	■	■
Water as needed								■	■	■	■
Disbud for larger flowers								■	■	■	■
Deadhead faded flowers								■	■	■	■
May											
Plant container roses	■	■	■	■	■	■	■	■	■	■	■
Plant bare-root roses	■	■	■	■							
Fertilize roses	■	■	■	■	■	■	■	■	■	■	■
Apply supplemental liquid fertilizer								■	■	■	■
Weed rose beds								■	■	■	■
Weed; apply preemergent herbicide	■	■	■	■	■	■	■				
Apply summer mulch	■	■	■	■	■	■	■				
Begin regular spraying	■	■	■	■	■	■	■				
Continue regular spraying								■	■	■	■
Water as needed	■	■	■	■	■	■	■	■	■	■	■
Disbud for larger flowers	■	■	■	■	■	■	■	■	■	■	■
Deadhead faded flowers								■	■	■	■
June											
Plant container roses	■	■	■	■	■	■	■	■	■	■	■
Fertilize roses	■	■	■	■	■	■	■	■	■	■	■
Apply supplemental liquid fertilizer	■	■	■	■	■	■	■	■	■	■	■
Weed rose beds								■	■	■	■
Weed; apply preemergent herbicide	■	■	■	■	■	■	■				
Apply summer mulch	■	■	■	■							
Continue regular spraying	■	■	■	■	■	■	■	■	■	■	■
Water as needed	■	■	■	■	■	■	■	■	■	■	■
Disbud for larger flowers	■	■	■	■	■	■	■	■	■	■	■
Deadhead faded flowers	■	■	■	■	■	■	■	■	■	■	■

ROSE CARE MONTH BY MONTH

Zone	1	2	3	4	5	6	7	8	9	10	11
July											
Plant container roses	■	■	■	■	■	■	■	■	■	■	■
Fertilize roses	■	■	■	■	■	■	■	■	■	■	■
Apply supplemental liquid fertilizer	■	■	■	■	■	■	■	■	■	■	■
Weed rose beds	■	■	■	■	■	■	■	■	■	■	■
Continue regular spraying	■	■	■	■	■	■	■	■	■	■	■
Water as needed	■	■	■	■	■	■	■	■	■	■	■
Disbud for larger flowers	■	■	■	■	■	■	■	■	■	■	■
Deadhead faded flowers	■	■	■	■	■	■	■	■	■	■	■
August											
Plant container roses	■	■	■	■	■	■	■	■	■	■	■
Fertilize roses								■	■	■	■
Apply supplemental liquid fertilizer	■	■	■	■	■	■	■	■	■	■	■
Apply fertilizer for the last time	■	■	■	■	■	■	■				
Weed rose beds	■	■	■	■	■	■	■	■	■	■	■
Continue regular spraying	■	■	■	■	■	■	■	■	■	■	■
Water as needed	■	■	■	■	■	■	■	■	■	■	■
Disbud for larger flowers	■	■	■	■	■	■	■	■	■	■	■
Deadhead faded flowers	■	■	■	■	■	■	■	■	■	■	■
September											
Order roses for fall planting						■	■	■	■	■	■
Prepare soil for spring planting	■	■	■	■	■						
Plant container roses							■	■	■	■	■
Apply fertilizer for the last time								■	■	■	■
Weed rose beds					■	■	■	■	■	■	■
Continue regular spraying							■	■	■	■	■
Water as needed					■	■	■	■	■	■	■
Stop deadheading roses	■	■	■	■	■	■					

A pergola of climbers at David Austin's show gardens in Shropshire, England

ROSE CARE MONTH BY MONTH

Zone	1	2	3	4	5	6	7	8	9	10	11
October											
Apply winter protection	■	■	■	■							
Order roses for fall planting						■	■	■	■	■	■
Prepare soil for spring planting					■						
Plant container roses							■	■	■	■	■
Transplant roses					■						
Weed rose beds						■	■	■	■	■	■
Continue regular spraying							■	■	■	■	■
Water as needed					■	■	■	■	■	■	■
Stop deadheading roses							■	■	■	■	■
November											
Apply winter protection					■	■	■				
Order roses for spring planting	■	■	■	■	■	■	■	■	■	■	■
Prepare soil for spring planting						■	■	■	■	■	■
Plant container roses								■	■	■	■
Plant bare-root roses						■	■	■	■	■	
Transplant roses						■	■	■			
Spray as needed									■	■	■
Withhold water from established plants									■	■	■
December											
Order roses for spring planting	■	■	■	■	■	■	■	■	■	■	■
Prepare soil for spring planting								■	■	■	■
Plant container roses								■	■	■	■
Plant bare-root roses								■	■	■	■
Transplant roses								■	■	■	■
Spray as needed									■	■	■

Old garden roses in the nursery show garden of Heirloom Roses near St. Paul, Oregon

Pruning Roses

Many gardeners new to rose growing have no difficulty removing dead, damaged, diseased, or weak growth from a rosebush. But they do have trouble taking up pruning shears to cut away live, healthy growth. Experienced rose growers know, however, that pruning is essential to good growth and flowering.

Pruning is the science of removing growth to achieve one or more goals: keeping the plant healthy, making it more productive, controlling its size, or encouraging it to grow in a particular shape or direction. The amount, type, and timing of pruning depends on the type of rose, the hardiness zone of the garden, the amount of winterkill, the condition of the plant, and what you want from your roses.

A rose that is not pruned well will soon grow tall and lanky, and its flower production will be poor. Pruning stimulates new growth, an important factor in flowering because many varieties produce flowers only on new canes.

Roses vary in their need for pruning. All hybrid teas, floribundas, grandifloras, and miniatures require heavy annual pruning to keep them in top shape. Climbers may need heavy pruning or only a light shaping, depending on the time of year and other circumstances. Many shrub and old garden roses need only the annual light pruning you would give to other woody plants in the garden.

Summer pruning can be as simple as deadheading to encourage more blooms.

Study a pro's pruning technique

Watch an expert rose pruner at work and you will see several of these strategies in action. First, the pruner removes dead, damaged, or diseased canes (known among rose growers as the "Three Ds") and any crossing canes, to enhance the appearance of the plant and prevent chafing. Next, the pruner opens up the center of the plant to improve air circulation and admit more light, which keeps down mildew and diseases.

Further cuts encourage growth at desired points along the canes or at the base of the plant to stimulate growth and flowering. Still other cuts give the plant an overall shape or ease the burden on a newly transplanted root system.

Like other skills, pruning is mastered with practice. Proper tools, good timing, and understanding of the growth habits of roses are essential to perfecting this skill.

Mastering the correct way to cut is the first step toward pruning like a pro. The cut should be made about ¼ inch above a bud or a five-leaflet leaf set at a 45° angle sloping away from the bud or leaf petiole (see page 109).

When to Prune

Roses are generally pruned according to the climate and the calendar; the ideal time to start is when growth buds swell in the spring. However, pruning rules vary somewhat with the type of rose.

Depending on your climate, pruning time for all types of roses is generally between midwinter and midspring. Look for forsythia to guide you: When you see its yellow flowers start to appear, you know it's rose-pruning time. If there is no forsythia in your area, prune when new growth buds start to appear along the canes. Also refer to the charts on pages 100 to 103 for timing guidelines.

'Paul's Himalayan Musk Rambler' is a once-blooming rose that should be pruned back in spring right after it's through blooming.

In most parts of North America, rose pruning begins when forsythia blooms.

Modern bush roses

Modern bush roses, such as hybrid teas, floribundas, grandifloras, and miniatures, should be pruned annually when growth buds begin to swell but before they actually start to leaf out. In very warm climates where the roses may not lose their leaves, pruning should be done in midwinter to late winter. Because these roses bloom only from new wood, pruning is essential to stimulate a crop of new canes from which flowers can arise.

Take care with climbers

Climbers bloom on old wood—the previous year's canes. They should therefore not be pruned until after their first flush of bloom, or wood that will produce flower buds will be cut away. However, you can cut out dead, damaged, or diseased wood at any time. If plants need shaping, you can do this in spring or later in the season, as you wish.

Old garden and shrub roses

It may not be necessary to prune old garden and shrub roses every year. The need to prune them depends on their condition, size, and shape. If these plants are generally healthy and shapely, you may not have to prune them except to remove dead, damaged, or diseased canes.

If old garden or shrub roses are unshapely, too large, or transplanted, you should perform major pruning on them after the flowers fade. Exceptions to this general rule include hybrid perpetuals, noisettes, Chinas, repeat-blooming damasks, hybrid musks, repeat-blooming Portlands, and moss roses— all of which are pruned in early spring (if needed) in the same way that modern bush roses are. These old garden roses are pruned early because, unlike the other old garden roses, they bloom exclusively on new wood.

Tools

Although garden centers and hardware stores sell a wide variety of pruning implements, you need just three types for pruning roses: pruning shears, lopping shears, and a pruning saw. Invest in the best tools you can afford. Well-made tools are a joy to own, last longer, and make your work easier than do shoddy ones.

Pruning shears

Pruning shears come in a range of forms for general and specialized uses. The best all-around shears for removing rose stems, flowers, and leaves are the hook-and-blade type (also known as curved bypass shears), with two opposing curved blades. Choose the largest pair your hand can comfortably hold.

Anvil shears

Anvil shears—a general-purpose type with a straight blade that strikes against a blunt surface—are less desirable because they can crush stems as they cut. This may cause the stems to die back or become prone to invasion by insects and diseases. The only task suitable for the safe use of anvil shears is removing dead wood.

You may see other types of pruning shears for sale, including branch cutters, flower shears, fruit shears, and hedge shears. These specialized tools are not needed for rose pruning.

Lopping shears

Lopping shears—heavy-duty, short-bladed shears with long handles—easily cut out thick

canes and to prune large old garden roses, shrubs, and climbers. If canes are too thick to cut with lopping shears, use a special large-toothed pruning saw. The saws with a long, thin, curved blade are the easiest to handle. A pole saw or pole shears, the same types of tools but with extra long handles, may be necessary for pruning very tall bushes or climbers. Roses should never be trimmed with hedge clippers, even if they are grown as a hedge. These tools are designed for overall shearing, not the selective pruning that roses require.

Keep your tools sharp

Be sure to keep pruning shears and saws sharp. Dull shears and saws make pruning more difficult, and they leave jagged cuts that heal slowly and admit insects and diseases. If your tools become dull, touch up the blades of pruning shears with a sharpening steel, hone saw blades with a file, or have

both tools professionally sharpened. If necessary, buy a replacement blade (they are available for most saws).

Clean tools keep plants healthy

Make sure that your tools are kept clean; contaminated shears and saws can spread disease. Apply rubbing alcohol to disinfect pruning tools or make a solution of 1 part household bleach and 9 parts water. Using a clean cloth, wipe the tools with whichever disinfectant you choose or dip the tools in a container holding the liquid.

In areas of high humidity, wipe shears and saws dry after each use and store them in plastic bags to retard rusting. Rubbing a thin coat of oil on the blades also helps prevent rust. Pruning shears with a nonstick coating on the blades are not as likely to rust, but the bolt holding the blades together may be rust-prone.

When pruning roses, wear sturdy leather gloves, such as the gauntlet gloves shown above left, to protect against thorns. Other essential tools include bypass pruning shears with a curved blade for cutting canes of typical thicknesses (ones with a swivel handle will reduce wrist strain); small pruning shears for small roses and miniatures; long-handled loppers for heavy canes; and a pruning saw for cutting woody canes and dead wood.

How to Prune: The Basics

The technique of pruning varies with the type of rose and the landscape purpose for which it was planted, whether it's growing in the ground or in a container. Pruning can range from removing unwanted buds to severely excising canes. Proper pruning stimulates growth at the buds closest to the cut, which produces new flowering stems.

The first step in pruning any type of rose is to remove any dead, damaged, diseased, or weak and thin canes, cutting them off flush with the bud union or, in the case of own-root plants, flush with the crown. Look for any canes that are broken or wounded, or that have cankers (dark,

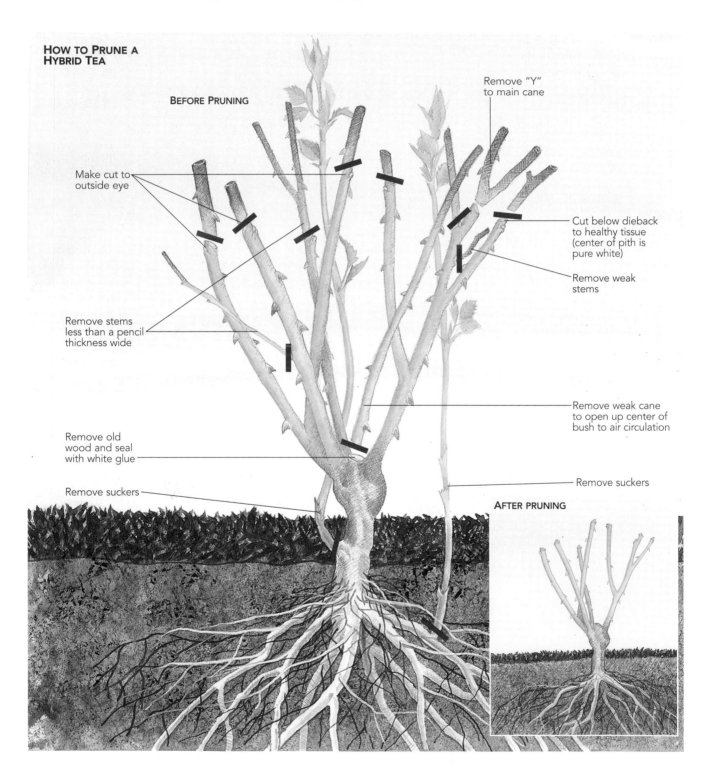

HOW TO PRUNE A HYBRID TEA

BEFORE PRUNING

Remove "Y" to main cane

Make cut to outside eye

Cut below dieback to healthy tissue (center of pith is pure white)

Remove weak stems

Remove stems less than a pencil thickness wide

Remove weak cane to open up center of bush to air circulation

Remove old wood and seal with white glue

Remove suckers

Remove suckers

AFTER PRUNING

sunken lesions caused by a fungus), and prune below the injury, at the highest point where the pith (the central portion of the cane) is healthy and white. Make the cut exactly ¼ inch above a growth bud. If the injury extends below that point, cut to a lower growth bud.

Next, remove canes that are growing into the center of the plant or those that cross each other. Canes that grow inward keep light and air from the center of the plant and will eventually cross, chafing one another. These abrasions can become entry points for insects and diseases. Using shears, cut these canes down to their origin, whether that is another cane, the bud union, or the crown. It is important to keep the center of the plant open to let in sunshine and allow air to circulate freely.

Always prune to an outward-facing bud so that canes do not grow into the center of the plant. Prune close enough to the bud that no stub remains to die off and

harbor insects or diseases but far enough away that the bud will not die. A good distance is about ¼ inch above the growth bud. Equally important, cut at the proper angle so that water runoff won't drip on the bud or collect in the cut and retard healing. The ideal angle is 45 degrees, slanted parallel to the direction of bud growth.

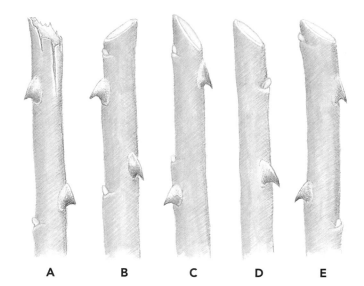

A   B   C   D   E

Make the right cut:
A: Damaged cut caused by blunt blades on old pruners.
B: Cut made at wrong angle.
C: Angle too steep.
D: Cut made too far above the bud eye.
E: The proper cut for a rose cane.

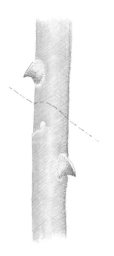

Find the dormant bud eye: Look for a slight swelling resembling a small pimple where the foliage has fallen off the cane. That's the dormant bud eye that will produce a new stem.

When the cut is made correctly—here, above an aging five-leaflet set with a dormant eye below (left)—the sap will rise from the rose cane and run down its opposite side (center). Remove the old leaf set just below the cut. Within a few weeks the dormant bud eye will begin to swell. In another three weeks the swelling will result in a young new stem (right) showing just a few foliage sets. Eventually that growth will become a stem and bloom.

How to Prune: The Basics

(continued)

Pruning in warm and cold climates

In warm climates where rose plants grow quite large, pruning to the recommended height is not desirable, because it will remove too much of the plant. Instead, prune away about one half to two thirds of the plant each winter or early spring by removing the older canes and shortening the remaining canes. In cold climates where there is a great deal of winter damage, pruning heights may be determined for you by the amount of winterkill. Prune canes down to where there is no more winter damage, even if it is almost to the ground.

The higher a plant is pruned, the earlier it will flower. But don't jeopardize the health and vigor of the plant by pruning too high just to have blooms a few days earlier. There is little advantage to pruning your roses lower than the heights prescribed above; unlike disbudding (see page 114), it will probably not make the plants produce larger flowers.

Preventing disease

Although black spot and other fungal diseases manifest themselves on leaves, their spores can overwinter on rose canes. If these diseases plagued your roses during the previous summer, you should prune them lower than recommended, thereby cutting away and discarding much of the source of the problem. Although you won't be able to see the spores on the canes, you can be assured that cutting off a few extra inches during spring pruning will reduce the number of spores somewhat. Never leave rose prunings on the ground. They look unsightly and harbor diseases and pests that may potentially reinfect the plant or spread to others. Refer to pages 116–127 for other methods of controlling diseases.

When to seal cuts

Pruning cuts more than inch in diameter can be sealed with pruning compound, orange shellac, or grafting wax (available at garden centers or hardware stores) if boring insects are a problem in your area. Pruning compound and orange shellac are the easiest to use because they can be painted on. Otherwise, sealing is not necessary. Some types of white glue, which is sometimes used as a sealant, are water soluble and will wash away with the first rain or watering; they should therefore not be used.

Timely inspection after initial pruning

Several weeks after you have pruned, take a second trip through the garden with your pruning shears. If you pruned early in the year, a late frost may have caused minor dieback on some of the canes. This dieback should be removed. Cankers that were not apparent at pruning time may be visible and should also be pruned away.

Don't be too harsh when pruning young plants. Until plants are well established

By fall, miniature roses have grown tall and leggy (left). Colder evenings produce ill-formed, mottled blossoms and yellowing foliage that often starts to fall off. Rose hips, which can interrupt the next blooming cycle, may result if spent blossoms are not removed. Pruning removes diseased, dead stems and canes as well as reducing the overall size of the plant (above center). The first spring bloom demonstrates how pruning results in an annual process of renewal (above right).

A modern rose bush before pruning (left) exhibits lopsided growth and a tangle of canes growing inward. Above center, lopping shears are used to

remove thick older canes (above center). Thinner canes (above right) are shortened or removed with hand pruners.

and have been growing robustly for two to three years, remove only weak, damaged, or dead wood. Shape and shorten the plants as recommended above without cutting away any of the older canes. In the following years, old canes can be removed as new ones develop.

Tips for pruning tall plants

New growth starts at the growing point immediately below a pruning cut. This is especially important to bear in mind when pruning back large, overgrown plants.

If your ultimate goal is a plant 6 feet tall or a climber trained to cover a section of fence 8 feet long, you must prune the plants shorter than the desired size in order to allow for new growth. For example, if your goal is a 6-foot-tall shrub rose, you should prune it to about 4 feet tall. Different plants have different growth rates, so gauge your pruning according to the past behavior of the plant.

How to prune roots

Roots can be pruned as well. When you plant or transplant a rosebush, prune off broken or damaged roots. Remove

about one-third off the tops of the canes to compensate for this root loss. Before transplanting a large rosebush, it is a good idea to prune the roots with a spade by digging in a circle around the plant (see pages 82–83 for instructions). Do this one to six months before the transplant so that the root ball will be more compact and easier to move.

Pruning can be a scratchy job, so wear gloves and a long-sleeved shirt or jacket to protect your skin against thorns. Some kinds of fabric, such as the nylon used in windbreakers, catch easily on thorns and can tear.

A pruning saw is used to cut away woody older growth.

After a severe pruning, four short canes remain evenly spaced around the plant.

A more moderate pruning has left a greater number of taller canes, which will produce higher, denser growth.

How to Prune Different Kinds of Roses

Just as roses vary, so do pruning methods. For exquisite blooms, apply the appropriate technique.

Hybrid teas, floribundas, and grandifloras

On hybrid teas, floribundas, and grandifloras, once you have pruned the diseased, damaged, weak, or excess canes, select three or four of the newest and healthiest remaining canes and cut off the rest flush with the bud union, using pruning shears or a saw if necessary. Next, prune the remaining canes of hybrid teas and floribundas to a height of 12 to 18 inches above the bud union, and those of grandifloras a few inches higher. Floribundas used as hedges can have five to six canes left on each plant, and can be pruned to 24 inches high so that they will grow denser and taller and produce more flowers.

Miniatures

Prune miniatures to about half their ultimate summer height.

Up to six strong new canes can be left on the plants after pruning; the more canes you leave, the fuller the plants will be.

Roses grown in decorative containers should be pruned so that they will be in proportion to the size of the container when they are in full bloom; this may mean shorter or higher pruning than is normally recommended.

Climbers

Because climbers bloom solely on old wood, they are pruned somewhat differently than bush roses. In early spring, while the plants are still dormant or have just started to grow, any dead or damaged canes can be removed, as can those that are too long or misshapen. However, leave all other pruning until after the plants first flower so that you do not remove any flower buds. This is especially important with climbers that bloom only once a year. Those that repeat their bloom may actually be encouraged to have a heavier

second bloom if they are properly pruned after the first bloom. The oldest canes should be removed to the bud union to leave room for new growth. Also thin out dense growth as well at this time.

Removing flowers as soon as they fade encourages some climbers that would not otherwise flower again to repeat their bloom during the summer. Climbers will bloom more heavily if trained along a fence or a trellis and if the ends of the canes are directed to grow down toward the ground. This forces the plants to produce more laterals. As new canes of climbers grow, they must be trained into position and tied to their supports with cord, string, or twist-ties.

Shrub roses and old garden roses

Shrub roses and old garden roses, including species roses, do not require severe pruning unless overgrown. In early spring, cut out weak, damaged, or dead wood. Prune only to shape the plant or control its size. Leave the plants as large and as natural looking as space permits. Perform heavy pruning either in early spring or after flowering, depending on the type of plant. Many old garden roses—albas, centifolias, and moss roses in particular—have long, supple canes that can be bent over and pinned to the ground. This practice makes these plants easier to control and gives them a bushier appearance. It also encourages the formation of new basal breaks (new canes that grow from the base of the plant). The canes often root at the point where pegged to the ground, and new plants that

When pruning floribundas, cut a little bit higher than for hybrid teas and leave as many canes as possible to produce lots of sprays.

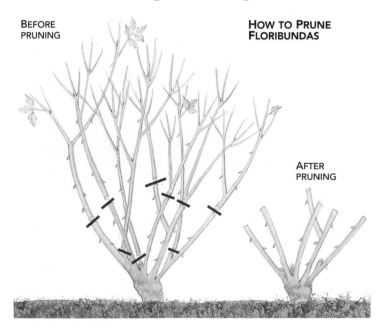

BEFORE PRUNING

HOW TO PRUNE FLORIBUNDAS

AFTER PRUNING

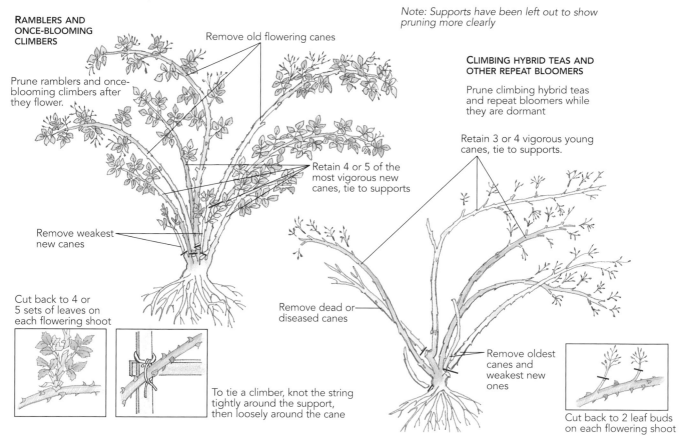

RAMBLERS AND ONCE-BLOOMING CLIMBERS

Note: Supports have been left out to show pruning more clearly

Remove old flowering canes

Prune ramblers and once-blooming climbers after they flower.

Retain 4 or 5 of the most vigorous new canes, tie to supports

Remove weakest new canes

Cut back to 4 or 5 sets of leaves on each flowering shoot

To tie a climber, knot the string tightly around the support, then loosely around the cane

CLIMBING HYBRID TEAS AND OTHER REPEAT BLOOMERS

Prune climbing hybrid teas and repeat bloomers while they are dormant

Retain 3 or 4 vigorous young canes, tie to supports.

Remove dead or diseased canes

Remove oldest canes and weakest new ones

Cut back to 2 leaf buds on each flowering shoot

form can be left in place or transplanted.

Polyanthas

Polyanthas are hardy plants that, like many old garden and shrub roses, seldom suffer winterkill. They are therefore pruned more like old garden and species roses than like hybrid teas, floribundas, and grandifloras. If they are not overgrown, trim only to remove old, damaged, or diseased canes. If they are overgrown, prune them in early spring, to about half their former height, and remove the oldest canes. Leave them on the bushy side.

Tree roses

Tree roses are pruned like modern bush roses, but they must be symmetrical to be most attractive. Prune canes to about 12 inches beyond the

bud union at the top of the trunk and leave them as evenly spaced around the plant as possible. Leaving four

to six canes on each tree rose will produce a full, attractive-looking plant.

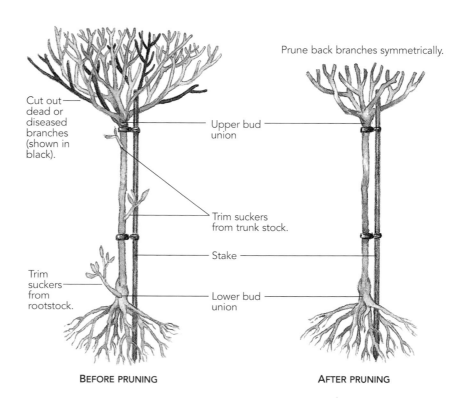

Cut out dead or diseased branches (shown in black).

Upper bud union

Trim suckers from trunk stock.

Stake

Trim suckers from rootstock.

Lower bud union

Prune back branches symmetrically.

BEFORE PRUNING

AFTER PRUNING

Disbudding

Disbudding is a type of pruning aimed at producing a single, large flower at the top of the cane or forming a more uniform spray. To produce a single, large flower at the top of a cane, you remove all flower buds below the top one. This forces the plant to devote all its energy to growing one flower that can bloom twice as large. Disbudding is necessary for producing show-quality hybrid teas, grandifloras, and climbing hybrid teas, which must be exhibited with one flower per stem in order to qualify for the highest awards. (For more information on exhibiting and judging roses, see pages 142–147.) Even if you never dream of exhibiting your roses, disbudding will help you achieve the largest flowers possible.

As soon as small secondary buds are visible around and below the central flower bud, remove them by rubbing them away with your fingers or the point of a small implement such as a toothpick. If you wait too long to disbud and the flower bud is an inch or more across, unsightly black scars will form and remain. Some roses naturally produce only one bloom per stem and will not require disbudding.

Roses that bloom in sprays, such as floribundas, grandifloras, climbers, and some miniatures, naturally grow in such a way that the central flower bud opens first. As it fades, the surrounding flower buds open. When the faded central flower is cut away, a large gap remains in the center of the spray. To prevent this, remove the central flower bud as soon as it appears. The remaining flowers will fill in the gap, coming into bloom simultaneously for a prettier effect, although flower size will not increase. Floribundas can be exhibited with one bloom per stem, but they are usually shown as sprays. The best floribunda in the show is almost always a spray. In the garden, allowing floribundas to bloom in sprays gives much more color and shows off their beauty more brilliantly.

Miniatures can be disbudded or not, depending on the effect you wish to achieve and whether you want large flowers on single stems or uniform sprays. Polyanthas, climbers, shrub roses, and old garden roses are rarely disbudded, as this would destroy their natural appearance. Their beauty rests in the large clusters of flowers they produce.

DISBUDDING

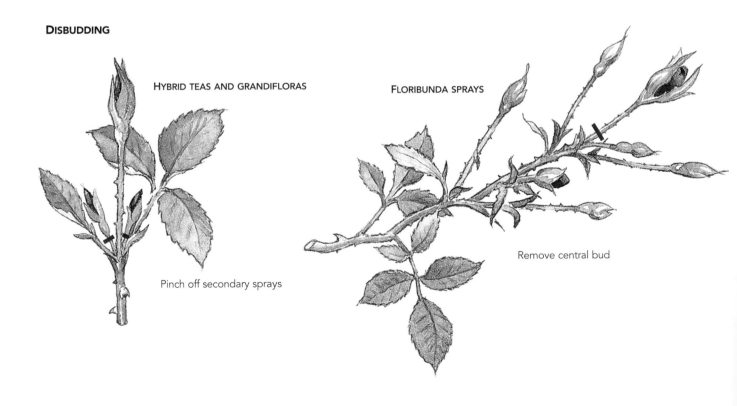

HYBRID TEAS AND GRANDIFLORAS

Pinch off secondary sprays

FLORIBUNDA SPRAYS

Remove central bud

Summer Pruning

Whether cutting single blooms or sprays, always cut to the nearest five-leaflet set that will support the next stem to sprout.

Flowers are produced at the ends of secondary stems, which grow from the main cane. Though you may not think of it as such, gathering these flowers is a form of pruning.

How to remove blooms

Whether you are cutting flowers for an arrangement or removing flowers that have faded (a technique known as deadheading), follow the same rule: Cut the flower stem no shorter than just above the first five-leaflet leaf below the flower you are removing. This is the point from which the next stem will grow and bloom. If you cut to a three-leaflet leaf instead, numerous small growth shoots will appear at the top of the stem but will never grow into sturdy, flower-producing stems.

When removing flowers from tall and vigorous roses, take the opportunity to shorten and shape them. Cut the stems down as low as you want them, but leave at least two five-leaflet leaves per stem to contribute to food production. Do not remove more than 25 percent of the foliage. If you do, you will send the plant into shock and a short dormant period. First-year plants should be pruned only slightly when removing faded flowers, to encourage growth and foliage production.

When to prune flowers

Old blooms past their peak should be pruned away as soon as possible. This not only keeps the plant looking neat and the ground free of fallen petals but also encourages new growth and flowers sooner.

To encourage repeat-blooming climbers to produce a heavy second bloom, prune and deadhead them as soon as the first flush of bloom is finished. Cut back the secondary stems, leaving two five-leaflet leaves on each. A new stem topped with a flower will grow from each leaf axil, the point where the leaf meets the stem.

Deadheading should cease as summer turns to fall because the new growth it encourages will probably not have time to produce flowers before the frost. The younger issue will also be more susceptible to damage from winter cold and wind. Leave the last roses of summer to fade naturally, and you will have plants that can better endure the rigors of winter. The only pruning that should be done in fall is to remove any tall canes that might be damaged by the wind or to shorten the canes enough to fit under rose cones or other winter protection (see pages 128–131).

Shrub roses, old garden roses, and climbers that bloom only once do not need to be deadheaded. After the flowers have faded, fruit known as hips will form. Rose hips can be harvested for cooking after they have ripened and turned yellow, orange, or red. You can also leave them as a treat for birds.

Eliminate suckers to protect plants

Throughout the summer be on the lookout for suckers, which are canes that grow from the understock to which the rosebush is grafted. Suckers are easy to recognize because they grow from below the bud union and because their foliage is different from that of the top of the plant. If suckers get to the blooming stage, you will see either small white flowers or nondescript red ones, depending on the type of understock used. If suckers are not removed, they will soon overpower the plant and cause the grafted part of it to be choked out and eventually killed by the understock's aggressive growth. As soon as you see a sucker, prune it away completely to its base.

It's important to remove root suckers from grafted roses right away. Here, the red-flowering 'Dr. Huey' understock will eventually overwhelm the white *Rosa soulieana* that has been grafted to it.

Protecting Roses

Even the most fastidious gardeners accept the reality that diseases, insects, and other inhabitants of the natural world will eventually inflict harm upon roses. But they take solace from the fact that few of these are devastating if prevented or treated in time. This chapter describes the major diseases and pests that can plague roses and ways to keep them in check.

Nature has a way of interfering with the desire to grow perfect roses. Choosing disease-resistant varieties, keeping plants well watered and nourished, and practicing good garden hygiene are vital steps in maintaining a healthy rose garden. But even the best-kept gardens are not invincible. Inevitably, some insects and diseases will attack.

Roses are especially susceptible to diseases, particularly powdery mildew and black spot. These are most severe where humidity or rainfall is high, or where air circulation is poor. Semitransparent aphids, iridescent Japanese beetles, and tiny spider mites are other common banes. Diseases and pests such as these can spoil or even kill your roses if not dealt with appropriately.

Fortunately, it is possible to prevent or cure many of the ills that can beset a rose garden. This chapter suggests ways to keep problems from starting and to solve them if they do.

A one- or two-gallon pressure sprayer is easy for most people to handle and allows you to apply pest or disease controls on up to 40 plants. Most sprayers of this size come with a 20-inch wand.

Before applying any pest or disease control it is essential to carefully read and thoroughly understand the label. (Opposite) Labels provide instructions for safe and effective use and should be followed to the letter.

DIRECTIONS FOR USE

It is a violation of Federal law to use this product in a manner inconsistent with its labeling.

SHAKE WELL

FOR BEST RESULTS

HOW TO APPLY
- Adjust spray nozzle to deliver a fine spray.
- Hold sprayer 12 inches from plant. Spray to uniformly cover upper and lower leaf surfaces, stems, and branches. When treating potted plants lightly spray the soil surface.

WHEN TO APPLY
- Spray when air is calm to avoid drift.
- Apply as necessary, waiting 7 to 14 days between each application. Hard to kill insects may require 2 to 3 applications.
- If temperature is expected to exceed 85° F, spray in early morning or late afternoon when it is cooler.

INSECTS CONTROLLED

Ants, aphids, armyworms, bagworms, black vine weevils, budworms, cabbage loopers, cankerworms, casebearers, catalpa sphins moths, caterpillars, cherry laurel leaftiers, crane flies, elm leaf beetles, fungus gnats, grasshoppers, greenbugs, green striped mapleworms, gypsy moths, hornworms, Japanese beetles, lacebugs, leafhoppers, leafminers, leafrollers, omnivorous leaftiers, maple shoot moths, mealybugs, mimosa webworms, mites (including spider mites), oak webworm, orange striped oakworms, poplar tentmakers, rose midges, sawflies, scales (crawlers), sod webworms, sowbugs, spittlebugs, spiders, sunflower moths, tent caterpillars, thrips, tip moths, webworms, weevils, willow leafbeetles and whiteflies

People and pets may enter treated area after spray has dried.

STORAGE AND DISPOSAL

STORAGE: Rotate nozzle to closed position. Store product in original container in a safe place. Keep from freezing.
DISPOSAL: Do not reuse container. Securely wrap partially filled or empty container in newspaper and put in trash.

PRECAUTIONARY STATEMENTS

HAZARDS TO HUMANS & DOMESTIC ANIMALS
CAUTION: Causes moderate eye irritation. Avoid contact with eyes or clothing. Wash thoroughly with soap and water after handling.
FIRST AID: IF IN EYES: Flush eyes with plenty of water. Call a physician if irritation persists. Note to Physician: Emergency Information call 1-800-225-2883.
ENVIRONMENTAL HAZARDS: This pesticide is extremely toxic to fish and aquatic invertebrates. Do not apply directly to water. Drift and run-off from treated areas may be hazardous to aquatic organisms in neighboring areas. Care should be used when spraying to avoid fish and reptile pets in/around ornamental ponds.

This product is highly toxic to bees exposed to direct treatment or residues on blooming plants. Do not apply this product or allow it to drift to blooming plants if bees are visiting the treatment area.

NOTICE: Buyer assumes all responsibility for safety and use not in accordance with directions.

Questions, Comments or Medical Information call 1-800-225-2883
www.ortho.com

?

Manufactured for
The ORTHO Group
P.O. Box 1749 Columbus, OH 43216
Made in USA

Form 008900
EPA Reg. No. 239-2668
EPA Est. 239-IA-3¹, 56100-LA-1G
Superscript is first letter of lot number

PRESS TO RESEAL

Controlling Diseases and Pests

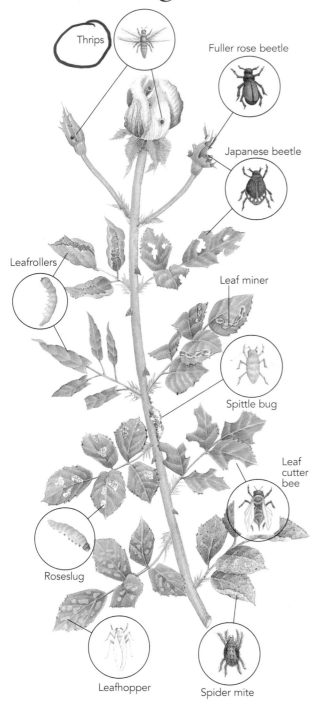

Thrips

Fuller rose beetle

Japanese beetle

Leafrollers

Leaf miner

Spittle bug

Leaf cutter bee

Roseslug

Leafhopper

Spider mite

Controlling diseases

Roses are susceptible to a variety of fungal, viral, and bacterial diseases whose effects can range from disfigurement of the leaves to outright killing of the plant. Because most diseases are hard to cure, it is usually easier to prevent them from taking hold in the first place.

Because well-maintained plants are less likely to succumb to diseases than weak ones, you can help ensure the health of your roses by caring for them properly. Follow the recommendations for watering (pages 86–89), fertilizing (pages 94–99), and pruning your roses (pages 104–115). If you live where one or more rose diseases are common, you may wish to plant only disease-resistant varieties; a list of these is on page 43.

Apart from practicing good garden hygiene and choosing disease-resistant plants, the best way to keep your roses from contracting diseases is to limit their exposure to the agents that spread them. Diseases are spread by air, water, and soil; by insects; and by direct contact with diseased plant material. Although you cannot completely protect your roses from these influences, you can at least exert some control over them. For instance, watering your roses by drip irrigation rather than by an overhead method can help control black spot and other fungal diseases, which quickly grow under moist conditions. If you must water from above, do so in the morning to give leaves and flowers a chance to dry by nightfall. Applying a mulch prevents water from splashing onto plants from the ground during rain or irrigation and contaminating them with disease spores from the ground.

Good air circulation can also hold back mildew and other diseases by keeping plants dry and not allowing disease spores to take hold.

To enhance air circulation, do not plant your rosebushes too close together (see pages 67–68 for spacing guidelines), and do not let them grow into one another if they become large. It also helps to keep the centers of the plants open through pruning.

Weeds can harbor many diseases, such as black spot and mildew, and disease-carrying insects, such as Japanese beetles and leafhoppers. You can eliminate this potential breeding ground by keeping weeds in check. If your garden has a large number of weeds, use a mulch or pre-emergent herbicide to control them; see pages 92–93 for information. Insects known to be disease carriers can be eradicated with sprays or, if practical, picked from plants by hand or knocked off with a jet of water.

To keep diseases from spreading among your roses by direct contact, prune away and destroy diseased parts of plants. Pick up diseased leaves as soon as they fall.

Some diseases, such as crown gall, are soilborne. Many have no means of prevention or cure so, when a rosebush becomes infected, the only remedy is to replace both it and the surrounding soil. Diagnosis and treatment of specific diseases are described later in this chapter, beginning on page 122.

Controlling insects and other pests

Hundreds of kinds of insects live in a typical garden, but only about a dozen regularly cause damage to roses. Indeed, some, such as ladybugs (also called lady beetles), are beneficial because they consume harmful insects. Although the variety of attackers is small, the damage they do can be extensive. Left unchecked in a rose garden, these insects can chew holes in leaves and flowers, suck vital juices from the plants, spread diseases, and even kill the plants. Insect control is therefore essential to a healthy, productive rose garden.

As with diseases, the best way to reduce the chance of an insect attack is to practice good garden hygiene. Insects often live and lay eggs in weeds, so it is vital to keep the garden free of these breeding sites. Cleaning up garden debris as it accumulates and destroying it each fall so that insects and their eggs cannot overwinter also reduce the insect threat. Even the tidiest garden can harbor destructive insects, so keep an eye out for early signs of infestation. Catching a problem early can save your garden from serious damage.

Once you have identified an insect problem, you may choose to fight back with insecticides. Some insects, such as aphids, can be dislodged from the plants by a jet of water, but application of insecticides is almost always a necessity at some time. Some of these insecticides, such as insecticidal soaps and pyrethrin sprays, are biological in origin. Others are synthetic formulations. These are usually stronger and longer lasting than organic agents, and should be used with care around birds and pets.

Insecticides of both types are classed as either contact or systemic. Contact

insecticides are absorbed through the insects' bodies and must be sprayed onto them directly. Horticultural oil and insecticidal soap are types of contact insecticide that kills insects by smothering them or their eggs with a film. Systemic insecticides are applied to plants and taken up through their roots or leaves; insects are poisoned as they feast on plant parts. The type of insecticide you choose depends to a great extent on what works best in killing the insect that is causing the problem; see the recommendations on pages 122 to 127. Some insecticides, such as Orthene®, work both systemically and by contact.

In addition to insecticides, you may need to use miticides in your garden. These are formulated especially to control spider mites—tiny eight-legged relatives of spiders that disfigure leaves and flower buds with grayish webs. Like spiders, mites are technically not insects. Although some insecticides are effective against them, miticides are usually applied to kill them.

Insecticides and miticides are best used at the first sign of infestation. Spraying to prevent attack rarely works and is costly as well. It also can destroy natural predators and other beneficial insects. These products can unnecessarily cause pests to build up an immunity so that these controls will not work when you need them.

Some rose growers prefer not to use any chemicals in their gardens and instead rely on natural predators to control destructive insects. Helpful species include ladybugs, assassin bugs, green

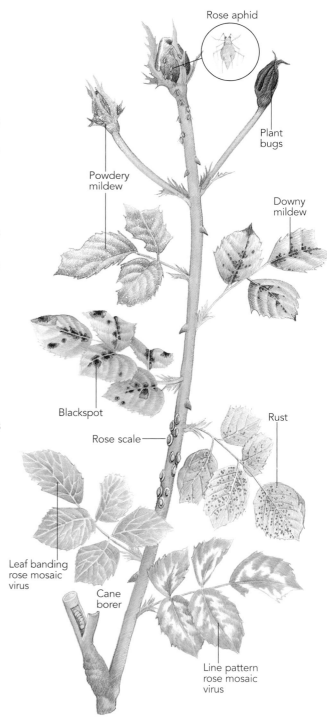

Rose aphid

Plant bugs

Powdery mildew

Downy mildew

Blackspot

Rust

Rose scale

Leaf banding rose mosaic virus

Cane borer

Line pattern rose mosaic virus

lacewings, praying mantids, parasitic wasps, and predatory mites. The drawback to these insects is that, once they have eaten the pests in your garden, they will move on to other gardens in search of food. Their overall effectiveness may not last long.

Sprayers

Although a few insecticides and fungicides are poured onto the ground or spread on in dry form, most are applied directly to the foliage as a spray. Ready-to-use products often come with built-in sprayers, but for larger gardens it is more economical to purchase a sprayer and chemical concentrates to dilute yourself.

There are several different types of sprayers, all widely available at garden centers and hardware stores. A compression sprayer has a tank for the spray solution (usually holding 1½ to 2 gallons), a plunger to compress air into the container, and a piece of tubing with a nozzle at the end. Pressure in the tank delivers a spray. Both metal and plastic types are available; plastic ones are lighter in weight and resist corrosion, which makes them easier to clean. All in all, compression sprayers are the most convenient and popular type.

Some small sprayers are driven by rechargeable batteries that eliminate the need for hand pumping. Overnight charging will power most of these for 45 minutes—enough time to spray the average garden. Some older types of aerosol sprayers have plungers that are operated by hand; these do not deliver as even a spray as the compression or battery-driven sprayers.

Other kinds of sprayers, called hose-end sprayers, are designed to be attached to the end of a garden hose. Most consist of a nozzle and a detachable plastic bottle that holds a concentrated solution of insecticide or fungicide. Water from the hose siphons and dilutes the concentrate and propels the mixture through the nozzle. This is the least convenient sprayer to use, because you must drag around a hose, which becomes inconvenient in a large or crowded garden. This type of sprayer may also distribute the concentrate unevenly. Siphon injectors, the type used to apply large amounts of liquid fertilizer, can also be used to apply spray materials.

Some sprayers have long, tubular or sliding attachments called trombones that make it easy to spray tall rose plants that are trained on trellises and arbors. These trombone-action sprayers are pumps, not compression sprayers, and pump solution out of a bucket. Tank sprayers that roll on wheels are also available and are convenient in very large gardens. Some have motorized compressors.

Garden centers also sell dusters for applying powdered insecticides and fungicides. These are tubular devices with a plunger at one end. However, in recent years they have given way to sprayers, as spraying liquid is a more even and effective way to apply materials.

SPRAYING TIPS

Before you use a sprayer for the first time, be sure to read the instructions accompanying it. Sprayers differ in design and operation, so it is important to follow the instructions carefully. Here are some general pointers:
■ Make sure plants are well watered before you spray since damage is more likely to occur to dry leaves than to moist, turgid ones. Never spray on a windy day as too much spray will be blown away, perhaps onto plants that may be damaged by the product.
■ Spray both the upper and lower leaf surfaces until the spray starts to run off the leaf. Nozzles on some sprayers can be adjusted to produce different droplet sizes; the finer the spray, the more even the coverage.
■ When applying dormant sprays, make sure the canes are completely covered. Also cover the ground around the bases of the plants.
■ When using a compression sprayer, you will need to repump it once or twice to keep the pressure high enough to deliver a fine spray.
■ If the sprayer contains powdered material in suspension, you may need to shake it several times during spraying to keep the material evenly dispersed. Adding a squirt of liquid dish detergent to the water in the sprayer if powdered material is being used, either in suspension or in solution, helps it to adhere to the plants leaves. Liquid pesticide concentrates often contain a material that helps the active ingredient to adhere to the leaves, so liquid dish detergent is usually not necessary when using them.
■ When spraying a chemical that is toxic (the label will give this warning), wear a mask, gloves, and protective clothing. Change your clothes and take a shower as soon as you have finished the job.
■ Never apply insecticides or fungicides with a sprayer that has been used to apply weed killers. Residues of weed killer remaining

Applying Pesticides

Once you have diagnosed your insect and disease problems, you can determine what spray material to use by studying the listings in this chapter, asking at your local garden center, or consulting your county agricultural extension service. Some of these products are sprayed directly onto the plants; others are applied to the ground.

Dormant sprays are applied in early spring before the plants show signs of life. Other formulations are applied throughout the growing season at intervals specified on their labels.

Insecticides, fungicides, and other chemicals are usually available wherever gardening supplies are sold. Many are concentrates that must be diluted with water before you use them. Some of these are liquids. Others are powders or granules that either dissolve in water or go into suspension. Several products come fully diluted and ready to use, and

in the sprayer can harm or kill your plants. To avoid this possibility, it's a good idea to have a separate sprayer for weed killers.

■ Keep your sprayer in good working order by cleaning and maintaining it properly. Nozzle apertures are small and clog easily. After each use, fill the sprayer with plain water and spray it through the nozzle to flush out any residue. If the nozzle becomes clogged, clean it by poking a thin wire through it. If you have a compression sprayer, you may need to apply a light oil to its pump cylinder from time to time to keep it working smoothly.

are convenient if you have only a few plants. For large gardens, however, concentrates are much less expensive.

When working with concentrates, read the label carefully and dilute the substance exactly as directed. Determine how much water you will need and add one-quarter of it to the empty sprayer (hot water works best to dissolve dry materials). Then add the concentrate and mix well by agitating the sprayer. Pour in the remaining water and mix again, making sure the ingredients are fully dissolved or suspended before spraying. The label also tells you how often to repeat treatment. Fungicides are usually needed every 7 to 10 days throughout the growing season. Apply all sprays—including insecticides and fungicides—as directed on the label. Spraying should usually stop when there are no more signs of infestation.

It is possible to mix different products together—for example, an insecticide and a fungicide—so that more than one treatment is applied at a time. Before mixing two products, however, make sure that the directions on both labels recommend this. If the mixing directions seem too complicated, you may choose to apply the products separately. If you are combining a powder and a liquid, add the powder first to one quarter of the total water needed. After mixing, add the liquid before adding the rest of the water. Label

instructions give dilution rates in units (such as tablespoons) per gallon of water. When combining products, dilute each one as if it were the only ingredient; do not increase the total amount of water.

Always mix chemicals outdoors in a well-ventilated area. Do not eat, drink, or smoke while handling them. When using hazardous chemicals (a hazard warning appears on the label), wear gloves, goggles, and protective clothing. As soon as you have finished spraying, remove the safety gear and take a shower. Never reuse a spray solution; mix only what you need for one application. Do not dispose of leftover pesticide in the trash. If you have finished spraying your roses, you can spray the remainder on other plants that are listed on the product label. Always wrap empty containers in newspaper and discard them in the trash; never burn or incinerate them.

Most fungicides work better in water that is slightly acidic. You can determine the pH of your water with a pH test kit available from swimming pool suppliers or by calling the local water authority. If your water is neutral or alkaline, you may wish to adjust it. Adding 1 to 2 tablespoons of white vinegar per gallon will lower its pH toward the slightly acid range (6.0 to 6.5).

Do not buy more pesticides than you will use in a year or two because chemicals can lose their effectiveness over time. Always store products in the original container where children cannot reach them. If possible, lock them away. Also keep them out of the sun and heat.

Ortho's Rose Problem Solver

Planting disease-resistant varieties that are hardy in your climate and keeping them vigorous with good gardening practices such as regular watering and feeding will give you an excellent chance to enjoy a lifetime of healthy, colorful roses with few serious problems. Yet periods of drought and inattention are sometimes difficult to avoid, and they can pave the way for disease. Even the most disease-resistant rose can suffer damage from insects.

This section will help you solve the most common problems you might encounter with growing roses. It is based on *The Ortho Problem Solver*, a professional reference tool for solving plant problems. Here you will find the experience of many experts, most of them members of research universities and cooperative extension services of various states.

To use this rose problem solver, examine pages 122–127 and select the picture that looks most like your problem. The map under the photograph shows how likely the problem is to affect your part of North America. If your region is red, the problem is common or severe. If it is yellow, the problem is occasional or moderate. If it is white, the problem is absent or minor.

The problem section describes the symptom or symptoms. The analysis section describes the organisms or cultural conditions causing the problem. The solution section tells you what you can do immediately to alleviate the problem. Then it tells you what changes you can make in the environment or in your gardening practices to prevent the problem from returning.

When you use chemical sprays make certain that roses are listed on the product label. Always read pesticide labels carefully and follow label directions to the letter.

Flower thrips

Flower thrips damage.

PROBLEM: Young leaves are distorted, and foliage may be flecked with yellow. Flower buds are deformed and often fail to open. Petals of open blossoms, especially those of white or light-colored varieties, are often covered with brown streaks and red spots. If a deformed or streaked flower is pulled apart and shaken over white paper, tiny yellow or brown insects fall out and are easily seen against a white background.

ANALYSIS: Flower thrips *(Frankliniella tritici)* are the most abundant and widely distributed thrips in North America. They live inside the buds and flowers of many garden plants. Both immature and adult thrips feed on sap by rasping the tissue. The injured petal tissue turns brown, and the young expanding leaves become deformed. Injured flower buds usually fail to open. Thrips initially breed on grasses and weeds. When these plants begin to dry up or are harvested, the insects migrate to succulent green ornamental plants. Adults lay eggs by inserting them into plant tissue. A complete life cycle may occur in 2 weeks, so populations can build up rapidly. Most damage to roses occurs in early summer.

SOLUTION: Thrips are difficult to control because they continuously migrate to roses from other plants. Immediately remove and destroy infested buds and blooms. Spray with Ortho® Systemic Insect Killer or Ortho® Bug-B-Gon Multi-Purpose Insect Killer Ready-Spray three times at intervals of 7 to 10 days.

Midges

Rose midge damage.

PROBLEM: The buds are deformed, or black and crisp, and stem tips are dead. This condition develops rapidly. Tiny whitish maggots may be seen feeding at the base of buds or on the stem tips.

ANALYSIS: The rose midge *(Dasineura rhodophaga)* is the larva of a tiny ($\frac{1}{20}$-inch), yellowish fly that appears in mid- or late summer. The females lay their eggs in the growing tips, flower buds, and unfolding leaves, often twenty or thirty eggs to a bud. The eggs hatch in about 2 days, and the maggots feed, causing the tissue and buds to become distorted and blackened. When mature, the larvae drop to the ground to pupate. New adults appear in 5 to 7 days to lay more eggs. When infestations are severe, most or all of the buds and new shoots in an entire rose garden are killed.

SOLUTION: Cut out and destroy infested stem tips and buds, and spray with Ortho® Rose & Flower Insect Killer or Ortho® Orthenex Garden Insect & Disease Control. Repeat the spray if the plant becomes reinfested.

Black spot

Black spot.

PROBLEM: Circular black spots with fringed margins appear on the upper surfaces of the leaves in the spring. The tissue around the spots or the entire leaf may turn yellow, and the infected leaves may drop prematurely. Severely infected plants may lose all of their leaves by midsummer. Flower production is often reduced, and quality is poor.

ANALYSIS: Black spot is caused by a fungus (*Diplocarpon rosae*) that is a severe problem in areas where high humidity or rain is common in spring and summer. The fungus spends the winter on infected leaves and canes. The spores are spread from plant to plant by splashing water and rain. The fungus enters the tissue, forming spots the size of a pinhead. The black spots enlarge, up to ¾ inch, as the fungus spreads; spots may join to form blotches. Twigs may also be infected. Plants are often killed by repeated infection.

SOLUTION: Spray with Ortho® RosePride Rose & Shrub Disease Control or Ortho® Orthenex Garden Insect & Disease Control. Repeat the treatment at intervals of 7 to 10 days for as long as the weather remains wet. Spraying may be omitted during hot, dry spells in summer. Prune off infected canes. Avoid overhead watering. In the fall, rake up and destroy the fallen leaves. After pruning plants during the dormant season, spray with a lime-sulfur solution. The following spring, when new growth starts, begin the spray program again. Plant resistant varieties.

Powdery mildew

Powdery mildew.

PROBLEM: Young leaves, young twigs, and flower buds are covered with a layer of powdery grayish-white material. Infected leaves may be distorted and curled, and many may turn yellow or purplish and drop off. New growth is often stunted, and young canes killed. Infected flower buds don't open properly. In late summer, tiny black dots (spore-producing bodies) may be scattered over the powdery covering like ground pepper.

ANALYSIS: Powdery mildew is a plant disease caused by a fungus (*Sphaerotheca pannosa* var. *rosae*). It is one of the most widespread and serious diseases of roses. The powdery covering consists of fungal strands and spores. The spores are spread by the wind to healthy plants. The fungus depletes plant nutrients, causing distortion and often death of the leaves and canes. It may occur on roses any time when rainfall is low or absent, temperatures are between 70° and 80°F, nighttime relative humidity is high, and daytime relative humidity is low. In areas where there is high rainfall in spring and summer, control may not be needed until the drier months of late summer. Rose varieties differ in their susceptibility to powdery mildew.

SOLUTION: Apply Ortho® RosePride Rose & Shrub Disease Control or Ortho® Orthenex Garden Insect & Disease Control at the first sign of mildew. Repeat the spray at intervals of 7 to 10 days if mildew reappears. Rake up and destroy leaves in the fall.

Rust

Rust.

PROBLEM: Yellow to brown spots, up to ¼ inch in diameter, appear on the upper surfaces of leaves, starting in the spring or late fall. The lower leaves are affected first. On the undersides of leaves are spots or blotches containing a red, orange, or black powdery material that can be scraped off. Infected leaves may become twisted and dry and drop off the plant, or they may remain attached. Twigs may also be infected. Severely infected plants lack vigor.

ANALYSIS: Rose rust is caused by several species of fungi (*Phragmidium* species) that infest only rose plants. Rose varieties differ in their susceptibility to rust. Wind spreads the orange fungal spores to rose leaves. With moisture and moderate temperatures (55° to 75°F), the spores enter the tissue on the undersides of leaves. Spots develop directly above, on the upper surfaces. In the fall, black spores develop in the spots. These spores can survive the winter on dead leaves. In spring, the fungus produces the spores that cause new infections.

SOLUTION: At the first sign of rust, pick off and destroy the infected leaves and spray with Ortho® RosePride Rose & Shrub Disease Control or Ortho® Orthenex Garden Insect & Disease Control. Repeat at intervals of 7 to 14 days for as long as conditions remain favorable for infection. Rake up and destroy infected leaves in the fall. Prune off and destroy infected twigs. Apply a lime-sulfur solution during the dormant season. Plant resistant varieties.

Ortho's Rose Problem Solver
(continued)

Spider mites

Spider mite damage and webbing.

PROBLEM: Leaves are stippled, bronzed, and dirty. A silken webbing may be on the lower surfaces of the leaves or on new growth. Infested leaves often turn brown, curl, and drop off. New leaves may be distorted. Plants are usually weak. To determine if a plant is infested with mites, examine the bottoms of the leaves with a hand lens. Or hold a sheet of white paper underneath an affected leaf and tap the leaf sharply. Minute specks the size of pepper grains will drop to the paper and begin to crawl around. The pests are easily seen against the white background.

ANALYSIS: Spider mites, related to spiders, are major pests of many garden and greenhouse plants. They cause damage by sucking sap from the undersides of leaves. As a result of their feeding, the plant's green leaf pigment disappears, producing the stippled appearance. Spider mite webbing traps cast-off skins and debris, making the plant messy. Many leaves may drop off. Severely infested plants produce few flowers. Mites are active throughout the growing season but are favored by hot, dry weather (70°F and up). By midsummer, they have built up to tremendous numbers.

SOLUTION: Spray with Ortho® Orthenex Garden Insect & Disease Control or Ortho® Systemic Insect Killer when damage is first noticed. Cover the undersides of the leaves thoroughly. Repeat the application two more times at intervals of 7 to 10 days.

Leafhoppers

Damaged leaf. *Inset:* Leafhopper (2× life size).

PROBLEM: Whitish insects, up to ½ inch long, hop and fly away quickly when the plant is touched. The leaves are stippled white. Severely infested plants may be killed.

ANALYSIS: The rose leafhopper *(Edwardsiana rosae)* is a serious pest of roses and apples and infests several ornamental trees as well. It spends the winter as an egg, usually in pimplelike spots on rose canes or on apple bark. When the weather warms in the spring, young leafhoppers emerge and settle on the undersides of leaves. They feed by sucking out the plant sap, which causes the stippling of the leaves. The insects mature, and the females produce a second generation of leafhoppers. Eggs may be deposited in the leaf veins or leaf stems of the rose, or the leafhopper may fly to another woody plant to lay her eggs. This second generation of leafhoppers feeds until fall. By feeding on the leaves and laying eggs in the rose canes, they may kill the plant.

SOLUTION: Spray with Ortho® Systemic Insect Killer or Ortho® Bug-B-Gon Multi-Purpose Insect Killer Concentrate when damage is first noticed. Cover the lower surfaces of leaves thoroughly. Repeat the spray if the plant becomes reinfested.

Viruses

Virus disease.

PROBLEM: Yellow or brown rings or yellow splotches appear on the leaves. The uninfected portions remain dark green. New leaves may be puckered and curling; flower buds may be malformed. Sometimes there are brown rings on the canes. The plants are usually stunted.

ANALYSIS: Several viruses infect roses. The viruses are transmitted when an infected plant is grafted or budded to a healthy one. This generally occurs in the nursery where the plant is grown. Some plants may show symptoms in only a few leaves. The virus is throughout the plant, however, and further symptoms may appear later. Most rose viruses are fairly harmless unless there is extensive yellowing or browning. The virus suppresses the development of chlorophyll, causing the splotches or rings. Food production is reduced, which may result in stunted plant growth.

SOLUTION: No cure is available for virus-infected plants. Rose viruses rarely spread naturally; therefore, only weak plants need to be removed. When purchasing rose bushes, buy only healthy plants from a reputable dealer.

Rose aphids

Rose aphids (8× life size).

PROBLEM: Tiny (⅛-inch), green or pink, soft-bodied insects cluster on leaves, stems, and developing buds. When insects are numerous, flower buds are usually deformed and may fail to open properly. A shiny, sticky substance often coats the leaves. A black, sooty mold may grow on the sticky substance. Ants may be present.

ANALYSIS: Rose aphids (*Macrosiphum rosae*) do little damage in small numbers. Plants can tolerate fairly high populations without much effect. The aphids are extremely prolific, however, and populations can rapidly build up to damaging numbers during the growing season. Damage occurs when the aphid sucks the juices from the rose stems and buds. The aphid is unable to digest all the sugar in the plant sap and excretes the excess in a fluid called *honeydew,* which often drops onto the leaves below. A sooty mold fungus may develop on the honeydew, causing the rose plants to appear black and dirty. Ants feed on the sticky substance and are often present where there is an aphid infestation. When aphid populations are high, flower quality and quantity are reduced.

SOLUTION: Spray with Ortho® Systemic Insect Killer, Ortho® Bug-B-Gon Multi-Purpose Insect Killer Ready-To-Use, or an insecticidal soap when clusters of aphids are noticed. Repeat the treatment if the plant becomes reinfested.

Leafrollers

Rolled leaves.

PROBLEM: Leaves are rolled, usually lengthwise, and tied together with webbing. The rolled leaves are chewed, and the plant may be defoliated. When a rolled leaf is opened, a green caterpillar, ½ to ¾ inch long, may be found inside, surrounded by silky webbing. Flower buds also may be chewed.

ANALYSIS: Several different leafrollers feed on rose leaves and buds. They may also feed on many other plants in the garden. Leafrollers are the larvae of small (up to ¾-inch) brownish moths. The larvae feed on young foliage in the spring, sometimes tunneling into and mining the leaf first. They roll one to several leaves around themselves, tying the leaves together with silken webbing. The leafrollers feed very little once the leaves are rolled. The rolled leaves provide protection from weather, parasites, and chemical sprays. Some leafrollers mature in summer and have several generations during the growing season. Other leafrollers have only one generation per year.

SOLUTION: Spray with Ortho® Bug-B-Gon Multi-Purpose Insect Killer Ready-To-Use, Ortho® Systemic Insect Killer, or the bacterial insecticide *Bacillus thuringiensis* (Bt) in the spring when leaf damage is first noticed. For the insecticide to be most effective, it should be applied before larvae are protected inside the rolled leaves. Check the plant periodically in spring for the first sign of infestation.

Caterpillars

Beet armyworm (life size).

PROBLEM: Holes appear in the leaves and buds. Leaves, buds, and flowers may be entirely chewed off. Worms or caterpillars are feeding on the plants.

ANALYSIS: Many species of these moth or butterfly larvae feed on roses and other garden plants. The adult moths or butterflies of most species start to lay their eggs on garden plants with the onset of warm spring weather. The larvae that emerge from these eggs feed on the leaves, flowers, and buds for 2 to 6 weeks, then pupate in cocoons attached to leaves or structures or buried in the soil. Adult moths and butterflies emerge the following spring.

SOLUTION: Spray infested plants with Ortho® Ready-To-Use Rose & Flower Insect Killer or Ortho® Systemic Insect Killer. The bacterial insecticide *Bacillus thuringiensis* (Bt) may also be used to control caterpillars, especially when they are small.

Ortho's Rose Problem Solver
(continued)

Roseslug

Roseslug (life size).

Scales

Rose scale (life size).

Beetles

Fuller rose beetle (4× life size).

PROBLEM: The upper or lower surfaces of leaves are eaten between the veins; the lacy, 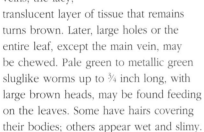 translucent layer of tissue that remains turns brown. Later, large holes or the entire leaf, except the main vein, may be chewed. Pale green to metallic green sluglike worms up to ¾ inch long, with large brown heads, may be found feeding on the leaves. Some have hairs covering their bodies; others appear wet and slimy.

ANALYSIS: Roseslugs are the larvae of black-and-yellow wasps called *sawflies*. The adult wasps appear in spring and lay eggs between the upper and lower surfaces of leaves along the edges with a sawlike organ. Depending on the species, some larvae exude a slimy substance, giving them a sluglike appearance. Others are hairy. The roseslugs begin feeding on one surface of the leaf tissue, skeletonizing it. Later, several species of these slugs chew holes in the leaf or devour it entirely. When they are mature, the larvae drop to the ground, burrow into the soil, and construct cells in which to pass the winter. Some roseslugs pupate, emerge as sawflies, and repeat the cycle two to six times during the growing season. Severely infested roses may be greatly weakened and produce fewer blooms.

SOLUTION: A small number of roseslugs can be picked off by hand. For larger numbers, spray with an insecticide containing *acephate* or *carbaryl* when damage is first noticed. Repeat as necessary if the rose becomes reinfested.

PROBLEM: White, cottony masses; brown or black crusty bumps; or clusters of flattened 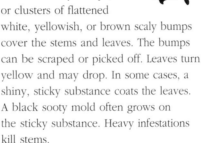 white, yellowish, or brown scaly bumps cover the stems and leaves. The bumps can be scraped or picked off. Leaves turn yellow and may drop. In some cases, a shiny, sticky substance coats the leaves. A black sooty mold often grows on the sticky substance. Heavy infestations kill stems.

ANALYSIS: Many types of scales infest roses. They lay eggs on the leaves or canes, and in spring to midsummer the young scales, called *crawlers*, settle on the leaves and twigs. These small (¹⁄₁₀-inch), soft-bodied young feed by sucking sap from the plant. The legs usually atrophy, and with some types, a shell develops over the body. The types of scales that do not develop shells are conspicuous. Females of the cottony cushion scale are covered with a white, cottony egg sac containing up to 2,500 eggs. Scales covered with a shell are less noticeable. Their shell often blends in with the plant, and the eggs are hidden beneath their covering. Some species of scales are unable to digest fully all the sugar in the plant sap, and they excrete the excess in a fluid called *honeydew*.

SOLUTION: Control with Ortho® Systemic Insect Killer or Ortho® Bug-B-Gon Multi-Purpose Insect Killer Concentrate when the young are active. To control overwintering insects, treat with Ortho® Volck Oil Spray in the spring.

PROBLEM: Holes appear in the flowers and flower buds; open flowers may be entirely eaten. Affected buds often fail to open, or they open deformed. Stem tips may be chewed, or the leaves may be notched or riddled with holes. Red, green-spotted, brownish, or metallic green beetles up to ½ inch long, are sometimes seen on the flowers or foliage.

ANALYSIS: Several beetles infest roses. They may destroy the ornamental value of the plant by seriously damaging the flowers and foliage. The insects usually spend the winter as larvae in the soil or as adults in plant debris on the ground. In late spring or summer, mature beetles fly to roses and feed on the flowers, buds, and sometimes leaves. Punctured flower buds usually fail to open, and flowers that do open are often devoured. Many beetles feed at night, so their damage may be all that is noticed. Female beetles lay their eggs in the soil or in flowers in late summer or fall. The emerging larvae crawl down into the soil to spend the winter, or they mature and pass the winter as adults. The larvae of some beetles feed on plant roots before maturing in the fall or spring.

SOLUTION: Spray with Ortho® Systemic Insect Killer or Ortho® Ready-To-Use Rose & Flower Insect Killer when damage is first noticed. Repeat the spray if the rose becomes reinfested.

Crown gall

Crown gall.

Stem canker and dieback

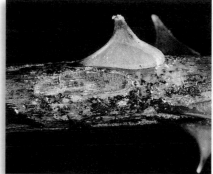

Stem cankers.

Borers

Carpenter bee larvae (3× life size).

PROBLEM: Large, corky galls up to several inches in diameter appear at the base of the plant and on the stems and roots. The galls are rounded, with rough, irregular surfaces, and may be dark and cracked. Plants with numerous galls are weak; growth is slowed and leaves turn yellow. Branches or the entire plant may die back. Plants with only a few galls often show no other symptoms.

ANALYSIS: Crown gall is a plant disease caused by a soil-inhabiting bacterium (*Agrobacterium tumefaciens*) that infects many ornamentals and fruit trees in the garden. The bacteria are often brought to a garden on the stems or roots of an infected plant and spread with contaminated pruning tools and soil. The bacteria enter the plant through wounds in the roots or the stem. They produce a compound that stimulates rapid cell growth in the plant, causing gall formation on the roots, crown, and sometimes branches. The galls may disrupt the flow of water and nutrients up the roots and stems, weakening and stunting the top of the plant. Galls do not usually cause the death of the plant.

SOLUTION: Crown gall cannot be eliminated from a plant. An infected plant may survive for many years, however. To improve its appearance, prune out and destroy galled stems. Disinfect pruning shears after each cut. Destroy severely infected plants. The bacteria will remain in the soil for 2 to 3 years. If you wish to replace the infected roses soon, select other plants that are resistant to crown gall.

PROBLEM: Yellowish, reddish, or brown sunken areas develop on the canes. The sunken areas may have a purple margin, or they may be cracked. The leaves on affected canes are sometimes spotted, yellow, or wilting. Stems may die back.

ANALYSIS: Several fungi cause stem cankers on roses, with the *Coniothyrium* species being most common. During wet or humid weather, the fungi enter the plant at a wound caused by the thorns, or at a cut stem. A canker develops and expands through the tissue in all directions. The fungus may cut off the flow of nutrients and water through the stem, causing the leaves to wilt or yellow and the twigs to die back. Rose plants that are infected with black spot or in a weakened condition are more susceptible to invasion by stem canker fungi.

SOLUTION: Cut out and destroy cankered canes at least 5 inches below the infected area. Disinfect pruning tools after each cut. After pruning, spray the canes with a fungicide containing lime sulfur. Sprays aimed at controlling black spot will help control canker. Or spray with Ortho® Garden Disease Control starting in the spring. Repeat every 7 to 10 days for as long as the weather is wet or humid. Keep the plants vigorous by feeding, watering, and pruning properly.

PROBLEM: Several or all of the larger canes and stems wilt and die. If the bark is peeled back or if dying stems are sliced open, white to yellowish worms or legless grubs up to ¾ inch long may be revealed. Affected stems may be swollen at the base.

ANALYSIS: Many kinds of insects bore into rose stems. They include certain sawflies, beetles, horntail wasps, and solitary bees. Some of these attack old, weakened plants or plants that are under stress from recent transplant or improper care; such borers often attack at the base of the plant. Other borers attack healthy rose plants, either traveling in a spiral pattern just under the bark or burrowing down through the center of the rose stems. Most rose borers produce one generation per year.

SOLUTION: Prune and destroy infested rose stems. Make the cut several inches below the point where the stem is wilted or swollen. If an insect has tunneled a hole through the center of the stem, keep cutting the stem lower to the ground until you find and destroy the insect or see the end of the tunnel. If this is a problem year after year, seal rose canes immediately after pruning with Ortho® Pruning Sealer or with a thumbtack to prevent borers from penetrating the soft tissue in the center of the stem. Keep rose plants in good health.

Winter Protection

Protect the cold-sensitive bud union by mounding soil over the bases of the canes in fall. To avoid exposing tender roots near the surface, do not take soil from around the plant.

In all but the mildest climates, most roses need some measure of winter protection. The degree of protection your roses need depends on how cold your area gets and on how hardy your roses are. The zone map on page 244 shows the distribution of average minimum temperatures within the continental United States.

Hardiness is the ability of a plant to maintain dormancy and not die during cold weather. When a plant is dormant, it is in a state of suspended animation, so to speak, with no growth occurring above or below ground. Tender plants are those that cannot adapt in this way to the cold.

Roses vary widely in their degree of hardiness. Although no one has ever compiled a zone-by-zone hardiness rating for each variety, some generalizations can be made. Typically, old garden roses, miniatures, and shrubs are inclined to be hardy whereas many teas, Chinas, noisettes, and modern bush roses are tender. If you live in Zones 9 to 11, where it rarely freezes, none of your roses will need winter protection. But if you live in Zones 1 to 8, where freezing is common, some or all of your roses will need buffering against the cold, depending on the zone and the type of roses you are growing. See the list on the opposite page.

The "Gallery of Roses" starting on page 168 provides a hardiness zone range for each variety listed. But bear in mind that the survival of individual plants will vary to some degree with the microclimate. For instance, a rose growing against a sunny southern wall may thrive without winter protection even if similar roses in your zone normally need it. If you live by a lake, winter winds sweeping across it may make your roses more vulnerable to damage from the cold.

Natural winter protection

Perhaps the best shelter against winter extremes is the one that nature provides—a thick blanket of snow. Snow keeps temperatures beneath it

HARDY ROSES FOR COLD CLIMATES

Many old garden roses, species, shrubs, and miniature roses are hardy. In addition, the following are especially hardy for their class:

'Blanc Double de Coubert'
Carefree Beauty ('BUCbi')
Carefree Wonder ('Meipitac')
'Distant Drums'
'Dortmund'
'Earth Song'
Escapade ('HARpade')
'F. J. Grootendorst'
'Frau Dagmar Hartopp'
'Golden Unicorn'
'Hansa'
'Henry Hudson'
'Henry Kelsey'
'Jeanne LaJoie'
'Jens Munk'
'John Cabot'
'Lavender Lassie'
'Little Darling'
Marie-Victorin ('AC Marie Victorin')
'Martin Frobisher'
'Morden Amorette'
'Morden Blush'
'Morden Snowbeauty'
Mountbatten ('HARmantelle')
'Nearly Wild'
'New Dawn'
'Paul's Himalayan Musk Rambler'
'Prairie Flower'
'Prairie Harvest'
'Stanwell Perpetual'
'The Fairy'
'Therese Bugnet'
'William Baffin'

from dipping too far below freezing and from rising so high or so fast that plants are fooled into premature growth. Snow also blocks the wind, which can break branches and rob moisture from the canes and the soil. But snow can also be destructive, its weight breaking or deforming the branches of larger roses. After a snowfall, brush off branches that are sagging. If you live where heavy snowfall is common, you may want to tie large plants together with string to support them against the weight of the snow.

Additional winter protection

In most areas snow is neither deep nor frequent enough to provide constant insulation, so you need to rely on additional means of winter protection. These include covering plants with an insulating material, burying them partially or completely, or, in the case of container-grown roses, moving them indoors before the frost. The time to apply winter protection to outdoor plants is in fall, right after the first normal hard freeze has shocked them into dormancy. Any covering you apply should remain in place until spring and should be removed gradually if possible as warming accelerates to reduce potential losses from an unexpected late freeze. When removing a winter covering, be very careful to not break new canes that may have emerged since you last saw the entire plant.

Winter makes demands on both roses and gardeners. In cold climates, it may be easier to grow only cold-hardy varieties that can survive without special protection.

Winter Protection
(continued)

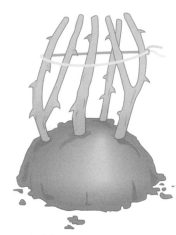

ROSE-CONE FOR WINTER PROTECTION

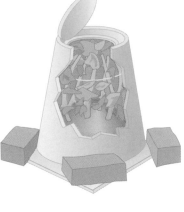

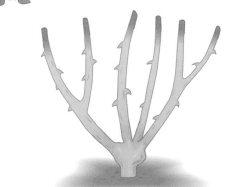

Trim, defoliate, and mound up the bush with about 12 to 24 inches of soil and mulch. Tie up canes, place protective cone, and weigh it down. After last frost, uncover to reveal dieback, which should be pruned off.

Mounding soil

The traditional method of protecting roses over the winter is to mound soil over the bases of the canes, to a height of about 12 inches, to protect the frost-vulnerable bud union. It is important that the mounding soil be brought from another area of the garden because removing soil from the immediate vicinity of the plant will expose its feeder roots to the cold air, damaging or killing them.

Winter mulch

Although highly effective, the mounding technique requires a lot of work, as you must move soil into the garden in fall and remove it in spring. A less arduous method is to apply to the same depth a layer of lightweight, nonabsorbent organic material, sometimes called winter mulch. Good materials for winter mulch are shredded oak leaves, straw, or evergreen limbs from unsold or discarded Christmas trees that are available after the holidays. When spring comes you can either remove the

MULCHING FOR WINTER PROTECTION

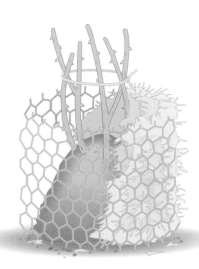

Using a collar of chicken wire, mound the rose bush with soil and mulch. Next, fill in the space between the canes with leaves, straw, and mulch. Any canes protruding from the chicken wire collar may die back and can be removed during pruning. Remember, this is not necessary for areas in southern Zone 8 and higher.

mulch or work it into the soil to improve it. The main drawback of this method is that it will usually not provide enough protection in areas colder than Zone 6.

Rose cones

In Zones 1 through 5, a useful technique is to cover roses with special caps known as rose cones, which are sold at large garden centers and hardware stores. Made of thick-walled expandable polystyrene, rose cones are usually rounded or multisided containers that taper toward the top and have flanges at the bottom that can be weighted or pinned to the soil. Some have solid tops; others have covers that can be removed on warm days to keep plants from breaking dormancy too soon. Venting the cones with holes provides additional air circulation that may reduce the growth of molds.

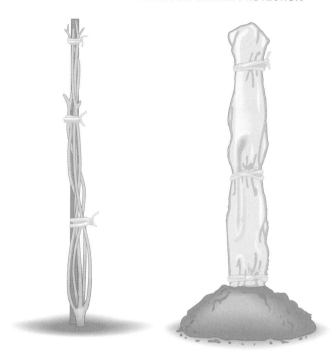

Trim, defoliate, and tie canes up into a neat vertical bundle. Wrap the bundle with burlap, canvas, or a similar fabric (never plastic), and tie down for security. Mound up the base of the plant with a mixture of mulch and soil.

Rose cones come in two sizes: an economical 12-inch height and an 18-inch height for gardeners who don't want to prune their roses excessively to fit underneath. However, even with the taller cones, larger plants need to be cut back somewhat to fit. Tying rose canes together with string before covering them with a cone also helps them fit better. Rose cones can be stacked and stored over the summer and reused from year to year.

BURYING A TREE ROSE FOR WINTER PROTECTION

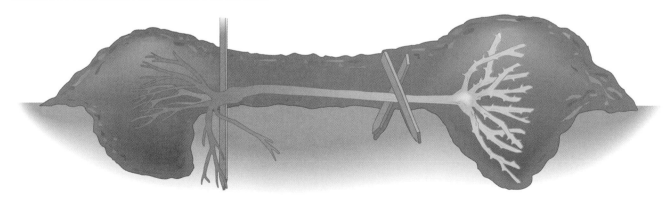

Trim and defoliate the bush and partially uncover the root system to allow the tree to lay on its side. Hold the entire plant in place with crossed stakes, and cover it with a mixture of soil and mulch.

The Pleasure of Roses

Growing roses can be a satisfying hobby, but many rose lovers delight in finding other ways to spend time with their favorite flower. Arranging, exhibiting, and photographing roses pass many enjoyable hours. Roses can also be preserved and included in recipes. Here is a potpourri of ideas for enjoying roses, both in and out of the garden.

The elation you feel as you walk through your rose garden, savoring its sights and fragrances, might seem to be pleasure enough. But your enjoyment of roses can go far beyond mere appreciation as you discover where else they can lead you. If you want to indulge your creative side, you can learn to use roses in arrangements. If you desire recognition for gardening skills, you may wish to exhibit your roses. If your interest is crafts, you'll find roses quite accommodating. Many unusual recipes feature roses, and roses can be preserved in dried arrangements or fragrant potpourris.

If you enjoy photography, you may want to combine this with your love of roses. And as you plan your vacation, you might consider heading for one of the rose festivals that take place annually around the country.

Whatever your interest, roses can take you in a new, productive, and stimulating direction. This chapter describes some of the many paths you can explore.

Potpourri is easy to make and a delightful way to enjoy the pleasure of roses.

A simple collection of modern English roses and old garden roses illustrates the ease of blending color and form into a masterpiece for the indoors: Golden Celebration (cupped yellow), Evelyn (flat, creamy white), 'Baronne Prevost' (quartered, medium pink), and 'Salet' (light pink).

Roses as Cut Flowers

Many gardeners like to enjoy their roses twice—first in the garden, then indoors as cut flowers. By choosing the right roses, cutting them at the proper time of day, and conditioning them after cutting, you can enjoy your cut roses for the longest possible time—up to five days or more after cutting.

When to cut roses

In general, the more petals a rose has, the slower it will open and the longer it will last. Thus the best roses to use as cut flowers are the fully double varieties. Flowers with fewer petals open quickly and need to be replaced more often. Old garden and shrub roses generally wilt rapidly because their petals lack the substance (thickness and sturdiness) of modern roses and thus do not make good cut flowers.

In addition to the form of a rose, you should consider its blooming stage. A rose will last longer if it is cut when the sepals have separated from the bud and have turned downward, and when the bud has softened but before the stamens are visible. If you squeeze the bud and it is still hard, wait a day or two before cutting it, or it may not open after it is cut.

Roses should be cut from a well-watered plant, late in the afternoon when the sugar and nutrient content of the plant is highest. This provides the bloom with ample energy to develop and open normally, and to stay open longer without wilting. During hot weather, when there is chance that a flower may be dehydrated by late afternoon, water the plant well several hours before cutting.

How to cut roses

Using pruning shears or flower-cutting shears, cut the stem at a 45-degree angle, no shorter than just above the first five-leaflet leaf below the flower. You may cut a stem as long as you like, provided that at least two sets of leaves are left on the main stem to act as food producers for future growth and flowering. Carry a bucket of water with you into the garden so that you can place the cut stems in the water immediately. The flowers will last much longer if the uptake of water is not interrupted for too long and the stems do not dry out. It is all right to submerge the leaves temporarily as they too will absorb moisture.

Although you will not harm a plant if you cut off all its flowers at one time, you may want to leave a few on the plant for garden color. Cutting roses, whether new or faded, encourages the plants to grow and rebloom quickly.

After you have cut the roses, recut the stems at a slant, underwater, to permit maximum water absorption.

How to condition roses

Place the bucket of water containing the cut roses in a cool, dark place, such as the basement, to allow the roses to become conditioned before arranging them in a vase. Conditioning roses allows them to get used to being detached from the plants and slows down the respiratory rate of the leaves. Leave them for at least several hours or preferably overnight.

You can condition cut flowers in a refrigerator, as long as the refrigerator is intended only for roses and not for food. Many types of fruit stored in a refrigerator release ethylene gas, a ripening agent that causes cut flowers to open prematurely.

Water for cut flowers is best if it is slightly acidic because acid breaks up air bubbles in water by neutralizing the carbon dioxide gas. Air bubbles may clog capillaries in the stem and prevent water from reaching the flowers and foliage. Water also travels more quickly up a stem when the water is acidic. If you're not sure whether your water is acidic, ask your water company. If it is not acidic, add lemon juice to acidify it. You should not use artificially softened water; it contains sodium, which is toxic to plants. In most cases, use cold water; it slows down the respiratory rate of the leaves. However, if the flowers have wilted because they have been out of water too long or because the stems were not

GOOD ROSES FOR LONG-STEMMED CUTTING

Barbra Streisand ('WEKquaneze')	Moonstone ('WEKcryland')
Bride's Dream ('KORoyness')	New Zealand ('MACgenev')
Crystalline ('ARObipy')	Peter Mayle ('MEIzincaro')
Elina ('DICjana')	'Royal Highness'
Jardins de Bagatelle ('MEImafris')	Toulouse Lautrec ('MEIrevolt')
Kardinal (KORlingo')	Valencia ('KOReklia')
Love & Peace ('BALpeace')	Veteran's Honor ('JACopper')

cut underwater soon enough and the stem ends have become clogged, hot water will revive them faster than cold water. The stems absorb hot water more quickly.

How to prepare roses for the vase

Before placing the roses in a vase, remove any leaves and thorns that will be below the water after arranging, because these will quickly disintegrate, foul the water, and shorten the life of the cut flowers. Thorns can be snapped off by hand or with a special thorn-stripping tool sold by florist supply stores. Then clean the remaining foliage with soap and water if necessary to remove dirt or spray residue,

and make the leaves shine by rubbing with a paper towel, a soft cloth, or a nylon stocking. If any of the leaves are ripped or chewed, they can be manicured with small scissors.

MORE TIPS: If the roses you have picked are fragrant, handle them gently. The petals of fragrant roses have more scent-emitting glands than do those of less-fragrant kinds, and they therefore tend to bruise more easily.

To lengthen the life of your cut roses, always use a clean container for the flowers, and add a floral preservative to the water. Because they are acidic, contain sugar, and include a bacteria-retarding agent, floral preservatives provide some nutrients and restrain the growth of bacteria

that will shorten the life of the flowers. These preservatives can be purchased at a flower shop. If you can't buy one, mix any clear citrus-based soft drink containing sugar with three parts water; or mix 2 tablespoons lemon juice, 1 tablespoon sugar, and ½ teaspoon household bleach in 1 quart of water.

Keep the container filled with water to reduce the chance that it will evaporate or be consumed by the roses. If possible, change the water daily, recutting the stems underwater each time. Or check the level every day and add water as needed. To prolong the life of cut roses, keep cool and away from drafts, air-conditioners, radiators, and full sun.

Display the splendor of single rose stems in simple vases. When enjoying blooms from first-year roses, it's usually better to cut short stems.

Arranging Roses

Arranging your roses is a matter of taste. An arrangement can be as simple as one long-stemmed rose in a bud vase or a large flower floating in a shallow bowl, or as elaborate as a massive arrangement of hundreds of flowers.

You can display your roses in all-rose arrangements or combine them with other flowers from the garden. Try asters, astilbe, chrysanthemums, delphinium, gladiolus, iris, lilies, peonies, snapdragons, stock, or veronica, depending on the season and the color harmony you wish to create. Foliage, too, can come from plants other than roses. For a tall, spiked look, use the leaves of iris, gladiolus, or canna. For more graceful, lower arrangements, use the variegated leaves of hosta.

Old roses balance their limited array of colors with an astonishing variety of perfumes, from musk and citrus to spice and pure rose.

After cutting roses and other flowers and greenery in the garden, assemble everything you need to make arrangements: vases and bowls, florist foam, pinholders, flower-cutting shears, florist wire and tape, gloves for handling thorny stems, and a thorn stripper.

For a delicate look, snip a few fronds of ferns. Broad-leaved evergreen leaves can impart shininess; for a silvery look, try a few stems of dusty miller or artemisia.

The flowers and foliage you combine with roses should be appropriate for the type of arrangement. For example, peonies and irises can be used in formal arrangements whereas daisies look better in informal ones. Spiked foliage is often used in modern designs because of its strong lines. Similarly, curved branches of plants such as flowering cherries are often incorporated in oriental designs, with or without foliage. (See Styles of Design on pages 140–141.)

Containers and accessories

When choosing a container for your arrangement, keep two things in mind. First, the container should be in proportion to the height of the roses: Long-stemmed roses call for a tall, elegant container whereas roses with shorter stems are delightful in a low container, a rounded teapot, or a sugar bowl. Second, consider the material from which the container is made. Formal arrangements look more refined in china, silver, or glass containers whereas informal arrangements are appealing in earthenware vessels or straw baskets. You can arrange miniature roses in any small container you happen to have around—a thimble, a shot glass, a perfume bottle, or a seashell, for example.

Many arrangements are made without vases or containers and are instead

placed in shallow trays, bowls, or other vessels. To anchor the flower and foliage stems and to provide them with a source of water, set them in either floral foam or pinholders. Both are available from crafts stores and florist supply stores.

Floral foam looks like soft Styrofoam; it is sold in blocks that can be cut with a knife to the correct size. In addition to holding the stems in place, it absorbs and stores water to supply them with moisture. If you use foam, be sure to soak it completely in water before plunging the stems into it. The disadvantage of foam is that it can be reused only once or twice.

A pinholder consists of a thicket of pointed pins sticking up from the bottom of a small receptacle that can hold water. Floral foam and pinholders can be used with dried as well as fresh arrangements; in the case of dried arrangements, of course, you would not need to worry about watering.

When making an arrangement with foam, cut the foam to size according to the number of stems to be inserted into it, soak it in water, and fasten it to the container or vessel with floral tape. When using a pinholder, first anchor it to the vessel with floral clay before inserting the stems. Both floral tape and floral clay are available at florist supply stores. Whichever anchoring device you use, be sure to keep the water supply steady by making sure the foam is always moist or the pinholder is filled. Because foam and pinholders can dry out quickly, be sure to check the water frequently. If the

A moss-lined wire urn makes a surprising "container" for a big bouquet of roses—with an ordinary jar full of water tucked inside the urn. The moss hides the jar, and the arrangement looks good in any setting.

container does not hide the anchoring device, conceal it with foliage, pebbles, marbles, shells, or other accessories.

Floral wire is thin and flexible and is often wrapped around stems to strengthen them or to give them a curved shape. Wire can also be used as a substitute for a stem if you dry flower heads only. (See Dried Flowers on pages 148–149.) The wire can be wrapped in a self-adhesive green tape to camouflage it. Both wire and tape are available at flower shops and florist supply stores. To cut stems while making arrangements, you can use pruning shears or flower-cutting shears. You can strip thorns off by hand or with a thorn-stripping tool.

Arranging Roses
(continued)

A cut glass vase holds peppermint-striped 'Variegata di Bologna' (Bourbon) and rich pink 'Madame Berkeley' (Tea).

Elements of design

Although there are many styles of flower arranging, all employ the same basic elements to create an appealing result. These elements are space, line, form, pattern, texture, and color. A successful flower arranger builds with these elements to achieve inspiring balance, dominance, contrast, rhythm, scale, and proportion.

Although a flower arranger may not be consciously aware of these components, they are important ingredients in any harmonious and expressive arrangement.

SPACE refers to the height, width, and depth to be filled by the flowers and their container. Before creating an arrangement, imagine a picture frame around it and make the proportions of the frame fit the intended setting. For example, an arrangement for a serving table or atop a mantle should be horizontal, whereas one for a pedestal should be vertical.

LINE is the route your eyes follow from one part of an arrangement to another. It may be long or short, straight or curved, delicate or bold, horizontal or vertical; but line must be there. A horizontal line imparts an air that is restful and static. A vertical line is dramatic and inspiring. Diagonal lines create a feeling of surprise or movement. Curved lines are graceful.

FORM is the shape with which an arrangement occupies space. A flower arrangement is a kind of sculpture, and as such it must harmoniously occupy its setting. For example, an arrangement for the center of a table might have great depth, whereas one placed against a wall might be relatively flat. The form of an arrangement also depends on whether it will be viewed from all sides or seen only from the front.

PATTERN is the organization of shapes and colors in an arrangement. A pattern is established by using the same color, size, or variety of flower in several places or by placing the flowers of a small arrangement in a structured grouping.

TEXTURE encompasses the tactile and visual qualities not only of your roses but also of the container, the foliage, and the other flowers that may be present. Textures can harmonize or contrast. For example, a delicate arrangement of pale roses with ferns harmonizes well with a fine porcelain vase, whereas a bold arrangement of brightly colored roses, black-eyed Susans, and coarse foliage contrasts well with a black metallic bowl.

COLOR is one of the most important elements of design because it engenders a strong emotional reaction. Red, hot pink, bright yellow, and orange are dazzling and exciting; mauve, pale pink, pale yellow, and white are more calming. Formal arrangements are best made with a single color or with closely related subtle colors; informal arrangements can use a kaleidoscope of brighter colors. An appealing technique is to combine complementary colors, such as violet with yellow, or blue with orange. The split complementary harmony of blue with red or pink is also attractive. Try to fit the colors to the mood of the occasion.

If the arrangement is intended to be viewed from a distance, colors that reflect the most light are the best choices for it. These include bright red, yellow, orange, pink, and white. Blue and violet appear as shadows or voids from 15 feet or more away. Dusky and subdued colors, such as smoky whites, salmon, and dusty pinks, do not project well because they absorb more light than they reflect.

Accomplished floral arrangers use the elements described above to achieve balance, dominance, contrast, rhythm, scale, and proportion.

BALANCE is not necessarily symmetry; rather it is equilibrium, visual stability. To achieve balance, place buds at the top of the arrangement and large open flowers at the bottom. Use lighter colors at the top, and weight the bottom with darker colors. If the container has an irregular shape, skew the arrangement in the same fashion.

DOMINANCE is control of the design by one of its elements: space, line, form, pattern, texture, or color. A design that lacks dominance is nondescript; it makes no definitive statement. After you have decided on a theme for your arrangement, select one of its elements and emphasize it, making all of the other elements work with it.

CONTRAST is the placement of elements to emphasize their difference—for example, tight buds with open flowers or tall stems with short ones.

RHYTHM, a lively interaction of the parts, is also the hallmark of a good design. In a rhythmical arrangement the eye is constantly moving from element to element, savoring what it sees.

SCALE refers to the size of an arrangement. Large arrangements provide drama; small ones are good for close viewing or intimate effects.

PROPORTION is the relationship between the scale of an object's parts and the space it occupies. Good proportion means good fit—internally, between the scale of the flowers, foliage, and container used for an arrangement, as well as externally, between the scale of the finished arrangement and the scale of its setting.

Arranging Roses
(continued)

Styles of design

There are probably as many styles of flower arranging as there are people who arrange them. But over the years a number of traditional styles have evolved. The most common styles used by arrangers in the United States, and displayed at rose and flower shows, are mass, Williamsburg, Victorian, line, line-mass, Hogarth curve, modern, and Asian. These are described here as models that you can vary according to your taste, mood, and the materials you have to work with.

A MASS ARRANGEMENT, as its name implies, consists of a large number of flowers massed together in one container. It may be formal or informal. Large mass arrangements in fine china vases are generally seen at formal occasions and in formally decorated rooms whereas smaller mass arrangements in low bowls are often centerpieces in informal settings. To achieve the correct balance and proportion, the height of a mass arrangement must be one and a half times the height and width of the container added together. Otherwise the arrangement will look too "squat."

A mass design is symmetrical and takes a geometrical shape, such as a fan, a pyramid, a globe, or an oval. To avoid a hodgepodge effect, have in mind a well-coordinated color scheme and a structured pattern.

A WILLIAMSBURG ARRANGEMENT is a type of mass arrangement that originated in colonial times and can be seen extensively throughout the restored homes in Williamsburg, the historical district of Virginia's former capital. Williamsburg arrangements are usually large and are used in formal settings. The key to making a good Williamsburg arrangement is to use roses and containers that are in keeping with the colonial era; for example, orange hybrid teas would be out of place because these did not exist in colonial days. Old garden roses would naturally be more fitting, and you would likely see them in a pewter vase. Williamsburg arrangements can take the symmetrical shape of any mass arrangement, with oval or pyramidal shapes the most common. In addition to being symmetrical in form, the colors of one side mirror those on the other.

A VICTORIAN MASS ARRANGEMENT, from Victorian England, is similar to a Williamsburg arrangement but has its colors placed in asymmetrical drifts rather than in a mirrored pattern. Like a Williamsburg arrangement, it is formal in character, and any flowers other than roses should also be formal in appearance. Containers are ornate, such as highly decorated china vases or urns on pedestals.

When making any type of mass arrangement, first decide what shape and size it will take. Then place the flowers to form the outer perimeter of the design. Next, fill in the rest of the roses, other flowers, and foliage.

LINE AND LINE-MASS ARRANGEMENTS are both distinguished chiefly by a strong, simple line. This is created by either plant material or accessories, such as small statuettes. Line arrangements use only three to five flowers; line-mass arrangements may use many more. A line arrangement has very little depth and is placed against a wall rather than displayed as a centerpiece; a line-mass arrangement is somewhat deeper and can be used in either setting. The container should be small enough that it does not distract from the line; it can actually be a part of the line. Because only a few flowers may be used in either arrangement, it takes practice to learn how to position them in a graceful line rather than in a stilted row.

THE HOGARTH CURVE ARRANGEMENT, named for the 18th-century English artist William Hogarth, is a type of line-mass arrangement that features an S-shape curve. A typical container is a pedestaled vase, which allows the lower portion of the S-curve to extend below the container. It is usually placed against a wall rather than displayed as a centerpiece. Its swoop of line is exciting, emphasizing the fullest part of the design, usually where the stems emanate from the container. To create the curves necessary in this type of arrangement, you may need to wire some of the stems so that they can be bent to conform to the S-shape.

MODERN, OR ABSTRACT, 20th-century designs are bold, strong, and interpretive of a mood or feeling. Depending on the size and shape of a modern design, it can range from a centerpiece to a large accent piece in a room. Empty space is a deliberate part of the design, so typically this type of arrangement uses few flowers. Unlike traditional styles, where pattern and color are the more dominant elements, modern designs are held together more by their line. Containers match the theme of the design; for example, if the designer is creating an interpretation of motion, the containers could be hubcaps or air filters.

ASIAN DESIGNS come principally from the Japanese. There are several major styles, all employing asymmetrical lines that are simple, clean, and symbolic. Asian designs usually consist of three or fewer flowers although more can be added as long as there is an odd number. Containers are generally shallow bowls or dishes. Asian designs can be placed against a wall or can serve as a table accent.

The type of design you follow depends on your taste, the decor of the setting in which the arrangement will be placed, and the formality of the occasion. The color of the flowers should harmonize with the setting and fit the mood; for example, bright colors are appropriate for a child's birthday party and subdued colors for formal dinner parties. In large mass arrangements, some flowers can be removed as they fade without disturbing the overall design, but the arrangement should be started anew as the majority of the flowers fade.

Flower arranging is an art, not a science, even though structured principles are applied to it. Improvisation is more important than following strict rules. With a little trial and error, you'll soon be creating lovely arrangements to use in your home or to give to friends on special occasions.

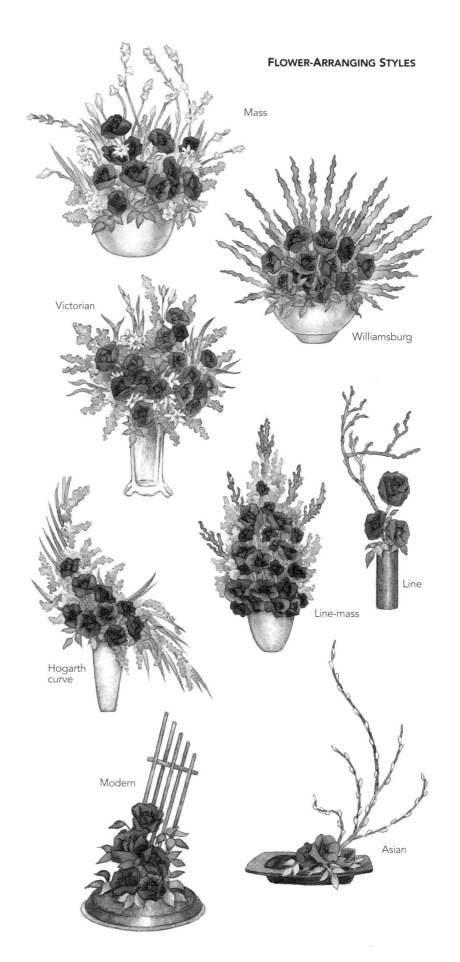

Mass

Williamsburg

Victorian

Line

Line-mass

Hogarth curve

Modern

Asian

The American Rose Society

Headquartered in Shreveport, Louisiana, the 20,000-member American Rose Society offers a wide range of member services throughout the United States, including access to a network of 2,800 local rose experts, as well as lists that rank and rate new roses.

People who enjoy the same hobby inevitably get together to discuss their activities, exchange information, and enjoy their hobby even more through their common bond. The American Rose Society (ARS) is a national organization with a membership of about 20,000. Founded in 1892 as an association of commercial rose growers, the ARS today is made up primarily of amateur rose enthusiasts. It is the only national rose association, and among flower-oriented groups its size is exceeded only by that of the American Orchid Society.

Joining the ARS is a step to becoming a better rose grower. As a member you receive a monthly magazine, *The American Rose,* which provides up-to-date information about rose care, new varieties, landscaping, and other topics. Yearly the magazine publishes the winning entries from its photographic slide contest.

Another publication that members receive is the *American Rose Annual,* a book that includes descriptions of all new roses that have been registered with the ARS during the past year as well as articles on various aspects of rose growing. Each annual contains a section called "Roses in Review," a compilation of ratings and comments about new rose varieties from gardeners all over the country. This section's "show me" attitude makes it an invaluable guide in weighing the promotional claims of nursery catalogs.

Members also receive the yearly "Handbook for Selecting Roses," a buyer's guide to more than 3,000 commonly available varieties. Each rose in the handbook is assigned a rating from 0 to 10, based on a survey of ARS members taken every three years. This small booklet contains a wealth of information, such as type of rose and color, to help you select new varieties for your garden.

The ARS maintains a lending library at its headquarters, and as a member you are entitled to borrow any of its more than 5,000 books, films, video tapes, and slide shows on roses, by mail or in person. Write for a description of what's available. On the grounds of the Shreveport, Louisiana, headquarters is a magnificent rose garden; for the address, see page 243.

Twice each year the ARS holds national conventions. Each convention features a rose show, garden tours, educational programs, and good "rose talk." Many professional hybridizers and rose producers attend, giving you a sneak preview of what's to come in the world of roses.

In addition to the conventions, the ARS sponsors tours and cruises to faraway places, and seminars on special topics. Once every three years members join with rose growers from all over the world at the meeting of the International Federation of Rose Societies. The meetings are held at a different location each time and are organized by volunteers from the host country.

The ARS maintains a number of committees to help members better know and grow roses. Staffed by volunteers from all over the country, these committees specialize in a variety of subjects. For instance, the Trial Grounds committee tests new varieties of large roses at the ARS gardens in Shreveport. The Miniature Rose Testing committee evaluates new miniatures in Shreveport and at several other locations. The New Products Evaluation committee reports on new insecticides, fungicides, sprayers, and other garden products. The Rose Registration committee approves all new variety names submitted by commercial hybridizers to make sure the name has not been used before and, if it has, that the older rose is out of commerce. You can receive a detailed listing of these and other committees by contacting ARS headquarters.

One of the ARS's most valuable activities is the Consulting Rosarian program, in which outstanding rose growers who are active ARS members serve as advisers-at-large to the rose-growing community. Consulting Rosarians share their knowledge and enthusiasm by giving talks, opening their gardens to visitors, and traveling to neighboring gardens to give advice.

If you are like many people who have become dedicated to the hobby of rose growing, eventually you may wish to exhibit your roses at ARS-sponsored rose shows. (See the next section for details.) And some ardent exhibitors go on to the next step by becoming a judge. The ARS trains and accredits rose judges from among its members in all areas of the country so that there will be no shortage of qualified judges for local rose shows.

In addition to the ARS's national activities, the 18 regional districts and their scores of local chapters sponsor events of their own. Every district has a yearly convention that includes a rose show, programs, tours, awards, and social events. Most districts publish newsletters, and many hold winter meetings to keep

enthusiasm high while roses hibernate under the snow. Many local chapters within each district are also active, sponsoring their own monthly meetings, newsletters, shows, and demonstrations. Their members often help out at public gardens; answer questions at flower shows, garden centers, and libraries; and do whatever else they can to foster interest in roses.

If you want to join a local rose group, which is separate from membership in the ARS, there is probably one less than an hour's drive from your home. If you can't locate one through community notices in your newspaper or on the radio, contact the ARS. It will put you in touch with the appropriate organization.

For membership or other information, contact the ARS. See page 243 for the address and telephone number.

The website of the American Rose Society (www.ars.org) is a rich source of information for rose lovers across the nation.

Exhibiting and Judging Roses

Most people who become active in rose societies eventually become interested in exhibiting their roses. The lure of ribbons and trophies, as well as the chance to compare their achievements with those of others, is hard to resist.

If you are interested in exhibiting your roses, you will find many opportunities. In addition to local, regional, and national shows sponsored by the ARS, many garden clubs and state fairs have rose sections in their flower shows. These can take place anytime during rose-blooming season and are often advertised in local newspapers and on the radio. The ARS publishes the dates and locations of its rose shows in its monthly magazine.

Rose shows are usually held indoors at shopping malls, schools, libraries, and other public buildings. Exhibitors arrive early in the morning, usually about 6 a.m., and spend three to four hours arranging tables and setting out cut roses in clear glass bottles or vases. Roses are often positioned alphabetically by class (such as floribunda, hybrid tea, and so on).

Judging the roses begins when the exhibits are ready and is closed to the public, if feasible. Judges, trained and accredited by the ARS, work their way among the entries, usually in teams of three. The number of teams depends on the size of the show. A large national show may have as many as two dozen teams. Judges award blue (first prize), red (second prize), yellow (third prize), and sometimes white (honorable mention) ribbons by variety within each class. Only one blue ribbon is awarded per

Judges at a rose show examine each entry carefully and rate it according to specific standards set by the American Rose Society.

class and variety, but there can be numerous second and third prizes if the entries warrant it. After the judging, the exhibitors and the public are allowed to view and enjoy the show.

After all the ribbons have been awarded, the blue-ribbon winners undergo a second round of judging. From among the one-bloom-per-stem, disbudded hybrid teas, grandifloras, and climbing hybrid teas, the judges select a grand-prize winner known as the Queen of the Show. Second- and third-place winners from these classes are often chosen as well and are usually called the King and the Princess of the Show. Together with the best floribunda spray, grandiflora spray, one-bloom-per-stem miniature, miniature spray, old garden rose, polyantha, climber, and shrub (which are ineligible for the grand prize), these winners are placed on a separate table known as the Court of Honor. The winners of the Challenge Classes (see page 145) are also exhibited on this table.

Judging criteria

To be a good exhibitor, you need to know what the judges look for when they choose winners. For hybrid teas, grandifloras, floribundas, and miniatures, there are two main sets of judging criteria: one for single blooms and another for multiple blooms. Polyanthas, climbers, shrub roses, and old garden roses are judged separately by class, without regard to the number of blooms. Additional categories called Challenge Classes evaluate groups of cuttings as a whole.

SINGLE BLOOMS: When judges turn a critical eye to roses that are eligible for Queen of the Show, they use the set of guidelines that follow—awarding up to the maximum number of points for each attribute. The flower with the most points is the winner. Miniatures, floribundas, and climbers (other than climbing hybrid teas) that are exhibited with single blooms are judged in the same way, although they are not eligible for Queen of the Show.

■ **Form—25 points:** An exhibition rose is in its ideal form when it is one half to three quarters open. When viewed from the top, the outline of the bloom is circular, with the petals arrayed symmetrically within the circle. The stamens at the center must not be visible. When the flower is viewed from the side, it should be triangular in form—pointed at the top and flat at the base.

■ **Color—20 points:** The rose must be as close to its ideal color as possible, free of the bleaching or darkening caused by adverse weather conditions or refrigeration. There should be no green or white streaks on the petals, and no marks or spots from rain or spray residue.

■ **Substance—15 points:** Substance refers to the crispness, texture, firmness, thickness, and toughness of the petals. A newly cut rose that has been properly conditioned will have excellent substance. As a cut rose ages, it naturally loses some of its substance and will not be as eligible for a high award as one that has been newly cut.

■ **Stem and foliage— 20 points:** The stem should be straight and strong, and the foliage free of dirt, disease, insect infestation, spray residue, and cuts and holes. The foliage should also be large and healthy-looking without being overgrown. There should be at least two five-leaflet leaves on the stem although there can be many more. The foliage should be evenly placed around the stem. If you look down on the exhibit, the foliage makes an evenly balanced background for the bloom.

■ **Balance and proportion— 10 points:** The size of the flower should be in proportion to the length of the stem. In other words, a small flower should not be shown on a very long stem, nor should a large flower be shown on a short stem. There are no exact rules here; evaluation is subjective.

■ **Size—10 points:** This refers to the size of the flower. The bigger the better.

MULTIPLE BLOOMS: More than one flower blooming on a stem is called a spray. Sprays are found on hybrid teas, grandifloras, floribundas, miniatures, polyanthas, and climbers. The individual flowers in sprays are judged by the same criteria as single flowers and additionally by how they appear in relation to one another.

Each flower on a winning hybrid tea or grandiflora spray must have the ideal form, color, substance, size, and so forth required of a one-bloom-per-stem specimen. What's more, all flowers in the spray must be arranged in a pleasing, balanced way. Judges look for how flowers open according to the variety. The flowers of some varieties open all at once whereas others open in stages.

The flowers in a floribunda spray should have an overall form, or outline, that is pleasing from the side. It may be rounded, flat, or dome shaped, but it should be symmetrical. No flowers in the spray should protrude above or beyond this outline. Sprays of polyanthas, climbers, and miniature roses are judged in the same way as floribundas.

Old garden and shrub roses may be exhibited either with a single bloom or with multiple blooms, depending on the way the plant naturally flowers. They are awarded blue ribbons if they have a fully open, circular form and if they are fresh and have good substance. Because most of these plants naturally have short stems, the "balance and proportion" category is not weighed as heavily as it is with modern roses. It is possible for a rose to have a large spray on a short stem and still win an award.

CHALLENGE CLASSES: Sponsored by rose societies, Challenge Classes usually call for a collection of roses, with each bloom standing in a separate container. In evaluating them, the judges first apply the criteria for judging individual flowers, sprays, or clusters, and then assess 10 additional points per bloom for how the collection looks as a whole. Winning entries are those collections whose roses have complementary colors and are ideally the same size and at the same stage of development. The more closely matched the individual flowers in the collection, the better the chance that the collection will win the trophy.

The "Court of Honor" at a rose show enables award-winners to enjoy their day in the sun.

Exhibiting and Judging Roses

(continued)

Readying roses for an exhibit

Producing show-quality roses takes effort. But once you have experienced the exhilaration of winning your first ribbon or trophy, you'll probably want to work even harder for the next one.

IN THE GARDEN: Exhibiting starts in the garden. If you do not grow healthy plants and give them the care they need, they will not produce award-winning roses. In addition to good plant care, serious exhibitors apply several techniques to improve their roses in the months and days before a show. If the spring has been cold, delay applying summer mulch until the ground has completely warmed so that growth will not be retarded. If you will be entering roses in competition for Queen of the Show, disbud hybrid teas, grandifloras, and climbing hybrid teas as soon as side growth appears (see page 114). About ten days before

Flowers on the bush can be covered with plastic bags to shield them from light rain just before a show.

the show, fertilize the plants with a water-soluble plant food. This will make the foliage healthier looking, give more color and substance to the flowers, and sometimes speed up their development.

If bad weather threatens just before a show, protect flowers by covering them loosely with a plastic bag and sealing it with a twist-tie.

THE DAY BEFORE A SHOW: The next step is to cut the flowers to take to the rose show. For advice on cutting, see page 134. Stems must have at least two five-leaflet leaves but may have many more, as long as the stem length is in proportion to the size of the flower. However, stems must be no longer than 18 inches from the base of the stem to the base of the flower. They can be cut from the garden a little longer than 18 inches, and adjustments made at the show. As you cut your stems, write the variety name on a tag of paper and attach it loosely to the stem. The tags can be attached with string, but the easiest way is to cut the tags into long, rectangular strips. Make a slit at one end of the strip, and pull the other end of the paper through the slit as you wrap the strip around the stem.

Cutting for a rose show usually takes place the day before the show, unless you have a refrigerator in which you can store your roses. Most refrigerated roses retain their show quality for up to about five days, as long as there is no food in the refrigerator. If food is present, especially fruit, roses will open more quickly and will not retain their show quality. Moreover, refrigeration can discolor some flowers,

primarily reds and oranges. If this happens, they will be penalized by the judges. Roses keep best if they are stored standing up in a bucket of water in a refrigerator. Do not submerge any leaves, which will foul the water.

If you have a large number of entries, you'll find it easier and more efficient to do most of the preparation at home during the days before the show. In addition to cutting and labeling your roses, you can clean the foliage and fill out the show entry tags at home. These tags are provided by the rose society or sponsor and can usually be obtained in advance of the show. Using waterproof ink, write in the name of the rose, the class in which it is being exhibited (hybrid tea, floribunda, for example), and your name. Each tag is tied to the neck of the bottle holding the rose and is folded over so that your name is not visible during judging.

At most rose shows, roses are exhibited in clear glass bottles. Find out whether the sponsor will supply the bottles or whether you must furnish your own. Bottles that are provided by the sponsor are often available before the show. You will save time by putting your rose specimens in the bottles at home. Be sure to fill the bottle to the neck to keep the specimen from drying out. A floral preservative can be added to the water (see page 135).

Rose shows always follow a schedule, which is usually available from the sponsor at least a month before the show. You must follow the instructions in the schedule to the letter, or your entry may be disqualified. For example, if the instructions say that a Challenge Class calls for three dark red hybrid teas, you cannot enter two dark reds and one medium red.

Other things that can disqualify a rose from competition include misnaming the rose on the entry tag; entering the rose in the wrong class, or section, in the show; employing cosmetic substances such as pigments, oil, glue, or wires; and showing roses not registered with the American Rose Society (this rule is often ignored at garden club and state fair shows). These and other rules are outlined in the instructions.

THE DAY OF THE SHOW: Rose shows always specify a time for making entries (for example, from 6 a.m. to 10 a.m.). Plan to arrive at the rose show early so that you will have enough time to place all of your entries on the show tables. It is also cooler in the early morning, so the roses will suffer less from heat in transit. If your car is air-conditioned, cool it off first and then keep the air-conditioner running as you drive to the show. Placing small plastic bags over the flowers (the bags do not need to be sealed) will help them retain moisture during the trip. If you must travel a long distance to the show, your roses will keep much better if they are transported in an ice chest or other insulated box containing frozen ice packs (be sure the blooms do not touch the ice). If the insulated box is not large enough to let roses stand up in their bottles, place each rose in an orchid tube. Orchid tubes, which are available from florist supply stores, are plastic or glass

tubes resembling test tubes. The stems are placed in water in the tubes and held in place by a rubber stopper, which has a hole for the stem. If you don't have an insulated box, place the stems in ice water before you transport them if the trip is long.

AT THE SHOW: As you make entries, keep the judging criteria in mind. If the form of a rose is not perfect, you may be able to groom it by removing one or two petals. It is possible to shift a petal around in front of another petal so that the form is more symmetrical. If a rose has not opened enough, you can usually open it more by warming the outside of the rose for a few minutes between your fingertips and then gently pulling the petals down. The rose will also open more quickly if you place it in the sun or in warm water, either at home or after you get to the show. Dust and insects can be cleaned away with an artist's brush. Torn or damaged foliage can sometimes be manicured with small scissors. Avoid smoking while getting your roses ready; cigarette smoke contains chemicals that cause flowers to open more quickly.

Sometimes a stem refuses to stand up straight in the bottle, which will detract from its beauty and probably cause the judges to bypass it. In such an instance, it is acceptable to wedge the stem with a piece of folded paper towel (as long as the paper does not touch and absorb water), a ball of aluminum foil, or wadded plastic wrap. If you must use a wedge, place it so that it does not protrude awkwardly above the lip of the bottle.

An exhibitor inserts cotton swabs between rows of petals to train them open in a desired shape.

After you have groomed the rose for exhibit, make sure that the paper identification tag placed on the rose at home is removed, that the entry tag is attached to the bottle with a twist-tie or rubber band, and that the rose is entered in the correct class in the show. In a few hours, after judging is over, you'll know whether your efforts have paid off.

Groomed to perfection, roses await judging at a national show.

Preserving Roses

Alas for rose lovers, the life of a cut rose is short and the time between blooming periods is often long. Fortunately, roses can be preserved in several ways to extend their beauty: They can be dried for arrangements, pressed for display in picture frames, or blended to make fragrant potpourris. All you need are a few simple ingredients and minimal tools and supplies. The results of your efforts can look and smell marvelous, and can last for years.

Roses for preserving can be picked anytime during the season and are best picked in the morning after the sun has dried the dew. You can cut and preserve roses all summer, and then make home decorations and gifts with them during the winter months. Flowers for drying should be at the peak of perfection when cut. Freshness is also critical with roses for pressing and for potpourri.

Dried flowers

Both the flowers and the foliage of roses can be dried to make charming arrangements for display around the house. Although many different types of roses can be dried, miniature roses are the most popular. Their small flowers dry more easily than larger roses and retain their shape and color better. Along with size, color is an important consideration when choosing roses for drying. Many white roses turn brown when dried, many red roses turn black, and some orange roses turn dark at the tips of their petals. Pinks and yellows are a better choice because most of them retain their original color. Even if fairly confident that you can anticipate the results, experiment with a few flowers before drying a large batch.

Silica gel is the material that dries roses best. It is a white, crystalline substance resembling table sugar and has the capacity to absorb large quantities of moisture. Sealed into small packets, it is the material sold by photo supply companies for protecting camera equipment. Larger quantities for flower drying are sold at craft and flower shops. A 1½-pound canister contains enough silica gel to dry several small flowers at once, and it may be reactivated and reused many times. Many brands of silica gel contain small blue indicator crystals that turn pink when it is time to reactivate the substance. To do this, simply spread the silica gel in a shallow, ovenproof container and bake it for 30 to 60 minutes at 250°F, until the crystals turn blue again. You can also dry it in the microwave for a minute or two.

To dry roses, choose flowers that are as perfect as possible, dry, free of insects and debris, and at the desired stage of development. If possible, cut the flowers with 2 inches of stem to make arranging easier. You can dry anything from tiny buds to fully opened flowers with leaves.

Then select a wide, flat-bottomed container with a tight-fitting cover, such as an imported-cookie tin, and spread a 1-inch layer of silica gel in the bottom. Lay the roses on top of it with the flowers facing up, cutting the stems if necessary so as not to bend the flowers over. Take care that the flowers don't touch one another. Foliage can be dried on the stem, but there is a chance it will break off later on. A better idea is to dry foliage separately from the flowers, laying it flat on silica gel beside them. Cover everything completely with more silica gel, making sure to fill in the flowers with silica gel, and then seal the container tightly for about a week. Flowers dry more uniformly if flowers of the same size are dried together. If you want to dry other types of flowers to use in arrangements with roses, such as zinnias, marigolds, or

Dried, preserved roses can combine with other dried flowers and herbs to create interesting, beautiful, and long-lasting arrangements.

asters, it is best to dry them separately, as drying times may vary.

When the roses and the leaves are fully dried, they will feel crisp or papery to the touch. Remove them carefully from the container and gently blow away any silica gel that has stuck to them. If any crystals remain, dust them away lightly with an artist's brush.

A few tricks will help you achieve better and longer-lasting results. Sepals curl as they dry, so if you cut them off before immersing the flowers in silica gel, the result will be more attractive. After a flower has dried, you can insert floral wire into its base and wrap it around the stem. This strengthens the stem and makes it easier to arrange the blooms. If you are leaving a stem on the flower, it's better to insert the wire through the stem before drying, as the stem is more likely to break after drying. To strengthen a dried rose, apply a few drops of white glue to the undersides of the outer petals to make them less likely to fall off. To make a dried rose less brittle and also less likely to reabsorb moisture, spray it with clear plastic available from art supply stores or dip it in warm, melted paraffin, which will give the rose a waxy coating.

You can also dry roses in a microwave oven; in fact, the resulting color and shape of the flowers will be better than if the roses are dried in a tin. It's best to dry only one flower at a time to avoid crowding and overdrying. First, dry and heat the silica gel at the high setting for about a minute. Then prepare the roses as described above,

using an uncovered microwavable container. (Omit metal floral wire, which may cause arcing.) Because microwave ovens vary in wattage, it is impossible to give exact times. Start with one minute at the high setting. If that is not enough, dry for another minute. If the microwave lacks a rotating platter inside, stop the oven after 30 seconds and rotate the container so that the flowers dry evenly. Let the flowers cool for 20 to 30 minutes, then remove them from the silica gel.

Dried roses are arranged in the same way as fresh roses, with several additional considerations. First, you do not need to worry about water; in fact, placing them in water will ruin them. Containers, floral foam, or pinholders can be used to support the stems. If the stems are weak and no supporting wire is in place, you can use wire to tie them to florist picks (pieces of wood that resemble large toothpicks, available at florist supply stores), or insert wire through the base of the flower and twist it around the stem. Wire and picks can be hidden if necessary with self-adhesive green tape.

Roses can be combined with many other kinds of dried flowers, as well as with other types of foliage. Dried roses can also be wired onto wreaths and garlands. A dried arrangement can last for many years, depending on the humidity in the room. If it gets dusty, brush the dust off gently with a feather duster or an artist's brush. In humid climates, protect the arrangement in a glass bell jar.

Flowers dried in silica gel can retain their color and shape for years.

Place roses in a one-inch bed of silica gel and then gently spoon more gel over each blossom (or sift it through your fingers). Cover container tightly. Most roses will be dry in a week (four days for miniatures).

Potpourri

Potpourri is a mixture of dried rose petals, aromatic oils, other scents derived from herbs or spices, sometimes other dried flowers, and a fixative to retain the aroma. Although potpourris can be made with flowers other than roses, roses are traditionally the main ingredient. Potpourri is a French term meaning "rotten pot," which derives from the original practice of placing rose petals in a container to ripen and age.

Although it is tempting to enjoy roses in the garden and then collect the petals for potpourri as they start to drop, this method is not satisfactory because the petals are past their peak and will not dry and retain their fragrance properly. Any type of rose of any color can be used to make potpourri; just be sure to use fragrant roses.

Today, potpourri is made by two methods—the dry method and the moist method. The dry method, which uses only thoroughly dried rose petals, makes potpourri to be displayed in glass bowls and in sachets to perfume lingerie drawers. Potpourri in glass bowls can last for 10 years or more whereas that in sachets usually loses its fragrance after two years or so. The moist method, using partially dried petals, creates potpourri that is less attractive to view but whose scent lasts much longer—up to 50 years. Moist potpourri is used in glass bowls as well.

Aromatic oils, fixatives, dried flowers, and other ingredients necessary to make potpourri are available from craft stores and specialty shops or by mail order.

Fragrance is personal. Different varieties of roses combine to create potpourri with unique scents. Be creative and experiment with different recipes to find your favorite.

DRY POTPOURRI: Gather petals from fragrant roses after the morning dew has dried, and spread them on an elevated screen out of the sunlight and in a warm, dry, airy place. Drying will take several days to a week, depending on heat and humidity. The petals should be dry enough that they break easily when bent. If you cannot dry enough petals at once, store the dried petals in an airtight glass jar until you have enough.

In a large glass or wooden bowl, mix 1 quart of dried petals with about 1 ounce of dried herbs or spices of the scent you desire—for example, allspice, cinnamon, cloves, lemon verbena, or mint. You may also add other dried flowers. Carnations, lavender, and orange blossoms are most common because they retain their scent long after drying. Place several drops of aromatic oil on 2 ounces of fixative such as orrisroot or benzoin (congealed resin from the styrax tree) and gently blend this into the rose petals and spice/herb mix with a wooden spoon. Use chunks of fixative rather than powder as the latter can cling to the container and cloud the glass. Aromatic oils of cinnamon, cloves, lavender, lemon, rose, and sandalwood are the ones most often used.

Store the mixture in a dark, cool place in an airtight container, stirring or shaking often. Test the scents periodically. They will naturally smell harsh at first; do not try to compensate by adding other fragrances to the mix. After 3 to 12 weeks aging will be complete, and the mixture will have a pleasant aroma. Place the potpourri in a covered glass container, adding other dried flowers for color. Remove the cover when you wish to scent the room.

There are thousands of potpourri recipes. From Caswell-Massey Co., Ltd., of New York, the country's oldest perfumer and purveyor of spices and essential oils, comes this recipe for dry potpourri. All plant material should be dried before use.

- 4 ounces dried rose petals (about 1 quart volume)
- 2 ounces dried lavender flowers or buds
- 4 ounces dried coriander leaves
- 4 ounces chopped dried orrisroot
- ½ ounce ground cinnamon
- ½ ounce ground mace
- ¼ ounce ground cloves
- ¼ ounce table salt
- ¼ ounce oil of lavender
- ¼ ounce oil of cinnamon
- ¼ ounce oil of cloves
- ¼ ounce oil of rose
- ½ ounce tincture of musk

MOIST POTPOURRI: To make moist potpourri, dry rose petals until they are limp but not completely dry. Mix them with the dried herbs and spices whose scents you desire, then place a 2-inch layer of the mixture into a ceramic or glass bowl. Add a

thin layer of noniodized salt, then 2 more inches of petals; repeat until the bowl is full. Press the mixture down with a weight, and mix daily. The mixture will completely age in about two weeks.

Fixative is not needed— the salt absorbs and retains the scents. If the mixture loses some of its scent, it can be revived with just a few drops of brandy.

There are many variations on the theme. The following is a 19th-century list of ingredients.

- 3 handfuls fragrant rose petals
- 3 handfuls orange blossoms or other fragrant flower
- 3 handfuls carnation petals
- 1 handful chopped marjoram leaves
- 1 handful chopped lemon thyme leaves
- 6 sweet bay leaves
- 1 lemon rind, grated
- 25 cloves, crushed
- 1 handful myrtle leaves
- ½ handful spearmint leaves
- ½ handful lavender flowers

Moist potpourri releases its wonderful scent whenever the lid is removed from its glass bowl.

Creating and Multiplying Roses

Have you ever wondered how the roses in your garden were created and marketed? Have you ever wanted to try your hand at hybridizing? As rose breeders are well aware, it is easy to produce a new variety but far more difficult to achieve real novelty. In these pages you will learn how professional hybridizers create new roses and how you can experiment with this fascinating process.

Most people who grow roses seldom stop to wonder where they came from; they are simply content to plant and enjoy them. But if you have been growing roses for a while, you may find that you are curious about how new roses are created, how they are named, and how they are grown for the market. You may even wish to try your hand at creating and multiplying roses of your own.

This chapter describes several methods of hybridizing and propagating roses for the home garden. It also takes you behind the scenes to learn how commercial growers create and produce roses in quantity. Lists of the best commercial roses follow, along with brief profiles of some of the outstanding hybridizers who created them.

Below: Rose test fields trial new Jackson & Perkins roses in Southern California. At right: The revolutionary Knock Out, developed by William Radler and introduced by Conard-Pyle in 2000, was bred for near-total disease resistance.

Hybridizing a New Variety

To prevent self-pollination, hybridizers have removed this rose's pollen-bearing male anthers before brushing its female stigmas with pollen from another plant.

People who grow roses often try to produce their own varieties, even if just for the fun of it. Although professionals estimate that the chance of creating a rose with commercial value is about 1 in 10,000, amateurs often derive sufficient pleasure from just trying. Some have actually gone on to see their varieties marketed.

The creation of a new rose variety begins with hybridizing fertilization of the female parts of one variety with the male pollen of another. Each seed produced by this union can grow into a plant resembling one or both of its parents, or possessing any combination of traits from its earlier ancestors. Because parent roses may themselves be the products of complex hybridization, there are millions of potential variations.

Both amateur and professional breeders apply the same techniques to create a new rose; the professional, however, will take this work several steps further, undertaking field trials to establish a performance record before the new variety goes on the market. If you would like to experiment with hybridizing, you can do so with minimal effort and little in the way of equipment or materials. If you make your crosses outdoors in early summer, you will have seeds by fall for planting the following winter or spring. If you are lucky enough to have a greenhouse, you will be able to make crosses and start seeds throughout the year.

Making a successful cross

Hybridizing roses is an unpredictable process. Because roses carry the genes for millions of traits, not all of which are expressed by the plant, it is impossible to tell in advance which set of traits a given offspring will manifest. A plant can exhibit the traits of one of its parents, both of them, neither of them, or a blending of the two. A dominant trait is one that will appear in offspring even if only one parent passes it on. A recessive trait is one that must come from both parents.

For example, fragrance seems to be a recessive trait (or possibly, some genes affecting fragrance are recessive). Thus a rose will be scented only if both of its parents have passed on the genes for fragrance. (The parents themselves need not be scented; they need only possess and transmit the fragrance genes.) The inheritance of color is more ambiguous. Two red roses crossed together usually produce red offspring; however, the color produced by crossing a red rose with a pink or yellow rose is anyone's guess. It can be a blending of the parents' colors, or it may be a completely different color.

A new generation of rose seeds matures inside the orange hips of *Rosa rugosa alba*. Each seed within them can give rise to a plant with different characteristics.

The hybrid tea Love & Peace ('BALpeace') is an All-America Rose Selection introduced in 2002. It was named in part after one of its parents, 'Peace', which was introduced by Meilland in 1945 to celebrate the end of World War II and is perhaps the most famous and beloved hybrid tea in the world.

Hybridizing a New Variety

(continued)

Pollen is removed from flowers of the plant designated as the father.

Botanists still do not know either the exact mechanisms by which rose genes are inherited and expressed or the roles that many rose genes play. Until rose genetics is better understood, creating new roses with the desired characteristics will remain a matter of trial and error. Hybridizing today is as much a matter of throwing out combinations that don't work as it is fostering combinations that do.

Selecting parents

Before making a cross, a hybridizer selects the parent plants, taking into account their color, form, hardiness, disease resistance, fragrance, and other characteristics. However, the presence of good traits in the parent plants is no guarantee that the offspring will exhibit them. Modern roses are of such complex and mixed ancestry that almost anything can happen and usually does.

With experience, hybridizers learn that some varieties make good female parents, others make better male parents, and still others can be used as either mother or father. The same variety is rarely used for both roles. After the parents are selected, the hybridizer removes the outer petals of the parent flowers in order to expose their reproductive organs.

To prevent self-pollination, which will interfere with the selected cross, the pollen-producing anthers are removed from the rose designated as the mother flower. This flower is then covered with a plastic bag to prevent cross-pollination by insects or the wind.

On the rose designated as the father, the stamens are picked off, labeled, and stored in an airtight container in a refrigerator. After about a day they release their pollen and can be discarded; the powdery yellow pollen remains in storage in the airtight container until used.

Pollination

About a day after the stamens have been removed from the female flower, a sticky substance appears on the stigma, a signal that the female is ready to receive pollen. The pollen of the selected male parent is then brushed onto the stigma with a fingertip or a small brush. A label detailing the parentage of the rose and the date of pollination is attached to the stem, and the pollinated flower is enclosed in a bag to protect it from further pollination. If fertilization occurs (it does not always happen), the ovary swells and the hip forms as the seeds develop. After the hip ripens in several months, it is harvested from the plant and its seeds are removed for germination. They can be planted right away, but more will germinate if you first subject them to stratification (see page 158).

Owing to the permutations of heredity, the new plants that grow from these seeds are usually as different from their parents as they are from each other. The first flowers of these new plants appear within seven months to a year after the initial cross has been made. But since early blooms are often slightly different in form from those of a mature plant, it is necessary to wait for several bloom cycles to determine whether a new rose has any potential.

If it does, an amateur hybridizer will either bud the rose or let it grow on its own roots. Professionals bud every variety that looks promising for two reasons: to test whether the new rose can be budded (a requirement for mass production) and to see how the rose grows and flowers after being budded, because budded roses may perform differently than those grown on their own roots. Successful crosses are selected for further testing.

Selected pollen is brushed onto the stigmas of a flower of the mother plant, which is tagged to identify the cross. Dustlike pollen grains grow pollen tubes to fertilize ovules in the ovary.

Starting Roses From Seed

Growing roses from seeds is not difficult and requires a minimum of equipment. This includes pots, sowing flats, and ideally a green house or fluorescent lights. If you do not own a greenhouse, you can grow seeds on a windowsill, under lights in the basement, or outdoors in containers or the ground.

About one year will have passed from the time a cross is made until the seedling of a new variety first blooms. For most growers the prospect of beholding a new and unusual variety makes the wait worthwhile.

Harvesting

To harvest the seeds from a rose plant, cut the hips from the plants when they are ready, wash them, and cut them in half with a knife. The round to oval, slightly pointed white seeds, which are about ⅛ inch long, can be easily removed. There may be 1 to 50 seeds in a hip. Next, wash the seeds in a kitchen strainer.

Although rose seeds can be sown as soon as they are harvested, germination is usually more successful if they are placed in the refrigerator in an airtight jar or plastic bag, between layers of moist sphagnum peat moss, moist paper toweling, or moist tissue, for six to eight weeks before sowing. This process, known as stratification, simulates the cold of a natural winter, priming the seeds to sprout. After the cold treatment, use tweezers to remove the seeds from the sphagnum peat moss or paper. Before sowing the seeds, you may wish to test them for viability, or the ability to germinate. To do this, place them in a container of water. Those that are not viable will float to the top and can be discarded.

Sowing

Seedlings often succumb to a disease known as damping off, caused by one or more fungi that are present in most garden soils. Seedlings that have succumbed to damping off suddenly wilt and fall over soon after they have germinated. There is no cure for damping off, so prevention is the only remedy. Use a sterilized, soilless sowing mixture.

Sow the seeds in a wide, shallow container filled with about 4 inches of medium, burying them ¼ inch deep. Rose seeds germinate best under greenhouse conditions; if you do not have a greenhouse, cover the seed flats with clear plastic or glass, or place the flat in a clear plastic bag to keep the medium moist and the humidity high until the seeds germinate. If condensation forms on the glass or plastic, remove the glass or plastic for a few minutes to dry out the medium slightly and to prevent diseases. Rose seeds germinate at highest rates at temperatures between 50° and 55°F but will germinate at temperatures as high as 60°F. Place the flats in bright light but not full sun for as many hours as possible, or keep them 6 to 10 inches below fluorescent lights that are kept on continuously until the seeds germinate.

Germination time can vary from three weeks to four months or longer. When you see short stems with two seed leaves called cotyledons, remove the plastic bag and move the containers into as many hours of full sun as you can provide or place under fluorescent lights.

After the seeds have germinated, check them every day to see if the medium is dry and if they need water. Avoid watering in any way that will dislodge or uproot young seedlings. A good method is to use a very fine mist or spray, or to set the container in a tray of water and let it soak up moisture from the bottom. Once all the seedlings are growing, ensure steady growth by adding soluble fertilizer such as 20-20-20 or 15-30-15 to the irrigation water once a week at one quarter the recommended strength.

Transplanting

When seedlings have produced three sets of compound leaves, they're ready to transplant into individual pots. First, moisten the medium in the original container. Then fill 2-inch plastic or peat pots with moistened growing medium and make a hole the depth of the roots at the center of pot. The ideal tool for this is a probe known as a dibble (available at garden centers and greenhouse supply stores), but a pencil will also work. With a wooden plant label or a spoon handle, gently lift out the tiny plants, disturbing the roots as little as possible.

Holding the seedling by the leaves—never by the stem— lower it into the pot and firm the medium gently around the roots. Continue to provide light, water, and fertilizer.

A more convenient alternative to sowing seeds in a large container is to plant them directly into individual 2-inch pots filled with growing medium. This saves a transplanting step and reduces the need to handle the delicate seedlings. It also usually produces larger plants by the end of the first year. When a plant is about 4 inches tall, transfer the entire soil ball to a 4-inch pot and fill the extra space with potting medium.

It is also possible to sow rose seeds directly into the garden. Prepare the soil and sow the seeds in late fall or in early spring for germination in mid- to late spring. The cold weather will not harm the seeds; in fact, it helps them germinate. Sow seeds ½ inch deep and 1 inch apart, in rows 2½ inches apart.

Make sure that the seed beds never dry out. Once the seeds have germinated, continue to water and start to administer light applications of soluble fertilizer such as 20-20-20 or 15-30-15, applied at one quarter the rate recommended on the label once a week, until the plants produce their first blooms.

Evaluating

The first flowers will appear by the time the seedling is 4 to 5 inches high, about six to eight weeks after germination. Don't be disappointed if the first flowers are not exciting as they are often not representative of mature blooms. After the plant has bloomed several times, you can decide whether you want to keep or discard it.

If a seedling shows promise—for example, if it is a color you like or has good flower form—it can be moved to a permanent place in the garden and left either to grow on its own roots or to be grafted to a more robust understock (see the next section). If practical, it's a good idea to let your rose grow from its own roots, for two reasons. First, own-root roses are never plagued by suckers that grow from the understock and steal the plant's energy. Second, vigorous and hardy varieties will often grow faster, bloom better, and survive winter more easily on their own roots than on the roots of an equally vigorous understock. On the other hand, roses that are tender or do not grow well on their own roots will thrive far better if budded. There's no way to predict whether a newly hybridized variety will be hardy or vigorous. If you grow it on its own roots and it does not grow well, try budding it and see what happens.

Seeds from a cross between two roses develop inside the ovary, which swells to form a hip. Seeds within a rose hip can range in size and number, depending on the variety. This hip contains just a few large seeds. If spectacular, plants from one of these seeds could reach the market in 7 to 10 years.

Propagating Roses

Propagating rose plants by budding

Budding is the method of propagation most often used to reproduce large modern bush roses. Unlike propagation by seeds, this asexual method produces a plant identical to the parent. Many roses are difficult to grow from stem cuttings (another asexual method, described in the next section), and many that do take root from cuttings will not be as vigorous or as hardy as those that are budded.

Budding is a type of grafting in which a growth bud (sometimes called a bud eye) from the variety to be reproduced is joined together with roots of a different variety, known as an understock. In the process of budding, one bud is grafted to the main cane of the understock at a point just above the ground. Budding increases the vigor and hardiness of a variety and is often the only reliable method of propagation. The only disadvantage of budding is that the process takes longer than rooting cuttings, requiring two years to produce a new plant. Two major understocks, 'Dr. Huey' and *Rosa multiflora,* are used in the United States because they thrive in the wide range of climates and soils. Two other understocks occasionally used are *R. manettii* and *R. × odorata.* 'Dr. Huey' and *R. multiflora* are rarely grown in their own right. The flowers of 'Dr. Huey' are undistinguished, and *R. multiflora,* although it produces pretty flowers, grows so rank that most people consider it a weed.

R. manettii is sometimes grown in gardens although it is quite large and unruly. *R. × odorata* is often seen in old-rose collections, as it is the original tea rose.

'Dr. Huey' grows best in the irrigated desert soils where most commercial roses are grown and is therefore the most popular understock by far. Its pliable bark makes budding easier, and it forms a good union with nearly all varieties. It produces a strong, hardy root system that tends to refrain from producing suckers (unwanted shoots from underground portions of the plant). It also has fewer thorns than *R. multiflora,* making it easier to work with.

R. multiflora is vigorous and is the hardier understock. It grows as well in Minnesota as it does in Arizona, and almost all roses bud well to it. It is the second most popular understock, mainly because 'Dr. Huey' grows better in commercial fields in irrigated dry areas, where most of the country's roses are produced. *R. multiflora* is used extensively in areas with acid soil, such as Texas and Oregon. Its major disadvantages are that it is harder to work with and more prone to mite infestation.

R. manettii and *R. × odorata* are extremely tender plants and can be used as understock only where there is no frost during the winter. However, they are excellent understocks for greenhouse roses.

In Europe and Canada some rose producers use *R. canina* as an understock because of its extreme cold-hardiness. However, it forms a brittle bud union and tends to dwarf the variety budded to it.

Amateurs who want to bud their own plants can purchase understock from a few retail mail-order nurseries (see page 243) or through a local rose society that can buy in quantity from a wholesale source. Once you have acquired understock, you can root it as you would any other rose (see the next section), and then either bud directly onto the rooted plants or save a plant or two to use as stock for future cuttings. If you don't wish to purchase understock, you can propagate it from any hardy, vigorous variety, preferably a species rose or other old garden rose that you may have in the garden. It is also possible to collect and grow rose seeds from the wild.

If understock is planted in the ground, leave 12 inches between plants in rows 2 feet apart. Many gardeners who like to bud roses find it is easier to grow the understock, do the budding, and grow the new plant to maturity in a container.

How to bud a rose

The best period for budding is from early to late summer because the bud has time to "take" before cold weather. Before budding, be sure to water the understock thoroughly so that it will contain enough internal moisture to allow bark to pull away easily. To prepare the understock, make an inch-long vertical cut into the bark of the main cane at the base of the plant, cutting through to but not into the wood. You can use any small, sharp knife or purchase a budding knife at a garden center. Then make a horizontal cut at the top of the vertical cut to create a T-shaped incision. The horizontal cut should reach about a third of the way around the cane. The bark should pull away from the wood easily. If it does not, it may be too early in the season; wait a few weeks and try again on the same cane. (The first cut will gradually heal itself; no sealant is needed.)

To prepare the bud, select a stem on the plant to be budded (called the bud wood) and, with a sharp knife, cut out a shield-shaped layer of stem containing a large bud. Cut through the bark and slightly into the wood, cutting from top to bottom and taking as thin a slice of wood as you can. The cut should extend from 1 inch above the bud to ½ inch below it, skirting the

bud eye by about ⅛ to 3⁄16 inch on each side. Then take the bud (often called the shield) and insert it into the T-cut you made in the under stock. If the shield is too long for this opening, trim the shield above the bud eye with scissors or a budding knife. Finally, bind the shield and understock together by wrapping electrical tape or a cut rubber band around the cane several times, leaving the bud eye exposed. Be sure to overlap the tape or rubber band to keep water from getting behind the shield. Keeping the soil moist after making the graft helps the bud unite with the understock.

The bud will lie dormant during the first season and will start to grow the following spring. When the bud starts to grow and a stem

starts to develop, remove the tape or rubber band.

All the top growth of the understock should be cut away at this time, to a point just above where the bud has started to grow. Now, only the grafted variety will be making top growth on its new roots.

Budding has not been successful if the bud does not grow. You can then try to rebud the plant on the opposite side of the cane.

It often happens that unwanted shoots called suckers will develop from the understock below the bud union, the point at which the budded variety starts to grow. These shoots must be removed as soon as they appear or the understock will eventually outgrow the plant that has been budded to it.

BUDDING

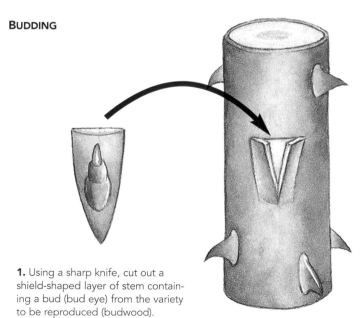

1. Using a sharp knife, cut out a shield-shaped layer of stem containing a bud (bud eye) from the variety to be reproduced (budwood).

2. Insert the bud into a T-cut made on the understock.

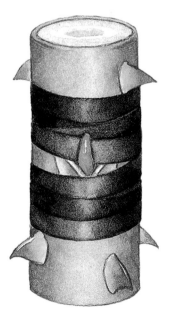

3. Bind the bud to the cane with electrical tape or a cut rubber band, leaving the bud eye exposed.

Propagating Roses
(continued)

Propagating roses from stem cuttings

One of the simplest techniques of propagating new roses is to cut off pieces of stem and plant them directly into a growing medium, where they will eventually take root. Commercial growers use stem cuttings primarily to multiply miniature and old garden roses, which take root readily by this method. However, some large modern bush roses, especially the larger and more vigorous varieties, can also be rooted from stem cuttings. Like budding, rooting stem cuttings is an asexual method of propagation that produces plants identical to the parent.

To take a stem cutting, use pruning shears to cut a 4- to 6-inch length of stem, making sure that the cutting has at least four five-leaflet leaves. Make the cut at a 45-degree angle, just above the highest leaf that will be left on the plant. It is sometimes possible to cut a longer stem and make two cuttings out of it, but the upper portion will usually root better.

The best time to take the cuttings is right after the flowers have faded, when the wood of the stem is neither too soft nor too hard and will thus take root readily. Remove from the cutting both the two lowest leaves and all its flowers and flower buds, then poke the cutting into a container of soilless medium. Make sure that the medium covers the two nodes from which leaves were removed. Use your fingers to firm the medium around the cutting.

Cuttings will root more quickly if you dust their bases with powdered rooting hormone before placing them in the medium. Rooting hormone is a powder available in packets or jars at garden centers. Cuttings that are started indoors will root faster if heated gently from the bottom. You can supply this warmth with a heating coil, a special electrical device sold at garden centers and through seed catalogs, or by placing the cuttings on top of a warm appliance.

If you are rooting cuttings in the house, place the container in a plastic bag and set it in bright light but not direct sun. Remove the plastic bag for a few minutes each day to circulate the air and prevent disease. After several weeks test the cutting for signs of root growth by tugging lightly at the stem. If it offers resistance, the cutting has rooted. Remove both the plastic bag and the source of heat. If the cutting pulls out freely, replace the bag and wait several weeks before testing the cutting again.

If you have access to a greenhouse, so much the better. Its moist environment is exactly what young cuttings need. You do not need to place them in plastic bags, but frequent misting helps them root more quickly.

Rose cuttings can also be rooted outdoors in beds of well-prepared soil, as long as the beds are not in full sun. Prepare the cuttings as you would for rooting in containers, and keep the air around them moist until they take root. You can do this by daily misting or by covering plants with plastic film stretched over a frame or glass jars. The plastic or glass will retain much of the soil moisture, but check for dryness and add water as soon as the ground starts to dry out. Test the cuttings for rooting as described above, and remove the plastic or glass when rooting is complete. Apply extra winter protection to get the plants through the first winter (see page 130), because young rooted cuttings are more vulnerable to the cold than mature plants. Cuttings can be moved to their permanent positions the following spring.

Growing new plants by layering

Layering is a method of asexual propagation in which the stems of roses with supple canes are buried underground until new roots grow from them. These canes are then severed from the parent plant. To propagate a plant by layering, choose one whose canes can be bent over to the ground. These will be primarily climbers or some of the old garden roses. Select a cane and mark a point about a foot in from the end, and notice where this point falls when you bend the cane to the ground. Here is where you will encourage the new roots to grow. Improve the soil in this area as if you were planting a new rose.

Next, just above a growth bud near the marked point on the cane, make a slanting cut halfway into the underside of the cane. Place a small piece of wood such as a toothpick or a matchstick into the cut to wedge it open. Apply rooting hormone to the cut, and remove any adjacent leaves. With a wire or a stick, firmly anchor the cut section of cane under about 3 inches of prepared soil, then cover the area with a mound of soil 4 inches high. Both ends of the cane should protrude from the mound. Keep the area moist until new roots grow. The time this takes depends on the variety of rose, but you can expect that a cane layered one summer will be ready to sever from the parent plant by the following summer. When new growth appears at the end of the cane, dig gently under the soil to see whether roots are growing. If they are, cut the new plant free with shears and transplant it.

Reproducing roses by division

Division is the least popular method of reproducing roses because it cannot be accomplished with budded varieties. However, it can be done with any rose that is growing on its own roots. A rose is divided by cutting it in half lengthwise, thus making two plants from one. Division can also be used to thin old, overgrown plants. Roses should be divided in early spring or late fall when the plants are dormant. In warm climates plants should be divided in winter.

To divide a rosebush, dig it from the ground after a thorough watering and examine it closely. The goal is to split the plant lengthwise so that each half will have an equal number of canes and roots. With a sharp knife or a pruning saw, carefully sever the plant in half by cutting through its crown. Then brush on tree wound paint or orange shellac over the exposed areas. Replant the two divisions as soon as the sealant has dried.

ROOTING STEM CUTTINGS INDOORS

1. Cut a 4- to 6-inch length of stem, making sure that the cutting has at least four five-leaflet leaves. Let the top two 5-leaflet leaves remain. Remove the lower leaves and all flowers and flower buds from the cutting. Dip in rooting hormone.

2. Set cuttings into damp premium potting mix that has been formulated for starting plants (a starting mix).

3. Cover the container in a plastic bag and set it in bright light but not direct sun. Remove the bag for a few minutes each day to circulate the air. After several weeks, test the cutting for signs of root growth by tugging lightly.

Commercial Production of Roses

The hybridizer of 'Chrysler Imperial', a 1952 hybrid tea, received a free automobile in return for helping promote the car line.

Tree roses take longer to mass-produce than bush roses because they involve two grafts: one to join the understock to a long stem, and another to graft the desired variety to the top.

Understanding the process of producing the millions of roses sold in North America leads to a new appreciation of roses for beginner and experienced enthusiast alike. Knowing how quality roses are produced can help gardeners make smart purchasing decisions. And it can even be instructive to amateurs who wish to propagate roses of their own.

A new rose hybrid passes through four phases of development before it reaches the market: field testing and stock buildup; naming; registration and patenting; and mass production. In addition, some nurseries test the market by distributing new roses to gardeners for evaluation.

Testing and stock buildup

For the professional rose grower, the first step after hybridizing is field testing and evaluation. Of the 100,000 different seedlings a professional may have hybridized in a year, only a thousand of the best varieties may be budded for field testing. After these have been evaluated, the best 50 to 100 varieties are chosen for further trials. This culling continues for at least two to four more years, after which one or two varieties might be commercially introduced.

Once a new variety has been selected for introduction, the next step is to build up enough plants for the market. This process may take as long as four years. In the first year, budwood from each plant remaining from the evaluation process will provide enough bud eyes to propagate 10 more plants. By the second year, the original plants will have grown larger, producing enough bud eyes for 20 plants. Their first offspring will each propagate 10 more plants. As the original plants grow in size, they can be counted on to produce enough bud eyes for 40 to 50 more plants, and each successive year their offspring will be able to produce more and more bud eyes. A large rose producer strives to have enough bud eyes to propagate 250,000 plants before introducing a new variety.

All told, the progress of a new rose from hybridization to market may take 7 to 10 years. Miniature roses take less time because they bloom and grow faster and because they don't need to be budded, but the procedure is similarly demanding.

Any amateur rose grower who thinks he or she has a rose worthy of introduction should contact one or more of the large rose nurseries for evaluation. It has happened more than once that an amateur has been successful in bringing a new rose to market.

Naming roses

Once a new variety has been selected for marketing and while the stock is being built up, an important next step is to give it a name. Because roses are sometimes sold in the dormant state when little about them looks appealing, a colorful name can make the difference between brisk sales and oblivion. For example, after the Jackson and Perkins Company first introduced the hybrid tea 'Jadis', it sold poorly and was taken off the market. About 15 years later it was renamed 'Fragrant Memory', returned to the market place, and sold well.

Most rose names fall into one of four categories, referred to by the trade as descriptive, complimentary, commemorative, and commercial. A descriptive name is apt, witty, or evocative, relating to some quality of the rose. Many descriptive names arise straightforwardly from the rose's color, scent, or form; for example, 'Crimson Glory' (a velvety red rose) and 'Dainty Bess' (a delicate five-petaled rose). Other names refer to these attributes indirectly—for example, 'Olé' (a ruffled orange-red) and 'Arizona' (a blend of desert-sunset colors).

Complimentary names honor prominent people in show business, the arts, politics, society, or the rose world itself. Others are named for people who are significant only to the namer of the rose. For example, well-known hybridizer Sam McGredy IV named a rose, 'Hector Deane', for the doctor who removed his tonsils.

Commemorative roses celebrate famous events. Examples are 'Sutter's Gold', commemorating the 100th anniversary of the discovery of gold at Sutter's Mill in California; and 'Diamond Jubilee', toasting Jackson and Perkins's 75th anniversary. Others, such as 'New Yorker', honor cities. A number of commemorative roses are

named for holidays, such as 'White Christmas' and 'Easter Morning'.

Commercial rose names are paid for by companies as a form of self-promotion—a practice that is now more common in Europe than in the United States. For example, 'Chrysler Imperial' was named for an American car model. Some European commercial names unfamiliar to Americans are changed when the roses are introduced in the United States.

Sometimes breeders nickname their roses as they evaluate them, and the names stick—for example 'Eiffel Tower' and 'Duet'.

Registration and patenting

While stock is building up and marketing plans are being drawn, the nursery does the paperwork to establish the rose as a commercial property. Although it is not a requirement, most hybridizers register their variety names with the International Registration Authority for Roses (IRAR), which is administered internationally by the American Rose Society. Registration was introduced to eliminate the giving of many names to the same rose—a practice that once confounded rose buyers. To be accepted for registration, a name must not be in use by another registered rose unless it can be proved that the older variety has become extinct. This is difficult to do since no one knows with certainty which older varieties are still growing in private gardens. Hybridizers make a point of registering their most promising new varieties because a rose must

be registered in order to be exhibited at rose shows.

In addition to registration with the IRAR, some variety names are trademarked. This practice is required in some foreign countries but not in the United States, although some U.S. growers do so anyway. Registering a name as a trademark legally precludes others from using it.

When hybridizers wish to protect the plant itself from unauthorized reproduction and sale, they obtain a patent. A patent gives patent holders sole rights over the variety for 17 years, during which they receive royalties on every rose of this variety that is sold.

The first step in patenting a rose is to obtain an application from the U.S. Patent and Trademark Office in Washington, D.C. On the application the patent seeker must state the name of the new variety and describe it completely enough to distinguish it from its ancestors and from all other known varieties. The patent seeker must also submit color photographs of the plant and declare that he or she did in fact hybridize it. There is also a substantial filing fee. It is also possible to patent a sport, or mutation, that has been discovered. In addition to supplying the information mentioned above, the patent seeker must describe the location and environment where the sport was found.

It is possible to patent a rose yourself but far easier to do so with the help of a patent attorney. However, you would undoubtedly not want to invest the time and expense to obtain a patent unless the variety showed strong commercial promise.

Commercial Production of Roses
(continued)

Mass-producing budded roses

Commercial rose growers harvest some fifty million modern bush roses and climbers each year from tens of thousands of acres of fields, primarily in Texas, California, Arizona, and Oregon. Production of these plants is a labor-intensive, multistep process that takes two years.

Preparing understock

A budded rose crop starts with the propagation and growth of the understock. In the fall, cuttings of understock are taken from stock plants or from the top growth of previously budded plants and prepared for rooting. During the preparation process, 9-inch lengths of stem are cut from the understock plants, and all but the top two or three buds are removed. Doing this helps discourage the understock from developing suckers after it has been budded. In early winter, the cuttings are planted into the fields where the budded varieties will be produced. Over late winter and early spring, the cuttings take root and start to grow vigorously.

Preparing budwood

While the understock is being readied, the budwood (cuttings from which buds will be taken) is harvested and prepared, and buds cut from it for future insertion into the understock. First, budwood is cut from stock plants during the fall in 10- to 12-inch lengths, wrapped in wet burlap, and placed in a cool room where workers remove the thorns and the foliage. The budwood is then dipped in fungicide, wrapped in wet newspaper, and wrapped again in dry newspaper and plastic. After being labeled with the variety names, the budwood is stored in a refrigerated room at 28 to 30°F until early the following summer. The budwood is then removed from storage, and the buds are cut from it. Amateurs who cut budwood in the fall can also use this method of storage.

Budding

The actual budding begins during the first summer. It is accomplished by a two-member team—one member who makes a T-shaped cut on each plant and inserts the bud to be grafted, and another who ties the bud firmly in place. A good team can bud 3,000 to 5,000 plants per day. After budding, the top of the understock plant continues to grow, storing food in the root system. In warm areas buds are left exposed over the winter, but in colder climates the grafts are covered with soil to prevent winter damage.

Buds usually start to grow vigorously at the beginning of the second season, at which time all of the top growth of the understock is removed. The budded portion of the

Left: Budwood is harvested for grafting. Above: Lengths of budwood are deleafed and dethorned.

A shield-shaped cutting from a length of budwood has been inserted into a T-shaped cut in the understock.

A newly inserted bud is wrapped and tied.

plant continues to grow energetically. During the summer months, the canes are pruned to prevent their tops from breaking off and to encourage them to branch. Plants also receive water, fertilizer, and protection against insects and diseases.

Harvesting

All roses are harvested in the fall. In some areas of the country, the leaves fall off naturally; in others, they are removed after harvesting. Digging is done by a machine with a large U-shaped blade that cuts at the required depth, loosens the soil, and lifts the plants out of the ground. Teams of workers follow the digging machine to pick up and bundle roses for delivery to cold storage.

At the cold storage facility, the roses are placed onto a conveyor belt where they pass before workers who grade them, label them, and tie them into bundles, usually of 10 plants. After bundling, the tops of the canes are cut to a uniform length with a band saw. Roses are then placed into bins and stored in warehouses that are held at 32 to 40 degrees F and kept very humid. At a major facility, approximately 140,000 rosebushes may be processed, graded, pruned, labeled, tied, and stored in one day. The plants remain in cold storage through the fall and winter until shipping begins in the winter or spring.

Shipping

The finished product is processed and delivered in one of several ways. Roses destined for sale as bare-root stock have their roots wrapped in moist sphagnum peat moss and plastic and are shipped directly to mail-order customers. A lesser number are sent to garden centers for sale. Roses that will be sold in containers are planted into boxes and shipped, mainly to garden centers. Although some other shrubs are produced as balled-and-burlapped plants, this method is rarely if ever used for roses.

Tree roses are complicated and time-consuming to produce, requiring two budding operations and a three-year growth period, which make them more costly than bush roses.

Onto a root of the same type of understock used for bush roses, growers bud a stem of *R. multiflora*, *R. rugosa*, or 'De la Grifferaie' (a robust variety of uncertain parentage that is believed to be a *R. multiflora* hybrid). These roses are used because they make strong, straight stems. Then stock from the variety that will produce the flowers is budded onto the top of the stem. This stock can be from any variety of bush rose. To harvest tree roses, growers use a special high tractor that can pass over the plants as it digs. These plants are stored, shipped, and sold in the same manner as bush roses.

Although most large modern rose bushes are currently propagated by budding, commercial growers hope to turn increasingly to cuttings and tissue culture (cloning of new plants from small pieces of plant tissue) for mass production. Propagation from cuttings is less laborious than budding, and tissue culture can yield more disease-free plants. For the moment, though, more research must be done before these methods can become economical.

Gallery of Roses

Flat ('Sally Holmes')

Classical high-centered ('Mister Lincoln')

Fully opened ('Frontier Twirl')

Globular (The Reeve)

Quartered ('Sombreuil')

Single: 5 to 12 petals (Pink Meidiland)

Rosette (Sexy Rexy)

Semidouble: 13 to 16 petals (Rosa Mundi)

Double: 17 to 25 petals (Showbiz)

Full: 26 to 40 petals (Fragrant Cloud)

Very full: 41 and more petals (America)

Illustrated here are examples of flower forms used in the descriptions in this chapter.

When you plant roses in your garden they will repay you with beauty and fragrance for many years to come. But which roses should you plant? The selections in this guide will help you answer that question. Here you will find described and illustrated 486 roses for every garden purpose. They represent the finest roses from more than 20,000 cultivars currently available. They were chosen based on these factors: ease of availability coast to coast; vigor, disease resistance, and hardiness; fragrance; variety of color and shape; ratings in nationwide evaluations; and, of course, personal experience. Each selection is alphabetized within categories modified from the rose group classifications of the American Rose Society. "In This Chapter," as shown at the lower left corner of this page, provides a complete picture of the categories and where to find them.

Roses arouse strong passions, and any list will be, at least in part, subjective. Some folks like their beauty, some their fragrance. There are so many characteristics from which to choose that choosing the best of thousands in a traditional rose class can be quite challenging, even for the experts. While many knowledgeable people across North America have contributed to the selections, the roses in this guide undeniably represent personal favorites. Never hesitate to experiment with other roses you find at nurseries and plant sales—there are thousands to learn about and enjoy in your garden.

Color Classifications of the American Rose Society

White, near white, and white blend (Irresistible)

Apricot and apricot blend ('Loving Touch')

Light pink ('Royal Highness')

Medium red (Olympiad)

Light yellow (Elina)

Orange and orange blend (Livin' Easy)

Medium pink ('Queen Elizabeth')

Dark red (The Prince)

Medium yellow (Toulouse Lautrec)

Orange-pink and orange-pink blend (All That Jazz)

Deep yellow (Goldmarie)

Russet (Hot Cocoa)

Deep pink ('William Baffin')

Red blend (Handel)

Yellow blend (Sheila's Perfume)

Orange-red and orange-red blend (Paprika)

Pink blend (Gemini)

Mauve and mauve blend (Intrigue)

How to Use the Selection Guide

With thousands of varieties available for sale, choosing the right rose need not be mind-boggling. The pages that follow describe the most outstanding roses that are commercially available in the United States and Canada. Roses are listed alphabetically within each class (such as hybrid tea or floribunda). Every rose described is illustrated with a photograph.

While the descriptions may seem brief, each is packed with useful information. The varietal names used in this book are the ones most likely to be encountered in nurseries and catalogs. Capitalized names enclosed in single quotation marks are officially registered cultivar names. Capitalized names not enclosed in single quotation marks are commercial names, many of which are trademarked or registered.

Each time a rose is listed in this book, its name is followed by its classification, the color class assigned to

the rose by the American Rose Society (essential if you want to exhibit roses), year of introduction, introducer or breeder, and, if applicable, important awards.

Next, you'll find a description of the variety, including a more detailed description of its color, the form of its flowers, and the number of petals. The term *high-centered* means that the center of the open flower is higher than the edges, forming a triangular shape when viewed from the side. This shape is sometimes referred to as classic, or exhibition form. The term *cup-shaped* means that the center of the flower is on an even plane with its edges, and that the outline is semicircular when viewed from the side. The word *flat* means that the flower has so few petals that when fully open it looks flat from the side. Cup-shaped and flat flowers are often referred to as decorative or informal. Roses are often described as having a *reverse*

of a different color. The reverse is the outside of a petal. A few roses are described as *quartered* because they appear to be divided into distinct quadrants. Most roses have *double* flowers (with 25 to 45 petals); a lesser number are *single* (with 5 to 12 petals), *semidouble* (with 13 to 25 petals), or *very double* (with over 45 petals).

Also listed are plant form and size, leaf color and texture, and any special characteristics such as disease resistance and thorniness. The sizes listed are the average for that variety under optimum conditions. The hardiness zones listed are from the USDA Plant Hardiness Zone Map (see page 244).

At the end of each listing, you'll find the Roses in Review (RIR) rating of the American Rose Society (ARS). The RIR ratings, which rate all-around performance, range from 0 to 9.9—the higher the rating the better the rose, in the opinion of this influential group and its members. If you stick with roses whose RIR rating is at least 7.0, you will rarely be disappointed. However, roses with lower ratings may still be worth growing for their historical or aesthetic interest.

Not all roses have an RIR rating. Some roses are too new to have ratings; others have been assigned a provisional rating until their evaluation is complete. For yet other roses, ARS survey takers received too few responses to determine a rating. And even established ratings are subject to change.

Use the photographs in this selection guide to help you choose roses for any color scheme. The cool austerity of this formal garden is delightfully warmed up by hot red roses.

ROSE AWARDS

Hot Cocoa, AARS 2003

ALL-AMERICA ROSE SELECTIONS (AARS)

The All-America Rose Selections (AARS) is a nonprofit organization of U.S. rose producers and introducers. It tests new rose varieties and recommends the best to the general public. Only a few outstanding varieties bear the title "AARS Winner" each year. This award is a hallmark of excellence, indicating that the variety can be grown in almost any climate. The testing protocol is rigorous. Varieties are evaluated for two years in two dozen specially designated AARS gardens throughout the United States that offer varying levels of heat, drought, cold winds, insects, and diseases. They must survive the harsh winters of Illinois, the subtropical climate of Florida, and the Mediterranean climate of California. Not all varieties chosen for this honor are exhibition roses. In many cases judges select good garden varieties for their abundant flowers or their speed of bloom cycle. Since this program began in 1940, nearly 200 varieties have received the award.

AWARD OF EXCELLENCE FOR MINIATURE ROSES (AOE)

Each year the American Rose Society (ARS) tests miniature roses. Entries are tested for two years. The ARS wants to foster the development of new and better roses in the United States, to establish gardens for testing new varieties, to acquaint people with worthy roses, to award superior new roses, and to publicize and recommend those award-winning varieties. The test gardens for miniatures are at the American Rose Society in Shreveport, Louisiana, and at six other locations throughout the country. Almost 70 miniature roses have received this award since the start of the program in 1975.

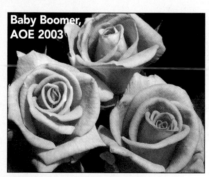

Baby Boomer, AOE 2003

ARS MINIATURE ROSE HALL OF FAME

This award program, established in 1999 by the American Rose Society, recognizes sustained achievement by a popular variety existing in commerce for more than 20 years. To date, there have been 10 recipients.

Starina, ARS Miniature Hall of Fame, 1999

WORLD FEDERATION OF ROSE SOCIETIES (WFRS ROSE HALL OF FAME)

Every three years the World Federation of Rose Societies votes on one rose to receive this title. To date 10 varieties have been honored.

Ingrid Bergman, WFRS Rose Hall of Fame

WORLD FEDERATION OF ROSE SOCIETIES (WFRS OLD ROSE HALL OF FAME)

Every three years the World Federation of Rose Societies votes on one old garden rose to receive this title. To date 11 varieties have been honored.

'Mme Alfred Carrière', WFRS Old Rose Hall of Fame

Hybrid Tea and Grandiflora Roses

Hybrid teas are repeat bloomers that create a striking display when massed in rose beds and borders. Because of their high-centered sculptural blooms that are long-lasting when cut, they are popular exhibition flowers in rose shows. Plants have an upright habit and reach 5 to 6 feet high and an average width of 3 to 4 feet by the end of the growing season. They typically produce one flower at the end of each long stem at regular intervals of 35 to 45 days. Spent flowers must be removed to induce the next flowering cycle. Deadheading is best done by cutting the stem to the nearest 5-leaflet set of foliage with a stem thickness greater than a pencil. Occasionally hybrid teas form clusters of flowers at the end of stems. Removing the side buds of the cluster encourages larger, more perfectly shaped single blooms on longer stems for cutting or exhibition.

Today the hybrid tea has become the most popular class of modern roses, easily recognizable by large symmetrically shaped flowers on long stems. Although the first hybrid tea was introduced in 1867, it wasn't until 1945 and the introduction of 'Peace' that hybridizing hybrid teas took off. There are now more than 10,000 hybrid teas in every color except true blue or black.

Breeders introduced the first grandiflora, an outgrowth of hybrid teas, in 1954. Grandifloras display the characteristics of a hybrid tea and also bear clusters, or trusses, of flowers. They grow to a commanding height of 6 to 8 feet tall.

Hybrid Tea and Grandiflora Roses

(continued)

■ Andrea Steltzer ('KORfachrit')
Hybrid tea, light pink, 1992, Kordes. Clear pink, large high-centered blooms (25 to 30 petals) on long straight stems. Light fragrance. Upright plants are 5 to 7 feet tall with glossy dark foliage. Protect from mildew. Zones 6–10. RIR=7.6.

■ Black Magic ('TANkalgic')
Hybrid tea, dark red, 1997, Tantau. Velvety black buds open to deep garnet-red blooms of exhibition form (30 petals, 4 to 5 inches across). Very long stems. Slight, sweet fragrance. Upright, 5 to 6 feet tall, with dark green leaves. Zones 5–10. RIR=7.7.

■ Artistry ('JACirst') Hybrid tea, orange-pink, 1998, Zary, AARS. Large double flowers (4 to 5 inches across, 30–35 petals), with good exhibition form, are coral-orange with a creamy coral reverse. Best color and form develop during periods of high heat. Only slight fragrance. Upright, tall plants have dark, semiglossy leaves. Zones 5–10. RIR=7.9.

■ Brandy ('AROcad') Hybrid tea, apricot blend, 1981, Swim & Christensen, AARS. Elegant pointed buds on long stems begin vivid deep apricot and fade to a rich warm apricot as the flowers open. Mild tea fragrance. Plants grow 5 to 6 feet tall with large glossy leaves. Good in warm climates. Zones 6–10. RIR=7.3.

■ Brigadoon ('JACpal') Hybrid tea, pink blend, 1991, Warriner, AARS. Double flowers (25 to 30 petals) of excellent form are creamy pink near the center blending to deep coral rose-pink at the edge. Vigorous, tall, upright plants have dark green semi-glossy leaves that can be quite large in cool climates. Zones 5–9. RIR=7.7.

■ Barbra Streisand ('WEKquaneze') Hybrid tea, mauve, 1999, Carruth. Lavender blooms are blushed with purple that deepens in cool climates. Strong sweet rose scent. Plants grow 3 to 6 feet tall with long stems and glossy dark foliage that is remarkably disease-resistant. Zones 5–10. RIR=7.2.

■ Bride's Dream ('KORoyness') Hybrid tea, light pink, 1985, Kordes. Long, elegant, angelic pastel pink blooms (30 to 35 petals) with porcelain look. Can grow 6 to 8 feet tall. Zones 5–10. RIR=8.1.

■ Cajun Sunrise Hybrid tea, pink blend, 2000, Edwards. Elegant high-centered blooms (25 to 40 petals, 4 to 5 inches across) are rich pink at the edge blending to creamy yellow in the center. Mild fragrance. Upright, 4 to 5 feet tall; lustrous dark foliage. Zones 6–10.

■ **Candelabra ('JACcinqo')**
Grandiflora, pink blend, 1998, Zary,
AARS. Clusters of long, pointed buds
open to 4-inch coral orange flowers
with a slight fragrance. Plants grow
4 to 5 feet tall with dark green,
glossy foliage. Zones 5–10. RIR=7.6.

■ **Caribbean ('KORbirac')**
Grandiflora, apricot blend, 1992,
Kordes, AARS. Borne in small
clusters, the large, double flowers
(30 to 40 petals) of exhibition high-
centered form are apricot, orange,
and yellow. Plants are upright
bushes 3 to 5 feet tall with large,
dark green, glossy foliage and
thorny stems. Zones 5–10. RIR=7.6.

■ **'Chrysler Imperial'** Hybrid tea,
dark red, 1952, Lammerts, AARS.
A classic favorite for its rich, velvety,
crimson red blooms with exhibition
high-centered form (45 to 50 petals)
and powerful, delicious fragrance.
Likes heat. Zones 5–10. RIR=7.7.

■ **'Captain Harry Stebbings'** Hybrid tea, deep pink, 1980, Stebbings.
Exhibition-quality blooms open from long, pointed buds into very large,
high-centered, deep pink flowers (40 to 45 petals) with a powerful fruity
fragrance. Plants are tall and slightly spreading, with large leathery leaves.
Zones 5–10. RIR=7.8.

■ **Cesar E Chavez ('JAColman')**
Hybrid tea, medium red, 2002, Zary.
Clear, bright red flowers of high-
centered exhibition form (4 inches
across, 30 to 35 petals) and excellent
substance, on long stems. 4 to 5 feet
tall; glossy dark foliage. Zones 5–10.

■ **'Classic Touch'** Hybrid tea, light
pink, 1991, Hefner. Large blooms are
a clear, light pink with a slight
fragrance. Plants are tall and upright
with large, medium green semi-
glossy leaves. Zones 5–10. RIR=7.5.

■ **Cherry Parfait ('MEIsponge')**
Grandiflora, red blend, 2003,
Meilland, AARS. White petals with
broad, bright red edges. Fast repeat.
Loose, spreading 3-foot plants good
for border, combined with
perennials. Zones 5–10.

■ **Crimson Bouquet**
('KORbeteillich') Grandiflora, dark
red, 1999, Kordes, AARS. Abundant
small clusters of large flowers (30 to
35 petals) that are a clear, bright
red. Slight fragrance. Flower size
is largest and petal count highest
in cool climates. Grows upright 4 to
5 feet tall with glossy, deep green
foliage that remains remarkably
healthy. Zones 5–10. RIR=7.7.

Hybrid Tea and Grandiflora Roses
(continued)

■ **'Crimson Glory'** Hybrid tea, dark red, 1935, Kordes. Velvety crimson blooms (30 petals) with a rich damask fragrance on straight stems. Vigorous, 4 to 6 feet tall, slightly spreading with leathery, dark, healthy foliage. Zones 5–9. RIR=7.3.

■ **Double Delight ('ANDeli')** Hybrid tea, red blend, 1977, Swim & Ellis, AARS, WFRS, James Alexander Gamble Fragrance Medal. High-centered flowers (30 to 35 petals) are creamy white blending to intense strawberry-red at the edge. Spicy fragrance. Upright, 4 to 6 feet. Needs full sun for best color. Prone to mildew. Zones 6–10. RIR=8.5.

■ **Crystalline ('ARObipy')** Hybrid tea, white, 1987, Christenson & Carruth. Originally bred for cut flowers. Weatherproof snowy white blossoms (30 to 35 petals) on long stems, often in grandiflora-like clusters. Spicy fragrance. Upright plants reach 5 to 6 feet tall. Excellent in hot climates. Zones 5–10. RIR=8.1.

■ **'Dublin'** Hybrid tea, medium red, 1982, Perry. Large, smoky red exhibition-form flowers (35 to 40 petals) borne on long straight stems. Intense raspberry fragrance. Plants are upright with large, matte-textured leaves. Needs humid warm evenings. Zones 5–10. RIR=8.3.

■ **Elegant Beauty ('KORgatum')** Hybrid tea, light yellow, 1982, Kordes. Large double flowers (30 to 35 petals) are pale yellow flushed with a hint of pink, on long stems. Plants are upright and bushy with large, dark, matte-textured leaves. Excellent for humid climates in the South. Zones 5–10. RIR=8.1.

■ **Diana, Princess of Wales ('JACshaq')** Hybrid tea, pink blend, 1998, Zary. Huge (4- to 5-inch) exhibition-form flowers on long, strong stems. Ivory petals (30 to 35) are overlaid with pink blush. Sweet fragrance. Has tendency to produce clusters. Zones 5–10. RIR=7.5.

■ **'Duet'** Hybrid tea, medium pink, 1960, Swim, AARS. Large 4-inch flowers (30+ petals) are light pink, deeper on the reverse. Slight tea fragrance. Often produces clusters. Good repeat; upright plants reach 6 to 8 feet tall with leathery, dark, glossy foliage. Zones 5–11. RIR=6.4.

■ **Elina ('DICjana')** Hybrid tea, light yellow, 1984, Dickson. White buds open to large, luminous, light yellow flowers (35+ petals) with deep cream centers. Light fragrance. Vigorous; reaches 6 to 8 feet tall in mild climates. Disease-resistant. Glossy dark foliage. Zones 5–10. RIR=8.7.

■ **'Elizabeth Taylor'** Hybrid tea, deep pink, 1985, Weddle. Shocking deep pink petals with smoky edges in flowers of exhibition form (30 to 35 petals). Prefers warm climates for best flower size. Light spicy perfume. Upright; dark, semi-glossy leaves. Zones 5–10. RIR=8.5.

■ **Fame! ('JACzor')** Grandiflora, deep pink, 1999, Zary, AARS. Double flowers (30 to 35 petals) of exhibition form are a deep shocking pink that is almost red, borne in small clusters. Slight fragrance. Full and bushy, 3 to 4 feet tall, with large, dark green foliage. Zones 5–10. RIR=8.1.

■ **'First Prize'** Hybrid tea, pink blend, 1970, Boerner, AARS. Classic high-centered blooms with ivory centers blending to pink on the edges of the petals. Mild tea fragrance. Vigorous, upright, with long, thorny stems and large, dark, leathery leaves. Zones 5–10. RIR=8.3.

■ **Folklore ('KORlore')** Hybrid tea, orange blend, 1977, Kordes. Large flowers of perfect exhibition form (40 to 45 petals, 4 to 5 inches across), with orange petals lighter on the reverse. Rich, intense fragrance. Tall, vigorous, upright growth with stems that tend to zig-zag. Glossy dark leaves. Zones 5–11. RIR=8.2.

■ **Fragrant Cloud ('TANellis')** Hybrid tea, orange-red, 1967, Tantau. Symmetrical, flaming orange-red flowers (about 30 petals) retain color without fading. Heavy, spicy-sweet perfume. Vigorous; grows 3 to 5 feet tall with large glossy green leaves. Can suffer from black spot in damp climates. Zones 5–10. RIR=8.1.

■ **Fragrant Plum ('AROplumi')** Grandiflora, mauve, 1990, Christenson. High-centered, lavender blooms age gracefully to smoky plum-purple toward edges. Fragrance is strong and fruity. Upright, bushy plants grow 4 to 6 feet tall. Zones 5–10.

■ **'Fragrant Hour'** Hybrid tea, orange pink, 1973, McGredy. Large, high-pointed, bronze-pink flowers (30 to 35 petals, 4- to 4½ inches across) have an intense, rich fragrance. Foliage is light green. Zones 5–10. RIR=7.4.

■ **Gemini ('JACnepal')** Hybrid tea, pink blend, 1999, Zary, AARS. Vigorous plant with symmetrical creamy blooms (35 to 40 petals) richly blushed with coral pink, on long stems. Sweet fragrance. Upright and spreading 5 to 6 feet tall with large, deep green, glossy leaves. Zones 5–10. RIR=8.1.

Hybrid Tea and Grandiflora Roses
(continued)

■ **Gift of Life ('HARelan')** Hybrid tea, yellow blend, 1999, Harkness. Soft yellow blooms with a hint of pink. Long stems. Grows 3 to 4 feet tall with large, glossy foliage. Raises funds for the Organ Donor Program and the National Kidney Foundation. Zones 5–10. RIR=7.6.

■ **Glowing Peace ('MEIzoelo')** Grandiflora, yellow blend, 1999, Selection Meilland, AARS. Yellow and orange flowers in small clusters. Fragrance is slight. Plants are upright and bushy with dark green, glossy leaves. Zones 5–10. RIR=7.5.

■ **Gold Medal ('AROyqueli')** Grandiflora, medium yellow, 1982, Christensen. Open trusses of deep yellow blossoms with burnt orange to red edge on the petals. Flowers last long when cut. Plants are vigorous, upright, and tall (5 to 7 feet). Zones 5–10. RIR=8.5.

■ **'Granada'** Hybrid tea, red blend, 1963, Lindquist, AARS, James Alexander Gamble Fragrance Award. A classic. Perfectly formed large flowers (4 to 5 inches) that blend orange-red and rose with lemon-yellow deep in the center. Heady damask-and-spice fragrance. Vigorous, upright with leathery, crinkled foliage. Zones 5–10. RIR=7.9.

■ **Helen Naude ('KORdiena')** Hybrid tea, white, 1996, Kordes. Large, very double blooms 4 to 5 inches across are white with a light blushing of pink. Bushes grow 3 to 5 feet tall with dull, medium-green foliage. Zones 5–10. RIR=7.7.

■ **Honor ('JAColite')** Hybrid tea, white, 1980, Warriner, AARS. Pure white blossoms of elegant sculptural form. Slight fragrance. Plants are tall and stately with long, straight stems and large, dark leaves that set off the flowers well. Excellent for Pacific Coast regions. Zones 5–10. RIR=7.7.

■ **Ingrid Bergman ('POUlman')** Hybrid tea, dark red, 1984, Olesen, WFRS. Powerfully fragrant, velvety red flowers (35 to 40 petals) are borne one to a stem and last long when cut. Color holds well, even in heat. Upright plants reach 5 to 6 feet tall, with dark, leathery, disease-resistant foliage. Zones 5–10. RIR=7.7.

■ **Hot Princess ('TANtocnirp')** Hybrid tea, deep pink, 2000, Tantau. Bred for the florist trade, with exquisite sculptural blooms of excellent substance and an almost porcelain quality. Deepest of deep pinks, nearly red. Quite tender; needs winter protection. Zones 7–10. RIR=7.9.

■ **Jardins de Bagatelle** ('MEImafris') Hybrid tea, white, 1986, Meilland. Perfectly formed creamy pink flowers tipped with pale pink, one to a stem. Strong rose bouquet. Upright plants grow 4 to 6 feet tall with medium green, semi-glossy foliage. Zones 5–9. RIR=7.4.

■ **'John F. Kennedy'** Hybrid tea, white, 1965, Boerner. Huge blazing white blooms of classic exhibition form (5 to 5½ inches across, 40 to 50 petals). Good substance resists heat and cold. Flowers sometimes have a greenish tint. Moderate licorice scent. Vigorous and upright with leathery, healthy foliage. Zones 5–10. RIR=6.2.

■ **Joyfulness** ('TANsinnroh') Hybrid tea, apricot blend, 1984, Tantau. Classic high-pointed form, large long-lasting blooms, a blend of apricot and orange blending to yellow at the base of the petals. Slight fragrance. Upright, 3 to 5 feet tall with glossy, dark foliage. Zones 5–10. RIR=8.1.

■ **'Just Joey'** Hybrid tea, orange blend, 1972, Cants, WFRS. Large, 5-inch, ruffled, loose double flowers are a rich apricot-buff-orange blend. Blooms are long-lasting. Powerful, rich fruity fragrance. Plants grow 5 to 6 feet tall with lush, glossy, leathery green foliage. Zones 5–10. RIR=8.0.

■ **Kardinal** ('KORlingo') Hybrid tea, medium red, 1986, Kordes. Elegant long stems support shapely buds opening to brilliant red blooms that last remarkably long when cut. Fragrance is light. Grows 4 to 6 feet tall with glossy, dark green foliage. Zones 5–10. RIR=8.6.

■ **Keepsake, Esmeralda** ('KORmalda') Hybrid tea, pink blend, 1981, Kordes. Deep pink flowers (40 petals) are blended with lighter shades of pink. Petals are reflexed. Moderate fragrance. Late bloomer in spring. Vigorous, spreading, disease-resistant bushes. Zones 6–10. RIR=8.1.

■ **'Louise Estes'** Hybrid tea, pink blend, 1991, Winchel. Exhibition-form flowers (40 to 45 petals) are medium pink with a white reverse to the petals, ruffled in some climates. Strong fruity fragrance. Plants are vigorous, tall, upright, resistant to mildew. Zones 5–10. RIR=8.2.

■ **Love & Peace** ('BALpeace') Hybrid tea, yellow blend, 2002, Lim & Twomey, AARS. Large symmetrical blooms (40+ petals) are yellow with deep pink to red blush. Mild fragrance. Best flower production is in humid climates. Color is most intense in moderate climates. Medium disease resistance. Grows 5 to 6 feet high. Zones 5–10.

■ **Lovers Lane** ('JACinber') Hybrid tea, medium red, 2000, Zary. Pure brilliant red blooms with a lighter reverse are large with classic exhibition form (35 petals, 4 to 5 inches across). Long-lasting in the vase. Vigorous, upright plants grow 4 to 5 feet tall with semi-glossy, dark green leaves. Zones 5–10.

Hybrid Tea and Grandiflora Roses
(continued)

■ **Lynn Anderson ('WEKjoe')**
Hybrid tea, pink blend, 1993, Winchel. White flowers edged in striking deep pink. Slight fragrance, few thorns. Upright, tall, bushy with large leaves. Zones 5–11. RIR=7.4.

■ **Mavrik** Hybrid tea, light pink, 1999, Edwards. Rich pink blending to cream in the center of huge blooms up to 6 inches across. Tender. Zones 7–11. RIR=7.7.

■ **'Marijke Koopman'** Hybrid tea, medium pink, 1979, Fryer. Clear pink flowers of classic high-centered form (25 petals) and moderate fragrance. Flowers are self-cleaning. Plants are vigorous, medium-tall, with dark leathery foliage. Disease-resistant. Zones 5–10. RIR=8.7.

■ **Memorial Day ('WEKblunez')**
Hybrid tea, medium pink, 2001, Carruth, AARS. Clear pink blooms washed with lavender are very large and full (up to 5 inches across, 50+petals). Powerful damask scent; long stems. Upright, 3 to 4 feet tall. Loves hot weather. Zones 5–10.

■ **Marilyn Monroe ('WEKsunspat')**
Hybrid tea, apricot blend, 2003, Carruth. Creamy apricot blooms washed with a hint of green are large, full (30 to 35 petals), and of exhibition form. Mild fragrance. Flowers last long in the vase. Upright, 4 to 5 feet tall, dark green leaves. The best apricot for hot climates. Zones 5–11.

■ **Midas Touch ('JACtou')** Hybrid tea, deep yellow, 1992, Christensen, AARS. Bright golden yellow color is nonfading. Lovely musk fragrance. Plants are upright and bushy with medium green, matte-textured foliage. Zones 5–11. RIR=7.4.

■ **'Mikado'** Hybrid tea, red blend, 1987, Suzuki, AARS. Brilliant scarlet flowers are yellow at the base of the petals; the two-toned effect is most intense at first flush in early summer and again in fall. Light spicy fragrance. Plants are upright and tall with medium green, highly polished foliage. Zones 5–10. RIR=7.3.

■ **'Mister Lincoln'**
Hybrid tea, dark red, 1964, Swim & Weeks, AARS. A classic, widely planted in spite of its susceptibility to mildew. Rich deep red flowers of exhibition high-centered form, with heavy damask fragrance. Plants are tall, vigorous, best where days are warm and nights cool. Zones 5–10. RIR=8.4.

■ <u>Moonstone</u> ('WEKcryland')
Hybrid tea, white, 1998, Carruth.
Symmetrical white blooms delicately
edged in pink. Mild tea-and-rose
fragrance. Vigorous, 5 to 7 feet tall
with large leaves and excellent
disease resistance. Stems are long
and straight. Zones 5–10. RIR=8.2.

■ **New Zealand ('MACgenev')** Hybrid tea, light pink, 1989, McGredy.
Soft, symmetrical creamy pink blooms (30 to 35 petals) of heavy substance.
Delicious honeysuckle fragrance. Largest bloom size occurs in cool climates.
Grows 4 to 6 feet tall with lush, dark, glossy foliage. Excellent disease
resistance. Zones 5–10. RIR=7.8.

■ **'Oklahoma'** Hybrid tea, dark red,
1964, Swim & Weeks. A classic, still-
popular dark red rose, with large full
blossoms (40 to 45 petals, 4 to 5
inches across) and intense fragrance.
Long, strong stems. Tall plants reach
5 to 6 feet, with dark, matte-textured
foliage. Zones 5–10. RIR=6.7.

■ <u>Olympiad</u> **('MACauck')** Hybrid
tea, medium red, 1982, McGredy,
AARS. Rich red flowers of exhibition
form (30 to 35 petals). Grows 4 to
6 feet tall with large, deeply veined
foliage that is highly disease-
resistant. Zones 5–10. <u>RIR=8.7.</u>

■ **Opening Night ('JAColber')**
Hybrid tea, dark red, 1998, Zary,
AARS. Large, brilliant, deep red
flowers sparkle atop long, strong,
straight stems ideal for cutting.
Plants are tall and slightly spreading
with dark, semi-glossy foliage.
Highly disease-resistant. Prefers
cooler temperatures. Zones 5–10.
RIR=7.8.

■ **Opulence ('JACosch')** Hybrid
tea, white, 1997, Zary. Bred for the
florist trade. Abundant creamy ivory
blooms (40 petals, 4 to 5 inches
across) of perfect exhibition quality
on long strong stems. Vigorous, 5 to
6 feet tall. Tender, but excellent for
mild climates. Zones 7–11. RIR=7.5.

■ **Papa Meilland ('MEIsar')** Hybrid
tea, dark red, 1963, <u>Meilland</u>, WFRS,
James Alexander Gamble Fragrance
Medal. Dark, velvety crimson flowers
of classic high-centered form are
intensely fragrant. Vigorous upright
plants have glossy olive-green
leaves. Zones 5–10. RIR=7.7.

■ **Paradise ('WEZip')** Hybrid tea,
mauve, 1978, Weeks, AARS. Very
large blooms are silvery-lavender
shading to ruby red at the edges
of the petals. Moderate fragrance.
Upright and tall with dark, glossy
leaves. In dry hot climates blooms
can lack substance and foliage can
burn. Zones 5–8. RIR=7.5.

Hybrid Tea and Grandiflora Roses

(continued)

■ **'Peace'** Hybrid tea, yellow blend, 1945, Meilland, AARS, WFRS. The classic that established the standards for hybrid teas in the 20th century. Huge fragrant blossoms up to 6 inches across (40 to 45 petals) with luminous colors blending cream, pink, and yellow. Tall, vigorous plants with large, dark, leathery, glossy leaves. Zones 5–9. RIR=8.2.

■ **Peter Mayle ('MEIzincaro')** Hybrid tea, deep pink, 2001, Meilland. Huge, deep reddish-pink flowers on strong straight stems are symmetrical and colorfast, holding well even in the hottest summers. Blossoms are intensely fragrant. Plants grow 4 to 6 feet tall with dark green foliage. Zones 5–10.

■ **Perfect Moment ('KORwilma')** Hybrid tea, red blend, 1989, Kordes, AARS. Dazzling red blooms (25 to 30 petals) with an electric yellow inner glow are large, weatherproof, long-lasting. Compact plants reach 4 to 6 feet with dark green, disease-resistant leaves. Zones 5–10. RIR=7.7.

■ **'Pink Parfait'** Grandiflora, pink blend, 1960, Swim, AARS. Produced in large clusters on long stems, flowers have outer petals of medium pink blending to pale orange in the center, with classic high-centered form (23 petals, 3½ to 4 inches across). Vigorous, upright, with semi-glossy leathery leaves. Good disease resistance. Zones 5–10. RIR=7.9.

■ **'Queen Elizabeth'** Grandiflora, medium pink, 1954, Lammerts, AARS, WFRS. The beloved first grandiflora that adorns gardens all over the world. Large trusses of shell-pink blossoms (about 35 petals); strong straight stems. Color is clear and weatherproof. Vigorous upright plants grow 6 to 10 feet high. Zones 5–10. RIR=6.3.

■ **Perfectly Red ('JACrove')** Hybrid tea, dark red, 1999, Zary. Dark red flowers are large (4 to 4½ inches across), borne one to each long straight stem. Plants are upright 4 to 5 feet tall with dark, semi-glossy leaves. Zones 5–10. RIR=7.6.

■ **Pristine ('JACpico')** Hybrid tea, white, 1978, Warriner. Sculptural, near-white flowers are delicately blushed with pink; the blooms are large and substantial (25 to 30 petals) with an almost porcelain effect. Flowers open quickly, last only a few days. Stems are long, strong, and very thorny. Upright with large, dark leaves; highly disease-resistant. Zones 5–10. RIR=8.7.

■ **Rina Hugo ('DORvizo')** Hybrid tea, deep pink, 1993, Dorieux. While officially classified as a hybrid tea, this variety produces large clusters of heavy blooms (40 to 50 petals) in an electric, deep pink hue. Zones 5–10. RIR=7.8.

■ **Rio Samba ('JACrite')** Hybrid tea, yellow blend, 1991, Warriner, AARS. Exhibition-quality blooms (15 to 25 petals) are a luscious medium yellow shading to peach-pink. Fragrance is slight. Plants are upright and bushy with dark, matte-textured foliage. Zones 5–10. RIR=7.3.

■ **'Royal Highness'** Hybrid tea, light pink, 1962, Swim & Weeks, AARS. The large, high-centered, pale pink blooms (43+ petals) are symmetrical and fragrant (sweet tea fragrance). Bloom size and color are best in moderate temperatures. Vigorous, upright (5 to 7 feet tall) with lustrous foliage. Highly disease-resistant. Zones 5–10. RIR=7.7.

■ **Secret ('HILaroma')** Hybrid tea, pink blend, 1992, Tracy, AARS. Light creamy pink flowers edged in deep pink are large and well-formed on strong stems. Intense sweet and spicy fragrance. Plants are 3 to 5 feet tall and bushy, with large, medium green, semi-glossy leaves. Zones 5–10. RIR=7.7.

■ **Sheer Bliss ('JACtro')** Hybrid tea, white, 1985, Warriner, AARS. Large, sculptural, high-centered flowers are white with a pink center. Spicy fragrance. Blooms can suffer in rain. Plants are upright with matte-textured foliage. Prone to mildew if not protected; best in dry sunny climates. Zones 5–10. RIR=7.8.

■ **Sheer Elegance ('TWObe')** Hybrid tea, orange pink, 1989, Twomey, AARS. Huge (4 to 4½ inches across) soft creamy pink blooms with darker pink edges. Musk fragrance. Tall upright bushes have large, dark green, glossy leaves. Best in cooler climates for maximum bloom size and color. Zones 5–10. RIR=7.6.

■ **Signature ('JACnor')** Hybrid tea, pink blend, 1998, Warriner. Brilliant deep pink blossoms blend to cream in the center. Sculptural, high-centered form (26 to 40 petals) in large 5-inch blossoms. Light fruity fragrance. Plants are tall (4 to 5 feet) and thorny, with large, dark, semi-glossy leaves. Zones 5–10. RIR=7.6.

■ **St. Patrick ('WEKamanda')** Hybrid tea, medium yellow, 1999, Strickland, AARS. Chartreuse buds open slowly into cool yellow flowers. In warm, humid climates the outer petals shade to green; in cool climates they show a touch of gold. Rounded bushes grow 4 to 5 feet tall with dark, matte-textured foliage. Highly disease-resistant. Zones 5–10. RIR=8.0.

Hybrid Tea and Grandiflora Roses
(continued)

■ **Stainless Steel ('WEKblusi')**
Hybrid tea, mauve, 1991, Carruth.
Large, elegant, well-formed blossoms
(5 to 6 inches across) borne in small
clusters are an unusual silvery-gray.
Intense sweet rose fragrance. Color
is best in cool climates. Upright and
tall, with semi-glossy foliage. Prone
to mildew. Zones 5–10. RIR=7.6.

■ **'Suffolk'** Hybrid tea, white, 1983,
Perry. Large, high-centered blossoms
are white with pink at the tips of
the petals. Upright plants have large,
medium green, matte-textured
leaves. Zones 5–10. RIR=8.3.

■ **Sunset Celebration ('Fryxotic')**
Hybrid tea, apricot blend, 1999,
Fryer, AARS. Large, creamy apricot-
to-amber flowers 4 to 5 inches
across hold their color well in heat,
although colors are deeper in cool
conditions. Sweet apple fragrance.
Upright and well-rounded, reaching
5 to 6 feet, with large, medium green
leaves. Zones 5–10. RIR=7.8.

■ **'Sutter's Gold'** Hybrid tea,
orange blend, 1950, Swim, AARS,
James Alexander Gamble Fragrance
Medal. A favorite for more than a
half-century due to its unusual color,
superb form, and intense fragrance.
Large flowers are golden orange,
often touched with red on the outer
petals. Vigorous, upright, with dark
leathery leaves. Zones 5–10.

■ **'Tiffany'** Hybrid tea, pink blend,
1954, Lindquist, AARS, James
Alexander Gamble Fragrance
Medal. Satiny, medium pink flowers
blending into yellow at the base
are large (4 to 5 inches across) with
powerful fragrance and superior
exhibition form. Long straight stems.
Grows 4 to 5 feet tall with dark
glossy foliage. Zones 5–10. RIR=7.8.

■ **Timeless ('JACecond')** Hybrid
tea, deep pink, 1998, Zary, AARS.
Long shapely buds slowly spiral
open to lustrous evenly dark pink
blooms (about 25 petals). Slight
fragrance. Plants grow 4 to 6 feet tall
with medium, dark green, semi-
glossy foliage. Zones 5–10. RIR=7.8.

■ **Toulouse Lautrec ('MEIrevolt')**
Hybrid tea, medium yellow, 1994,
Meilland. Although technically
classified as a hybrid tea, this
member of the Romantica series
looks and behaves more like an old
garden rose, with large, very double
and full yellow blossoms (90 petals).
Rounded, shrubby bushes reach
5 feet tall with dark green, glossy
foliage. Zones 5–9.

■ **Touch of Class ('KRIcarlo')**
Hybrid tea, orange-pink, 1984,
Kriloff, AARS. One of the most
highly rated exhibition subjects, with
medium pink flowers shaded with
coral and cream that keep their form
for weeks. Colors can fade in hot
sun. Grows 4 to 5 feet tall with
large, dark, semi-glossy leaves. Prone
to mildew. Zones 6–11. RIR=9.0.

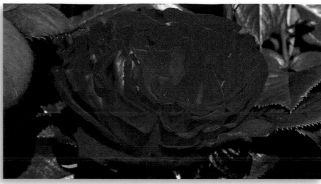

■ **Tournament of Roses ('JACient')** Grandiflora, medium pink, 1988, Warriner, AARS. Clusters of large, light coral pink flowers with a deep pink reverse. Good exhibition form. Color is deepest in warm weather. No fragrance. Upright and bushy with large, dark, semi-glossy leaves. Disease-resistant. Zones 5–10. RIR=8.3.

■ **Traviata ('MEllavio')** Hybrid tea, deep red, 1998, Meilland. Ruby red blooms are very full (100 petals) with a quartered form reminiscent of an old garden rose. Borne one to a stem, they last over a week in the vase. Rich fragrance. Bushy plants grow 4 to 5 feet tall with dark, disease-resistant foliage. Zones 5–10. RIR=7.7.

■ **Tropicana ('TANorstar')** Hybrid tea, orange-red, 1960, Tantau, AARS. Large, luminous, coral-orange flowers have excellent exhibition form and sweet, fruity fragrance. Vigorous upright plants have dark, glossy, leathery leaves. Best east of the Rockies. Zones 5–10. RIR=7.6.

■ **'Uncle Joe'** Hybrid tea, dark red, 1972, Kern Rose Nursery. A favorite in the Southeast. Extremely large, full blooms (80+ petals, 4 to 5 inches wide) of luscious red need high heat and humidity for best show. Large, vigorous, 6 to 8 feet tall. Leathery, dark leaves. Zones 5–10. RIR=8.0.

■ **Valencia ('KOReklia')** Hybrid tea, apricot blend, 1989, Kordes. Huge, full, high-centered flowers (30 to 40 petals) are pure copper-yellow. Sweet, enduring fragrance. Plants are somewhat angular, reaching 5 to 6 feet tall, with dark, large, leathery leaves that have good disease resistance. Zones 5–10. RIR=7.9.

■ **Veteran's Honor ('JACopper')** Hybrid tea, dark red, 1999, Zary. Sculptural 2-inch buds open into deep red flowers (25 to 30 petals) of excellent exhibition form. Color holds well in heat. Flowers survive for weeks in the garden. Vigorous, upright, 5 to 7 feet tall; dark, semi-glossy foliage. Zones 5–10. RIR=8.1.

■ **Whisper ('DICwisp')** Hybrid tea, white, 2004, Dickson, AARS. Creamy white blooms are large (5 inches across) and of exhibition form. Upright, 4 to 5 feet tall. Dark, semi-glossy leaves are highly disease-resistant. Zones 5–10.

■ **World War II Memorial Rose ('WEZgrey')** Hybrid tea, mauve, 2000, Weeks. Smoky blooms are soft white with gray and a tinge of lavender. Upright plants grow 4 to 6 feet tall. Zones 5–10. RIR=7.5.

Floribunda and Polyantha Roses

loribundas provide massive colorful, long-lasting garden displays. They make attractive low-growing hedges and excellent border accents. Second only to hybrid teas and grandifloras in popularity, floribundas grow 3 to 5 feet tall and bear flowers profusely in clusters, or trusses. More than one bloom in each truss is open at any given time. The distinct advantage of floribundas is their ability to bloom continually, whereas hybrid teas bloom in cycles of six to seven weeks. Floribundas often are hardier, easier to care for, and more reliable in wet weather than hybrid teas. Floribundas also offer a wider range of flower forms—single-petaled, semi-double, double, and rosette.

Polyanthas are sturdy plants that are smaller than floribundas. They produce large clusters of 1-inch flowers and have small leaves. Polyanthas and floribundas descend from *R. multiflora*, a wild rose with an abundance of little flowers. Breeders improved it for garden display because it has the advantage of producing clusters of flowers on one stem rather than a solitary bloom.

'Playboy', a floribunda developed in Scotland by Cocker and introduced in 1976, combines the simplicity of a single-petaled rose with rambunctious colors—orange and scarlet with a yellow eye.

Floribunda and Polyantha Roses
(continued)

■ **'Angel Face'** Floribunda, mauve, 1968, Swim & Weeks, AARS. Ruffled blooms (25 to 30 petals) with a strong aroma of sweet citrus appear continuously all season. Small plants grow 2 to 3 feet tall and wide. Zones 5–9. RIR=7.7.

■ **Amber Queen ('HARroony')** Floribunda, apricot blend, 1983, Harkness, AARS. Golden apricot flowers (30 petals, 2 to 3 inches wide, sweet and spicy scent) rarely fade, even in strong sun. Medium green foliage resists most diseases, even in partial shade. Plants grow 2 to 3 feet tall. Zones 5–10. RIR=6.8.

■ **'Anthony Meilland' (MEItalbaz)** Floribunda, medium yellow, 1994, Meilland. Elegant clusters of large, double (25 to 30 petals), nonfading flowers with a light fragrance. Mounded bush is vigorous, symmetrical, 4 to 5 feet tall. Zones 5–10.

■ **'Apricot Nectar'** Floribunda, apricot blend, 1965, Boerner, AARS. Large blossoms (30 to 40 petals). Glossy dark green, disease-resistant foliage, 3 to 4 feet tall. Fragrant. Zones 5–10. RIR=8.0.

■ **Betty Boop ('WEKplapic')** Floribunda, red blend, 1999, Carruth, AARS. Eye-catching blooms (6 to 12 petals) are ivory-yellow edged with red, borne in small clusters. Light fruity fragrance. Reblooms well, even without deadheading. Rounded plant grows 3 to 5 feet tall, covered with clean glossy leaves. Zones 5–10. RIR=8.0.

■ **'Betty Prior'** Floribunda, medium pink, 1935, Prior. A classic widely grown today for its nonstop blooms, vigor, versatility, and disease resistance. Immense clusters of modest-sized, single-petaled pink blooms (5 petals) that age to a deeper pink. Grows 4 to 6 feet tall. Zones 4–9. RIR=8.2.

■ **Bill Warriner ('JACsur')** Floribunda, orange-pink, 1998, Zary. Well-spaced clusters of large blooms in shades of salmon, orange, and coral. Pleasant, light fragrance. Grows 4 to 5 feet tall in moderate climates. Dense foliage is glossy dark green. Zones 5–10. RIR=7.8.

■ **Blueberry Hill ('WEKcryplag')** Floribunda, mauve, 1999, Carruth. Colorfast flowers (12 to 25 petals) with bright golden stamens. Blooms smell like freshly baked apple pie. Grows 3 to 4 feet tall with glossy, dark green leaves. Zones 5–10. RIR=7.8.

■ **Brass Band ('JACcofl')** Floribunda, apricot blend, 1993, Christensen, AARS. Large clusters of double blooms (30 to 35 petals) in a dazzling blend of melon, papaya, and apricot appear all summer and can last for weeks when cut. Fruity fragrance. In cool climates colors may be deeper. 4 to 5 feet tall. Zones 5–10. RIR=7.8.

■ **Brilliant Pink Iceberg ('PRObril')** Floribunda, pink blend, 1999, Weatherly. All the popular characteristics of its parent, Iceberg, but with a striking new flower color: bright cerise-pink painted onto cream. Color is more intense in cool climates. Mild honey scent. Zones 5–10. RIR=7.6.

■ **'Cherish' ('JACsal')** Floribunda, orange-pink, 1980, Warriner, AARS. Small clusters of perfect flowers (25 to 30 petals). Vigorous, disease-resistant. Good for cut flowers. Zones 4–11. RIR=7.6.

■ **'Circus'** Floribunda, yellow blend, 1956, Swim, AARS. Blooms (40 to 45 petals) appear in giant sprays on a 4- to 5-foot bush. Colors are brighter in cooler temperatures. Spicy fragrance. Zones 5–10. RIR=6.9.

■ **Columbus ('WEKuz')** Floribunda, deep pink, 1990, Carruth. Deep rose-pink hybrid-tea-size flowers (30 to 35 petals) in small sprays. Medium-rounded bush. Slight fragrance. Zones 5–10.

■ **Class Act ('JACare')** Floribunda, white, 1988, Warriner, AARS. Semi-double blooms (15 to 20 petals) in small clusters. Fruity fragrance. Weatherproof. Upright compact bush 4 to 5 feet tall. Zones 5–10. RIR=7.8.

Floribunda and Polyantha Roses
(*continued*)

■ **Confetti ('AROjechs')** Floribunda, red blend, 1980, Swim & Christensen. Yellow blooms deepen from blush to scarlet and finally to a dark red, with many colors on the bush at once. Old-fashioned tea rose fragrance. Plants grow 4 to 6 feet tall with long, arching canes. Zones 5–10. RIR=6.8.

■ **Constance Finn ('HAReden')** Floribunda, light pink, 1997, Harkness. Old-fashioned blooms (50 petals) reminiscent of pink cake icing. 4 to 6 feet. Zones 5–9.

■ **Day Breaker ('FRYcentury')** Floribunda, apricot blend, 2004, Fryer, AARS. Yellow blossoms (30 to 35 petals, 4 inches across) suffused with pink and apricot. Profuse blooms, fast repeat. Moderate tea fragrance. Upright, bushy plants are 4 to 5 feet tall with glossy dark green leaves. Zones 5–10.

■ **Dicky ('DICkimono')** Floribunda, orange-pink, 1984, Dickson. Large clusters of double (35+ petals) reddish salmon-pink flowers with a lighter reverse. Light fragrance. Zones 5–10. RIR=8.5.

■ **Cotillion ('JACshok')** Floribunda, mauve, 1999, Zary. Long-lasting, light lavender flowers have almost 40 petals. Rich, sweet fragrance. 5 to 6 feet. Zones 5–10. RIR=7.5.

■ **Escapade ('HARpade')** Floribunda, mauve, 1967, Harkness. Abundant, large sprays of semi-double flowers (12 petals). Blooms fade quickly in hot climates; in cool climates, color contrasts are dramatic. Low-growing plants reach 2 to 4 feet tall with dense, glossy, light green leaves. Zones 4–10. RIR=8.6.

■ **Easy Going ('HARflow')** Floribunda, yellow blend, 1999, Harkness. Descendant of Livin' Easy with peachy, golden-yellow blooms (25 to 30 petals). Glossy foliage, 3 to 4 feet tall. Zones 5–10. RIR=8.0.

■ **'Else Poulsen'** Floribunda, medium pink, 1924, Poulsen. Simple flower form (10 petals). Vigorous, 4 to 6 feet tall, always in bloom. Zones 5–10. RIR=8.1.

■ **Eureka ('KORsuflabe')**
Floribunda, apricot blend, 2003, Kordes, AARS. Full, 4-inch flowers in rich apricot-yellow with light fragrance. Vigorous bushy plants are 3 to 4 feet tall and wide, excellent as a hedge. Glossy, bright green leaves. Zones 5–10.

■ **'Europeana'** Floribunda, dark red, 1968, deRuiter, AARS. Huge sprays of red blossoms (25 to 30 petals) all summer. Glossy, dark, healthy foliage has a purple cast. Prefers heat. Zones 5–10. RIR=8.7.

■ **Fabulous! ('JACrex')** Floribunda, white, 2000, Zary. Sparkling white blossoms (25 to 30 petals) in exceptionally large clusters with light fragrance. 4 to 5 feet. Zones 5–10. RIR=7.8.

■ **'Fashion'** Floribunda, pink blend, 1949, Boerner, AARS. A classic favorite. Vigorous, medium-size bush with brilliant coral-peach blooms (20 to 25 petals), moderate sweet fragrance. Blooms are largest in cool climates. Zones 5–10. RIR=7.9.

■ **First Edition ('DELtep')**
Floribunda, orange-pink, 1976, Delbard, AARS. Small clusters of delicate blossoms (28 to 30 petals) in sparkling coral with shades of orange. Light tea fragrance. Glossy, dark green foliage. Compact medium-size bush, 4 to 5 feet tall. Zones 5–10. RIR=8.3.

■ **First Kiss ('JACling')** Floribunda, pink blend, 1991, Warriner. From a cross between Sun Flare and Simplicity comes delicate, mostly single (5 to 25 petals) pale pink flowers with a hint of yellow at the base. Compact bush, 3 to 4 feet tall. Best in cooler climates. Zones 5–10. RIR=8.2.

■ **Francois Rabelais ('MEInusian')**
Floribunda, medium red, 1998, Meilland. This Romantica-series rose combines the best of old-fashioned quartered flower form with superior recurrent bloom and compact size. Blooms (80+ petals) are the color of red wine. Slight cedar fragrance. Grows 3 to 4 feet tall. Zones 5–10. RIR=7.7.

■ **French Lace ('JAClace')** Floribunda, white, 1980, Warriner, AARS. Elegant pastel apricot to creamy off-white blooms (30 to 35 petals) in small sprays. Mild fruity fragrance. Produces best colors in cool temperatures. Upright, compact bush reaches 3 to 4 feet tall with dark, glossy leaves. Zones 6–10. RIR=8.1.

Floribunda and Polyantha Roses

(continued)

■ **'Gene Boerner'** Floribunda, medium pink, 1969, Boerner, AARS. Tall upright bushes with perfect deep pink blooms (35 to 40 petals) in large clusters. Deepest colors occur in spring and fall. Spicy fragrance. Zones 5–10. RIR=8.3.

■ **Goldmarie ('KORfalt')**
Floribunda, deep yellow, 1984, Kordes. The blooms (25 to 35 petals, larger in cool climates) are a long-lasting golden color with golden stamens. Large, tight clusters. Light, fruity fragrance. Compact, upright plants grow only 24 inches tall, with bright glossy foliage. Zones 4–10. RIR=7.4.

■ **'Gruss an Aachen'** Floribunda, light pink, 1909, Geduldig. Orange-red and yellow buds open to flesh pink blooms that fade to creamy white (40 petals, 3 to 4 inches wide, sweet fragrance). A small plant with rich foliage and nodding stems. 3 to 4 feet. Zones 5–9. RIR=8.3.

■ **Guy de Maupassant ('MEIsocrat')** Floribunda, medium pink, 1996, Meilland International. A Romantica-series rose with perfect old-fashioned quartered blooms in bright pink (90 to 100 petals). Great fragrance. Vigorous plant grows 4 to 6 feet tall. Zones 4–9. RIR=7.7.

■ **Honey Perfume ('JACarque')**
Floribunda, apricot blend, 2004, Zary, AARS. Luscious apricot-yellow blooms (25 to 30 petals, 4 inches across) with excellent spicy fragrance. Upright plants grow 3 to 4 feet tall with dark, glossy foliage that has good disease resistance. Zones 5–10.

■ **Hot Cocoa ('WEKpaltlez')**
Floribunda, russet, 2003, Carruth, AARS. Smoky orange flowers (3 to 4 inches across) washed with purplish cinnamon at the edge and rusty orange underneath. Upright, 4 to 5 feet tall, with dark, glossy foliage. Highly disease-resistant and heat-tolerant. Zones 5–11.

■ **Iceberg ('KORbin')**
Floribunda, white, 1958, Kordes, WFRS. Voted the world's most popular rose in 1983. Pure white flowers (20 to 25 petals) appear in open, airy sprays at the ends of long stems. Foliage is lush, glossy, and always healthy. In cool climates blooms can display an occasional flush of pink. Plant grows 3 to 4 feet tall. Zones 5–10. RIR=8.6.

■ **Impatient ('JACdew')** Floribunda, orange-red, 1982, Warriner, AARS. A low-maintenance shrub that provides fiery orange-red clusters all season. 25 petals. Warmer climates improve brightness of the color. Tall to medium upright plant, 4 feet high. Zones 5–10. RIR=7.8.

■ **Intrigue ('JACum')** Floribunda, mauve, 1982, Warriner, AARS. Buds are deep purple-red, opening to velvety plum flowers (30 petals) with a strong citrus perfume. Dark green foliage on 3- to 4-foot plants. Heat-tolerant; popular in warm climates. Zones 5–10. RIR=7.0.

■ **'Ivory Fashion'** Floribunda, white, 1958, Boerner, AARS. Large, eggshell white well-formed blooms (17 petals) in medium-size clusters. Dark leathery foliage. Vigorous. Nearly thornless stems. Best in cool climates. Zones 5–10. RIR=8.3.

■ **Johann Strauss ('MEloffic')** Floribunda, pink blend, 1994, Meilland. Exuding a delicious lemon scent with hints of apple, the candy pink flowers of this Romantica-series rose have an old-fashioned, globular form (100+ petals). Upright bushes grow 4 to 5 feet tall, with superb bronze-green foliage. Zones 5–10. RIR=7.8.

■ **Katherine Loker ('AROkr')** Floribunda, medium yellow, 1978, Swim & Christensen. Pointed buds open to perfectly formed, medium yellow blooms (28 petals). Non-fading color, even in strong sunlight. Cool temperatures improve color and size of blossoms. Dark green, healthy foliage. Zones 5–10. RIR=7.3.

■ **Lady of the Dawn ('INTerlada')** Floribunda, light pink, 1984, Interplant. Large, ruffled, semi-double flowers are a soft cream color edged in pink. Delicious fruity fragrance. Upright 4-foot plants have leathery, medium-green, matte-textured leaves. Zones 5–10. RIR=8.4.

■ **Lavaglut ('KORlech')** Floribunda, dark red, 1978, Kordes. Ruffled, velvety, nearly black-red to deep red blooms (25 petals). Lightly scented. Flowers last up to two weeks; color withstands heat and rain. Upright, spreading plants grow 3 to 5 feet tall with glossy, purplish-green foliage. Zones 5–10. RIR=8.7.

■ **Leonardo da Vinci ('MEIdeauri')** Floribunda, medium pink, 1994, Meilland. Flowers (25 to 30 petals) have the quartered and quilled form of old-fashioned roses. Fragrance is sweet and penetrating. Plant grows 3 to 4 feet tall, densely covered with medium green foliage. A Romantica-series rose. Zones 5–10. RIR=6.7.

■ **'Little Darling'** Floribunda, yellow blend, 1956, Duehrsen. Perfectly formed blossoms (25 to 30 petals) blended in yellow to salmon-pink are produced in clusters of 10 to 20. Plant can get 3 to 4 feet tall and wide in warm climates. Hardy: survives Great Lakes winters. Zones 4–10. RIR=8.2.

Floribunda and Polyantha Roses
(*continued*)

■ **Livin' Easy ('HARwelcome')** Floribunda, orange blend, 1992, Harkness, AARS. Showy clusters of frilly apricot-orange flowers (25 to 30 petals). Glossy foliage is highly resistant to disease, including black spot. Vigorous bushes grow 3 to 4 feet tall. Zones 5–10. RIR=8.1.

■ **Love Potion ('JACsedi')** Floribunda, mauve, 1993, Christensen. Deep purple blooms (20 to 25 petals) in clusters against shiny dark green foliage. Raspberry scent. 4 to 5 feet. Zones 5–10. RIR=7.7.

■ **Margaret Merril ('HARkuly')** Floribunda, white, 1977, Harkness. Long-lasting flowers are a ruffled satiny white. Intense citrus perfume. Habit is tall and upright, 4 to 5 feet high, with tough, disease-resistant, deep green foliage. Zones 5–11. RIR=8.3.

■ **Marina ('RinaKOR')** Floribunda, orange blend, 1974, Kordes, AARS. Massive sprays of clear orange blossoms (35 to 40 petals) with a mild fragrance. Flower size increases with cooler days. Vigorous, upright plants have dark, glossy, leathery leaves. Zones 5–10. RIR=7.4.

■ **Marmalade Skies ('MEImonblan')** Floribunda, orange blend, 1999, Meilland, AARS. Huge, bouquet-size clusters of brilliant tangerine-orange flowers (17 to 25 petals, 3 inches across) continuously cover this 3-foot rounded bush. Olive-green, semi-glossy foliage is disease-resistant. Excellent for hedges, massed in beds. Zones 5–10. RIR=7.7.

■ **Matador ('KORfarim')** Floribunda, orange blend, 1972, Kordes. Light scarlet and orange blooms (25 to 30 petals) with a gold reverse. Leathery, dark green foliage on vigorous upright bush. Prefers cool climates. Zones 5–10. RIR=6.4.

■ **Miami Moon** Floribunda, apricot blend, 2002, Carruth. Small clusters of ruffled shrimp-pink blooms with a spicy fragrance. Plant 30 inches apart. 4 to 5 feet. Zones 5–10.

■ **'Mlle Cécile Brünner'** Polyantha, light pink, 1881, Ducher. A classic with small silvery-pink flowers (30 petals) in large airy clusters. Spicy-sweet fragrance. 4 to 7 feet. Zones 6–10. RIR=8.4.

■ **Mountbatten ('HARmantelle')**
Floribunda, medium yellow, 1982, Harkness. Clusters of fully double primrose-yellow blooms sometimes edged with pink. 4 to 5 feet. Zones 4–10. RIR=7.0.

■ **'Nearly Wild'** Floribunda, medium pink, 1941, Brownell. Massive quantities of single-petaled pink blooms with a whitish eye cover this 2- to 3-foot-tall plant in the first spring flush. Distinct apple fragrance. Superb in cold-winter areas. Can suffer from occasional black spot if too crowded. Zones 4–9. RIR=7.7.

■ **Nicole ('KORicole')** Floribunda, white, 1985, Kordes. Large double blooms are white dramatically edged with deep cerise red, with golden stamens revealed at the fully open stage. Plants are vigorous, thorny, 4 to 7 feet tall, with excellent dark green foliage. Zones 5–10. RIR=8.9.

■ **Pink French Lace** Floribunda, light pink, 2000, Roses Unlimited. A sport of the popular French Lace with beautiful blush-pink flowers of full exhibition form (25 to 40 petals, 4 to 5 inches across). Mild fragrance. Grows 3 to 4 feet tall, with dark, lustrous, healthy leaves. Zones 6–10. RIR=7.7.

■ **'Playboy'** Floribunda, red blend, 1976, Cocker. A single-petaled rose with rambunctious colors—orange and scarlet with a yellow eye. Medium-size clusters of large flowers (smaller in hot climates) on strong, straight stems. Sweet apple fragrance. Grows 4 to 5 feet tall. Glossy green foliage is highly disease-resistant. Zones 5–9. RIR=8.4.

■ **Playgirl ('MORplag')** Floribunda, medium pink, 1986, Moore. Offspring of 'Playboy' with bright pink single flowers (5 to 7 petals), highlighted with golden stamens. Glossy foliage. Vigorous in most climates. Zones 5–10. RIR=8.3.

■ **Purple Heart ('WEKbipuhit')** Floribunda, mauve, 1999, Carruth. A modern rose with an old-fashioned look. The cupped, deep wine red blooms (30 to 35 petals) have a strong, spicy-clove perfume. Flowers are larger in cool climates. Foliage is matte green. Tends to weep if canes are not cut back to promote side growth. Zones 5–10. RIR=7.3.

■ **'Purple Tiger ('JACpurr')**
Floribunda, mauve, 1991, Christensen. Large, deep purple blooms (20 to 25 petals) with flecks and stripes of white are borne in small clusters on nearly thornless stems. Mild damask fragrance. Plants are vigorous, 3 to 4 feet tall, with medium green, glossy leaves. Zones 5–10. RIR=6.8.

Floribunda and Polyantha Roses
(continued)

■ **'Regensberg ('MACyoumis')** Floribunda, pink blend, 1979, McGredy. Striking pink flowers are edged in white and have a white eye. Cupped, semi-double flowers (21 petals) with bright yellow stamens. Sweet apple fragrance. Plants are compact. Zones 5–10. RIR=8.0.

■ **'Royal Occasion'** Floribunda, orange-red, 1974, Tantau. Brilliant orange-scarlet flowers open from long pointed buds into 3-inch, cup-shaped blossoms (20 petals) with a slight fragrance. Plants are upright, compact and bushy to 3 feet tall, with large, glossy, leathery leaves. Zones 5–10. RIR=8.6.

■ **Scentimental ('WEKplapep')** Floribunda, red blend, 1999, Carruth, AARS. Burgundy flowers striped with white, cream, and red—no two flowers are alike. Flowers have exhibition form (25 to 30 petals) with rich, spicy fragrance. Rounded, 3- to 4-foot bushes have medium green, matte-textured foliage. Best in cool climates. Zones 4–11. RIR=7.7.

■ **Sexy Rexy ('MACrexy')** Floribunda, medium pink, 1984, McGredy. Massive clusters of 20 or more blooms (40 petals) that look like camellias when fully opened. Flowers last for weeks. Pleasant fragrance. Small leaves are overpowered by large flower clusters. Upright, 4 to 5 feet tall. Zones 5–11. RIR=8.7.

■ **Sheila's Perfume ('HARsherry')** Floribunda, yellow blend, 1982, Sheridan. Powerful, delicious rose-and-fruit scent. Blooms are yellow brushed by deep pink and resemble hybrid tea flowers in size and form (25 petals). Well-rounded 3- to 4-foot plants have glossy, bright green foliage. Zones 5–11. RIR=8.2.

■ **Shocking Blue ('KORblue')** Floribunda, mauve, 1974, Kordes. Unusual lilac-mauve blooms (25 to 30 petals). Flowers are larger in cool climates. Strong citrus fragrance. Vigorous plants have dark, leathery, glossy leaves. Zones 5–10. RIR=7.3.

■ **Showbiz ('TANweieke')** Floribunda, medium red, 1983, Tantau, AARS. German variety with fire-engine red blooms in gigantic clusters (as many as 30 flowers on one stem). Foliage is glossy green and disease-resistant. 3 to 4 feet. Zones 5–10. RIR=8.4.

■ **Simplicity ('JACink')** Floribunda, medium pink, 1978, Warriner. One of the first roses developed to use as a hedge. Long pointed buds open to medium pink flowers (18 petals, 3 inches wide; blooms are larger in cool climates). Light fragrance. Vigorous and disease-resistant. 4 to 5 feet tall. Zones 5–11. RIR=7.6.

■ **Singin' in the Rain ('MACivy')**
Floribunda, apricot blend, 1994, McGredy, AARS. Superb, unusual color—flowers (25 to 30 petals) are apricot-copper to cinnamon-apricot-gold. Sweet musk fragrance. Upright plant grows 3 to 4 feet tall with dark green foliage. Zones 5–11. RIR=7.7.

■ **Summer Fashion ('JACale')**
Floribunda, yellow blend, 1986, Warriner. Radiant light yellow blooms (35 to 40 petals) are suffused with pink that deepens as they age. Heat intensifies the color. Fruity fragrance. Semi-glossy foliage is medium green. Zones 5–10. RIR=7.7.

■ **Sun Flare ('JACjam')** Floribunda, medium yellow, 1981, Warriner, AARS. A classic with lots of colorfast bright lemon blooms (20 to 30 petals) on a low, mounded bush. Light licorice fragrance. Glossy green leaves are small and disease-free. 3 to 4 feet. Zones 5–10. RIR=8.3.

■ **Sunsprite ('KORresia')**
Floribunda, deep yellow, 1977, Kordes. A classic, excellent as a low-growing hedge. Colorfast, deep yellow blooms (25 to 30 petals). Licorice scent. 3 to 4 feet. Disease-resistant. Zones 5–11. RIR=8.5.

■ **'Sweet Vivian'** Floribunda, pink blend, 1961, Raffel. Delicately colored semi-double blooms (12 to 15 petals) are pink blending to yellow in the center. Compact growth habit. Dark green, disease-resistant foliage. Best in moderate climates. Zones 5–10. RIR=8.2.

■ **'The Fairy'** Polyantha, light pink, 1932, Bentall. This award winner is the standard for low-maintenance, disease-resistant shrub roses used in landscaping projects. Seemingly never out of bloom, it has huge clusters of small, ruffled, soft pink flowers all summer. Little fragrance. Plant grows 3 to 4 feet tall. Zones 4–10. RIR=8.7.

■ **Trumpeter ('MACtrum')**
Floribunda, orange-red, 1977, McGredy. Cupped double blossoms (35 to 40 petals) are a clear orange-red and long-lasting on the bush. Light fragrance. Glossy foliage on dense, compact plants. Best in warm climates. Zones 5–10. RIR=8.2.

■ **Weeping China Doll; ('China Doll, Climbing')** Polyantha, medium pink, 1977, Weeks. The all-time favorite variety to use as a weeping tree rose (60-inch standard). Long thornless canes arch gracefully downward, covered with large trusses of small cupped flowers (20 to 25 petals) of rose-pink with a base of chrome-yellow. Slight tea scent. Foliage is narrow, leathery, and apple green. Zones 5–10. RIR=8.1.

■ **White Simplicity ('JACsnow')**
Floribunda, white, 1991, Jackson & Perkins. The next generation of the hedge rose Simplicity, with all the same traits. Double flowers—satiny white, with a touch of gold in the center when fully open—are weatherproof and can endure both strong sunshine and pouring rain. Grows 5 to 6 feet tall. Zones 5–10. RIR=7.9.

Miniature and Miniflora Roses

Miniatures and minifloras provide a dynamic display of color throughout the blooming season. They are ideal for edging beds, growing in containers and rockeries, and taking indoors as potted plants. They grow 15 to 36 inches tall and bear 1- to 2-inch flowers in small- to medium-size clusters. Bloom shapes include single-petaled, rosette, or classic hybrid tea form. Bushes are rounded and dense with leaves and flowers. Minifloras are between miniatures and floribundas in bloom size and foliage. The American Rose Society adopted this classification in 1999 to recognize another step in the evolution of the rose.

Right: The miniature rose Behold (flower detail shown above) makes an outstanding edging for a bed of hybrid tea roses.

Miniature and Miniflora Roses

(continued)

■ **American Rose Centennial** ('SAVars') Miniature, pink blend, 1991, Saville. Beautifully formed, very double blossoms (50 to 55 petals) are creamy white with a soft pink edge. Vigorous, compact bush. Dark green, semi-glossy foliage. Zones 5–10. RIR=7.2.

■ **Applause ('SAVapple')** Miniature, apricot blend, 1999, Saville, AOE. Beautiful coral flowers (17 to 25 petals) have a lighter reverse. Compact, low-growing plants with medium green, semi-glossy leaves. Zones 5–10. RIR=7.4.

■ **Autumn Splendor** ('MICautumn') Mini-flora, yellow blend, 1999, Williams, AOE. Sprays of flowers in brilliant yellow, gold, and orange, occasionally splashed with red. Petals reflex like a hybrid tea. 30 inches. Zones 5–11. RIR=8.1.

■ **Baby Grand** ('POUlit') Miniature, medium pink, 1994, Poulsen. Pure pink flowers with the quartered form of an old garden rose (30 to 35 petals). Slight apple scent. Compact, round habit, 12 to 16 inches. Zones 5–10. RIR=8.6.

■ **Baby Boomer (BENminn)** Miniature, medium pink, 2001, Bernardella, AOE. Large, clear pink blooms (2 inches across, 17 to 25 petals) of excellent exhibition form. 2-foot plants with good disease resistance. Zones 5–10.

■ **Baby Love ('SCRivluv')** Miniature, deep yellow, 1992, Scrivens. Single-petaled blooms (5 petals) are sunny yellow with golden stamens. Mild licorice scent. Plants grow 1 to 2 feet tall. Outstanding resistance to black spot, unusual for a yellow rose. Zones 4–11.

■ **'Beauty Secret'** Miniature, medium red, 1965, Moore, AOE. A classic miniature with brilliant red miniature hybrid-tea-like flowers on a small, healthy plant that requires little maintenance. 12 to 15 inches. Zones 4–11. RIR=8.0.

■ **Behold ('SAVahold')** Miniature, medium yellow, 1996, Saville. Clear bright yellow blooms (12 to 25 petals) with a lighter reverse. Holds color even in hot, sunny climates. Vigorous, upright plants 1 to 2 feet tall have matte-textured foliage. Protect from mildew in coastal climates. Zones 5–11. RIR=7.8.

■ Best Friends ('BRIfriends')

Miniature, orange blend, 2002, Bridges, AOE. Deep orange-pink washed with glowing yellow in the center and on the reverse of the petals. 15- to 20-inch mounds are very disease-resistant. Zones 5–10.

■ Black Jade ('BENblack')

Miniature, dark red, 1985, Benardella, AOE. An unusual color for a rose—nearly black buds open to deep blackish-red double flowers (35 petals) with contrasting yellow stamens. Tall, vigorous, upright bush. Zones 5–10. RIR=8.1.

■ Carrot Top ('POUltop')

Miniature, orange blend, 1991, Oleson & Mogens. Stunning clear orange blossoms (20 to 25 petals) on arching stems. Color lasts well. Vigorous, compact grower. Zones 5–10. RIR=7.7.

■ Child's Play ('SAVachild')

Miniature, pink blend, 1991, Saville, AARS, AOE. Porcelain-like white blossoms blend into pink at the edges, borne singly or in small clusters. Mild sweet fragrance. Upright with dark, matte-textured foliage. Zones 5–10. RIR=8.0.

■ Doris Morgan ('BRImorgan')

Miniature, deep pink, 2001, Bridges, AOE. Cerise-pink blooms glow with lighter pink highlights. Grows 2 to 3 feet tall and as wide, with healthy bright green leaves. Zones 5–10.

■ Fairhope ('TALfairhope')

Miniature, light yellow, 1989, Taylor. Light yellow flowers (16 to 28 petals) hold their color well without fading. Upright, bushy plants; semi-glossy foliage. Zones 5–10. RIR=8.1.

■ Figurine ('BENfig')
Miniature, near white, 1991, Benardella, AOE. Palest pink blooms blend to ivory white. Long stems are good for cutting. Plants are upright, 15 to 20 inches tall, with dark matte-textured foliage. Zones 5–11. RIR=8.0.

■ Giggles ('LYOgi')
Miniature, pink blend, 1982, Lyon. Medium pink semi-double flowers blend to white in the center. Plants are very dwarf and upright with small, semi-glossy leaves. Zones 5–10. RIR=8.9.

■ Gizmo ('WEKcatlard')
Miniature, orange blend, 1998, Carruth. Single-petaled scarlet-red flowers with a white eye completely cover this plant all summer. Blooms are long-lasting and resist fading even in hot sun. Plants are small (14 to 20 inches tall), healthy, and vigorous, with glossy green foliage. Mild apple scent. Zones 5–10. RIR=7.9.

Miniature and Miniflora Roses
(continued)

■ **Glowing Amber ('MANglow')** Miniature, red blend, 1996, Mander. Scarlet-red 1-inch double (26 to 40 petals) flowers with deep yellow undersides and golden stamens. Scarlet tones deepen with age. Upright compact plant grows 12 to 15 inches tall. Zones 5–10. RIR=8.0.

■ **Gourmet Popcorn ('WEOpop')** Miniature, white, 1986, Desamero. Semi-double (15 to 20 petals) pure white flowers with a light fragrance appear in big clusters. Upright and bushy, 2 to 3 feet tall. Foliage is dark green and disease-resistant. Zones 5–10. RIR=8.7.

■ **'Green Ice'** Miniature, white, 1971, Moore. Tiny white buds open slowly with a hint of pink to reveal soft white to green flowers. Relatively wide-spreading plants with arching canes, 2 to 3 feet tall, Glossy bright green foliage. Zones 5–11. RIR=7.9.

■ **Hot Tamale ('JACpoy')** Miniature, yellow blend, 1993, Zary, AOE. Yellow-orange blooms age dramatically to yellow-pink, even in hot climates. Compact, low-growing, 12 to 15 inches tall, with semiglossy dark green foliage. Zones 5–11. RIR=8.2.

■ **Incognito ('BRlincog')** Miniature, mauve, 1995, Bridges. Blossom color varies somewhat from dusty mauve to hints of yellow, pink, and russet. 25 petals, light fragrance. Vigorous medium-size bush. Zones 5–10. RIR=8.0.

■ **Jean Kenneally ('TINeally')** Miniature, apricot blend, 1984, Bennett, AOE. Tall, elegant sprays of exquisitely shaped apricot blossoms (25 petals). Thrives in just about all climates. Blooms are close to perfection. Zones 5–10. RIR=9.2.

■ **Irresistible ('TINresist')** Miniature, white, 1989, Bennett. Long-lasting white blooms with a creamy center are often produced in large "candelabras." Vigorous plants grow 2 to 3 feet high. Zones 5–10. RIR=9.1.

■ **June Laver ('LAVjune')** Miniature, deep yellow, 1987, Laver. Terrific exhibition form of blossoms (20 to 25 petals) and excellent dark yellow color on low-growing, short stems. Production can be lean. Not especially hardy. Zones 6–11. RIR=7.5.

■ **Jilly Jewel ('BENmfig')** Miniature, medium pink, 2000, Benardella. Elegant pure pink buds open slowly to flawless blooms (30 petals). Plants are strongly upright, 1 to 2 feet tall, with medium green, disease-resistant foliage. Zones 5–11. RIR=7.9.

■ **Kristin ('BENmagic')** Miniature, red blend, 1992, Benardella, AOE. Dramatic, deep pink edging on white petals (27 to 30 petals.). Color intensifies in hot climates; in cooler climates blooms tend not to open fully. Vigorous plants are disease-resistant. Zones 5–11. RIR=8.1.

■ **Lemon Gems ('JACmiryl')** Miniature, medium yellow, 1999, Walden, AOE. Profusion of colorfast blossoms in rich deep yellow. Zones 8–10. RIR=8.0.

■ **Little Flame ('JACnuye')** Miniature, orange blend, 1998, Walden, AOE. Big intense orange flowers last well and mature to rich burnt orange. Plants grow 1 to 2 feet tall. Zones 5–10. RIR=7.9.

■ **Little Tommy Tucker ('TUCtommy')** Miniature, medium yellow, 1998, Tucker, AOE. Classic, high-centered, hybrid tea form in medium yellow flowers (17 to 25 petals) with a lighter reverse. Plants are low-growing, 12 to 24 inches tall, with small, dark green, glossy leaves. Zones 5–10. RIR=7.6.

■ **Luis Desamero ('TINluis')** Miniature, light yellow, 1989, Bennett. Perfect pastel yellow blooms (28 petals) grow one to a stem. Tall, upright, healthy, and vigorous. Zones 5–10. RIR=7.9.

■ **'Loving Touch'** Miniature, apricot blend, 1983, Jolly, AOE. Deep apricot buds mature into a lighter hue at the edges of the petals as the flowers open. The fragrant 1-inch blooms (25 petals) have a sculptured, symmetrical form with a texture like fine porcelain. Bushes are rounded, 12 to 18 inches tall. Foliage is attractive and disease-resistant. Zones 5–10. RIR=8.3.

Miniature and Miniflora Roses
(continued)

■ **Magic Carrousel ('MORrousel')**
Miniature, red blend, 1972, Moore,
AOE. A classic. Double flowers are
creamy white with a vivid red edge
and well-formed high center. Fully
open they reveal contrasting golden-
yellow stamens. 1 to 2 feet tall.
Zones 4–11. RIR=8.6.

■ **Michel Cholet ('FOUmich')**
Miniature, apricot blend, 2001,
Jacobs, AOE. Luminous rich
apricot blends to creamy highlights
at the petal edges. Exhibition form.
Compact 2-foot plants with healthy
bronze-green foliage. Zones 5–10.
RIR=7.6.

■ **Miss Flippins ('TUCkflip')**
Miniature, medium red, 1997,
Tucker. Classic miniaturized hybrid
tea blooms in clear, bright red.
Strong stems, and glossy dark green
foliage. Long-lasting, unscented
flowers. Minimal fading in hot
weather. Upright plant reaches
2 to 3 feet tall. Zones 5–11. RIR=8.1.

■ **'Mary Marshall'** Miniature,
orange blend, 1970, Moore, AOE.
Abundant, fast-repeating blooms
(20 to 25 petals) are orange with
a yellow base. Moderate fragrance.
Dwarf, disease free. Zones 5–10.
RIR=7.6.

■ **Old Glory ('BENday')** Miniature,
medium red, 1988, Benardella, AOE.
Stunning bright red flowers age
gracefully to crimson red. Flowers
are like miniature hybrid teas.
Bushes are low-growing, 12 to
18 inches tall, with disease-resistant
foliage. Zones 4–10. RIR=7.9.

■ **Merlot ('BENfebu')** Miniature,
red blend, 2002, Bernardella, AOE.
Dark red bloom has a two-tone
effect with white center and reverse.
Large flowers (17 to 28 petals) are
2 inches across. Long stems. Grows
2 to 3 feet tall and as wide; disease-
resistant. Zones 5–10.

■ **Minnie Pearl
('SAVahowdy')** Miniature,
pink blend, 1982, Saville.
Elegant buds open slowly into
perfectly symmetrical, high-
centered, light pink flowers
(35 to 40 petals) with darker
undersides. Plants are
rounded, 12 to 24 inches tall.
In intense heat, color may
fade. Zones 5–10. RIR=9.1.

■ **'Orange Honey'** Miniature,
orange blend, 1979, Moore. Pointed
yellow-amber buds unfurl to
cupped, pure orange-yellow flowers
(23 petals) that develop reddish
color late in season. Fruity fragrance.
Spreading plants, 2 to 3 feet tall.
Zones 5–11. RIR=7.5.

■ **'Party Girl'** Miniature, yellow blend, 1979, Saville, AOE. Immaculate, well-formed, apricot-yellow blooms in gigantic clusters (18 to 24 blooms per stem). Growth habit is well-rounded and low, only 1 to 2 feet tall. Zones 5–11. RIR=8.3.

■ **'Peaches 'n' Cream'** Miniature, pink blend, 1976, Woolcock, AOE. Full blossoms (50+ petals) are a delicate blend of pale peach and pink. In cold, damp climates florets will not open fully. Vigorous, compact, spreading plants with dark green leaves. Zones 5–10. RIR=7.9.

■ **Petite Perfection ('JACrybi')** Miniature, red blend, 1999, Walden. Exquisite flowers of hybrid tea form, bright red with golden yellow reverse. Stunning against glossy dark foliage. Upright plants reach 2 to 3 feet. Zones 5–10. RIR=7.6.

■ **Pierrine (MICpie)** Miniature, orange-pink, 1988, William. Double (40 petals) medium pink flowers with a lighter reverse. Light damask fragrance. Upright plants; semi-glossy leaves. Zones 5–10. RIR=9.1.

■ **Pinstripe ('MORpints')** Miniature, red blend, 1985, Moore. Myriad fully opened, long-lasting blooms (35 petals), marked with red with white stripes. Low mounded habit. Disease-resistant foliage. Zones 5–10. RIR=7.7.

■ **Playgold ('MORplaygold')** Miniature, orange blend, 1997, Moore, AOE. Semi-double golden orange blossoms with yellow overtones. Vigorous plants grow 3 to 4 feet tall with small, glossy leaves. Zones 5–10. RIR=7.7.

■ **Rainbow's End ('SAValife')** Miniature, yellow blend, 1984, Saville, AOE. Double blooms (35 petals) start off deep yellow with a spectacular red edging on the outer petals, deepening with age to red in the heart. No fragrance. Plant is compact, 12 to 18 inches tall. Zones 5–11. RIR=8.8.

■ **'Rise 'n' Shine'** Miniature, medium yellow, 1977, Moore, AOE. Winner of the 1978 Miniature Hall of Fame. Brilliant, clear, timeless yellow blossoms with exhibition hybrid tea form (35 petals). Dark, glossy leaves. Zones 5–10. RIR=8.5.

■ **Ralph Moore ('SAVaralph')** Miniature, dark red, 1999, Saville, AOE. Rich vibrant red blooms in small clusters; reddish-green foliage. Zones 5–10. RIR=7.5.

Miniature and Miniflora Roses
(continued)

■ **Roller Coaster ('MACmnmo')**
Miniature, red blend, 1987, McGredy. Red-striped blossoms (6 to 14 petals) in small clusters. Dense upright plants with small, glossy leaves. Zones 4–10. RIR=8.2.

■ **Ruby ('BENmjul')** Miniature, deep red, 2001, Bernardella, AOE. Large, brilliant deep red blooms (2 inches across, 17 to 25 petals) seem to glow with a lighter reverse. Grows 2 to 3 feet high. Zones 5–10. RIR=7.6.

■ **Santa Claus ('POUlclaus')**
Miniature, dark red, 1991, Olesen. Large trusses of deep scarlet nonfading blooms (15 to 25 petals). Normally 1 to 3 feet tall, the bush can grow up to 4 feet tall in mild climates. Glossy dark foliage. Protect from spider mites in warm climates. Zones 5–10. RIR=7.7.

■ **Scentsational ('SAVamor')**
Miniature, mauve, 1995, Saville. Elegant buds open into perfectly formed blooms with a strong rose fragrance. In cool climates the mauve color deepens on the outer rim of the petals. The plant is low-growing. Zones 5–11. RIR=7.6.

■ **Sequoia Gold ('MORsegold')**
Miniature, medium yellow, 1986, Moore, AOE. Bright cheery yellow flowers mature to pale scintillating yellow. The 1-inch florets are double (30 petals) with decidedly fruity fragrance. Plants grow 1 to 2 feet tall. Zones 5–11. RIR=7.2.

■ **'Snow Bride'** Miniature, white, 1982, Jolly, AOE. Petals reflex to give porcelain-like qualities to marvelous white blooms (20 petals). Compact, low growing plants with semi-glossy leaves. Disease-resistant. Zones 5–10. RIR=8.7.

■ **Soroptimist International ('BENstar')** Miniature, pink blend, 1995, Benardella. Double bright pink and ivory blossoms open to a star-shaped bloom. Upright plants are 24 inches tall with dark, glossy leaves. Nearly thornless. Zones 5–10. RIR=8.0.

■ **Space Odyssey ('WEKsnacare')**
Miniature, light pink, 2001, Carruth. Semi-double (12 to 16 petals), bright red flowers with a white eye and reverse. Plants grow 15 to 20 inches tall with dark green, glossy leaves. Zones 5–10. RIR=8.0.

■ **Starina ('MEIgali')** Miniature, orange-red, 1965, Meilland. Miniature Rose Hall of Fame. Scarlet orange blooms (20 petals) appear singly or in small clusters of 3 to 5 florets. Dwarf habit with beautiful glossy leaves. Zones 5–10. RIR=8.4.

■ **Sun Sprinkles ('JAChal')** Miniature, deep yellow, 2001, Walden, AOE, AARS. Colorfast yellow blooms. Low-growing, ideal for edging. Zones 5–10. RIR=7.9.

■ **Sweet Caroline ('MICaroline')** Miniature, red blend, 1999, Williams, AOE. Double flowers of classic hybrid tea form (17 to 25 petals) are white with light to medium red in the outer petals. Plants are upright and slightly spreading, reaching 3 feet tall, with dark green, semi-glossy leaves. Zones 5–10. RIR=7.9.

■ **Sweet Chariot ('MORchari')** Miniature, mauve, 1984, Moore. Old-fashioned, deep lavender to royal purple flowers (40 petals) mature to lavender hues. Delicious, heavy damask perfume. Canes arch naturally downward, perfect for a hanging basket. Zones 5–10. RIR=8.4.

■ **Sweet Diana ('SAVdiana')** Miniature, deep yellow, 2002, Saville, AOE. Luminscent golden-yellow blossoms of good form (20 petals). No fragrance. Vigorous plants are 2 to 3 feet tall with excellent bright green foliage. Very disease-resistant and hardy. Zones 4–10.

■ **This is the Day ('SPRoday')** Miniature, russet, 2003, Sproul, AOE. Glowing orange-red blooms with a russet cast are abundantly produced on vigorous 30-inch plants. Excellent exhibition form. Good disease resistance. Zones 5–10.

■ **Why Not ('MORwhy')** Miniature, red blend, 1983, Moore. Upright bush. Fast rebloomer. Small single-petaled blooms (5 to 7 petals) are red with a yellow eye. Color fades after a few days. Light fragrance. Upright, bushy plants have matte-finish foliage. Zones 5–10. RIR=8.3.

■ **X-Rated ('TINx')** Miniature, pink blend, 1993, Bennett. Luscious plant with creamy, blushing, soft-pink-to-coral flowers in clusters. Slight fragrance. 2 to 3 feet. Zones 5–10. RIR=7.8.

■ **Y2K ('SAVyk')** Miniature, deep yellow, 1999, Saville. Deep yellow, colorfast blooms are splashed with coral. Good fragrance. Small plants reach 12 to 15 inches with glossy, dark green leaves. Superb disease resistance. Zones 5–10. RIR=7.4.

Classic and Modern Shrub Roses

Shrub is a generic classification given to a heterogeneous group of roses that don't fit neatly into any other category. Some are compact, growing no more than 3 feet tall; others sprawl to as much as 12 to 15 feet wide. What stands out about this class is its vigor, repeat cycles of bloom, disease resistance, and low maintenance. Some shrub roses make ideal hedges; others perform well as ground covers and in beds. There are five popular subdivisions—four classic and one modern—within this class.

HYBRID KORDESII: Evolutionary cross between *Rosa rugosa* and *Rosa wichuraiana,* resulting in very hardy large shrubs and climbers.

HYBRID MOYESII: Tall, stiff plants with repeat bloom, followed by hips (fruits) shaped like flagons.

HYBRID MUSK: Descendants of *Rosa moschata.* Tall, hardy, disease-resistant, and tolerant of some shade.

HYBRID RUGOSA: Dense low-growing plants with wrinkled foliage; more tolerant of wind and rain than most roses.

MODERN SHRUBS: The modern shrub category is known for its great diversity, versatility, and easy care in the landscape.

English roses are among the most popular modern shrub roses. Introduced by David Austin, like hybrid teas and floribundas they bloom repeatedly all summer, with many varieties possessing modern colors such as red, yellow, apricot, and salmon. Yet the flowers often have the romantic look and fragrance of old garden roses. Some have the added values of vigor, hardiness, and disease resistance. Since Austin premiered his revolutionary line of shrubs, other breeders have followed suit with equally appealing products. As a result, today you can enjoy a vast selection of modern shrubs. Many of the Generosa and Romantica roses from France and the Renaissance roses from Denmark fall in this group.

Some of the modern roses listed in this section are technically classified by their introducers as hybrid tea or floribunda roses. They are included here because by common agreement (usually in the nursery trade) their form and usage more clearly fit the shrub rose classification.

'Sally Holmes' is a large modern shrub that makes a superb subject to grow against a wall. In mild climates this rose can reach the dimensions of a small tree, with a trunk 4 inches or more in diameter.

Classic and Modern Shrub Roses
(continued)

■ **Abbaye de Cluny (MElbrinpay')**
Hybrid tea, apricot blend, 1996, Austin. Antique rose blooms (30 petals) are vibrant and fragrant. Repeat flowering is fast. Vigorous; 3 to 4 feet tall. Zones 4–9.

■ **Abraham Darby ('AUScot')**
Shrub, orange-pink, 1990, Austin. Small clusters of large cupped flowers in a peachy apricot blend. Pronounced fragrance. Rounded bush grows 4 to 6 feet tall—higher in warm climates—with dark, shiny, healthy foliage. Zones 4–9. RIR=7.8.

■ **All That Jazz ('TWOadvance')**
Shrub, orange-pink, 1991, Twomey, AARS. Plants covered with small sprays of semi-double coral-salmon florets. Bold damask scent. 4 to 6 feet. Zones 5–9. RIR=7.8.

■ **Alba Meidiland ('MEIflopan')**
Shrub, white, 1987, Meilland. Pure white double blossoms are medium size (1½ to 2 inches across), borne in profusion on vigorous, wide spreading shrubs excellent as a ground cover. No fragrance. Beautiful, glossy, medium green leaves. Zones 4–10. RIR=8.3.

■ **Ambridge Rose ('AUSwonder')**
Shrub, apricot blend, 1994, Austin. Large cupped blooms are rich apricot touched with gold. Strong stems. 4 to 6 feet. Zones 4–10. RIR=8.2.

■ **Astride Lindgren** Shrub, light pink, 1991, Poulsen. Large clusters of double, cupped, porcelain pink flowers appear continuously. A dense compact bush, 3 to 4 feet tall in warm climates. Zones 4–9.

■ **'Ballerina'** Hybrid musk, medium pink, 1937, Bentall. A profusely blooming rose with large clusters of medium pink flowers and a white eye. The first summer flush of flowers is so dense it often obscures the abundant green foliage. After a short pause the second flush nearly equals the first. Plant is a graceful, well-rounded bush, 3 feet tall. Zones 4–10. RIR=8.7.

■ **Belle Story ('AUSelle')**
Shrub, light pink, 1985, Austin. Large cupped flowers with contrasting yellow stamens. 4 to 6 feet. Zones 5–9. RIR=8.6.

■ **'Belinda'** Hybrid musk, medium pink, 1936, Bentall. Small, graceful, abundant flowers are a warm shade of rosy pink with small areas of white at the base. First flush of spring brings large clusters of 30 to 40 flowers; repeat bloom is less abundant but still showy. Light fragrance. Disease-resistant. 4 to 6 feet tall. Zones 5–9. RIR=8.5.

■ **'Blanc Double de Coubert'.** Hybrid rugosa, white, 1892, Cochet-Cochet. Delicate recurrent blooms (20 to 25 petals) with very sweet fragrance. Plants grow 5 to 7 feet tall with wrinkled foliage. Intermittent hips in the fall. Zones 3–9. RIR=8.3.

■ **Bonica ('MEidomonac')** Shrub, medium pink, 1985, Meilland, AARS, WFRS Hall of Fame. Small clusters of double clear pink flowers (40+ petals) cover this shrub all summer. Rounded, 3 to 4 feet tall; healthy foliage. Zones 4–10. RIR=8.4.

■ **'Buff Beauty'** Hybrid musk, apricot blend, 1939, Bentall. Apricot-yellow flowers (30 petals, 4 inches wide, moderate tea fragrance) in clusters of 12 florets on smooth arching canes. 4 to 5 feet tall. Dark green foliage. Zones 5–9. RIR=8.2.

■ **Cape Cod ('POUlfan')** Shrub, light pink, 1995, Poulsen. Large single-petaled flowers bloom profusely all summer. Medium-size shrubs 3 to 3½ feet tall with a wider spread; dense with small, semi-glossy leaves. Zones 4–10.

■ **Carefree Beauty ('BUCbi')**
Shrub, medium pink, 1977, Buck. Small sprays open to reveal large (4 inches wide, 10 to 20 petals), fragrant flowers of a rich pink color. Plant is upright (4 to 5 feet tall) with smooth, healthy, olive-green foliage. Orange-red hips fall through winter. Zones 4–10. RIR=8.7.

■ **Carefree Delight ('MEIpotal')**
Shrub, pink blend, 1994, Meilland, AARS. Small single-petaled blooms (5 petals), carmine-pink with a white eye, in large clusters (10 to 15 florets per stem). Unscented. Bright orange hips in winter. Vigorous plant, 4 to 5 feet tall, with exceptional disease resistance. Zones 4–10. RIR=8.2.

Classic and Modern Shrub Roses
(continued)

■ **Carefree Sunshine ('RADsun')** Shrub, medium yellow, 2002, Radler. This sister variety to Knock Out bears lightly fragrant, brilliant yellow flowers in abundance all summer. Excellent resistance to black spot, unusual for a yellow rose. Somewhat more upright than Knock Out, with glossy green foliage. Zones 4–10. RIR=8.1.

■ **Carefree Wonder ('MEIpitac')** Shrub, pink blend, 1990, Meilland, AARS. Large, double (20 to 25 petals), radiant pink flowers with a white eye and cream reverse are borne in small clusters. Superb disease resistance, hardiness, and neat growth habit. Zones 3–9. RIR=8.0.

■ **Charles Rennie Mackintosh ('AUSren')** Shrub, pink blend, 1994, Austin. Cupped lilac-pink, very double flowers (50 petals). Powerful fragrance. Vigorous and very thorny bush. Remove spent blooms to promote next cycle. 4 to 6 feet tall. Zones 4–9. RIR=7.9.

■ **Central Park ('POUlpyg')** Shrub, apricot blend, 1995, Poulsen. Compact clusters of warm peach flowers, yellow centers. This is a low spreading shrub only 2 feet tall with dense, small, glossy leaves. Zones 4–10.

■ **Cherry Meidiland ('MEIrumour')** Shrub, red blend, 1994, Meilland. Brilliant single-petaled red flowers (5 petals) with a white eye are abundantly borne in small clusters. Foliage is semi-glossy and dark green. Zones 4–10.

■ **Cliffs of Dover ('POUlemb')** Shrub, white, 1995, Poulsen. Many small clusters of white blooms with golden stamens. Arched canes. Zones 4–10.

■ **Colette ('MEIroupis')** Hybrid tea, light pink, 1996, Meilland. Strong climber covers itself and landscape with pink old-fashioned blooms (25 petals) in small sprays. Damask fragrance. 10 to 12 feet tall. Zones 4–9.

■ **Coral Meidiland ('MEIpopul')** Shrub, medium pink, 1994, Meilland. Small clusters of single flowers (5 petals) that are deep coral-orange with a white eye cover this plant in late spring and again in fall, with scattered blooms inbetween. No fragrance. Upright, bushy plants grow 4 to 6 feet tall with healthy, medium green foliage. Good choice for hedges. Zones 5–10.

■ **'Cornelia'** Hybrid musk, pink blend, 1925, Pemberton. Double rosette-shaped flowers in large trusses range from strawberry-flushed yellow to pale apricot-copper to salmon-pink with an orange base. Fragrance is a powerful sweet musk. Vigorous with 6- to 8-foot thornless canes. Glossy foliage is dark green tinged with bronze. Zones 4–10. RIR=8.8.

■ **'Country Dancer'** Shrub, deep pink, 1973, Buck. A dwarf shrub, 3 to 4 feet tall with large double rosy red blooms in clusters on dark green foliage. Light fragrance. Vigorous. Zones 4–9. RIR=8.5.

■ **Country Fair ('HARbanner')** Shrub, light pink, 1998, Harkness. Very large sprays of delicate pink blooms (40 to 50 per stem) mature to a lighter color with golden stamens. 25 to 30 petals. Well-rounded, medium-size bush, 4 to 6 feet tall. Zones 4–9.

■ **Country Lady ('HARtsam')** Hybrid tea, orange blend, 1987, Harkness. Fiery deep orange blooms (35 to 40 petals) with a light scarlet reverse change with age. They are borne one to a stem or in small clusters. Spicy fragrance. 4 to 6 feet tall. Zones 4–9.

■ **Country Life ('HARzap')** Floribunda, orange-pink, 1998, Harkness. Large fragrant tangerine blooms (30 to 35 petals) in small clusters repeat well in most climates. Good vigor and hardiness. 4 to 6 feet tall. Zones 4–9.

■ **Country Music ('HARcheer')** Shrub, pink blend, 1998, Harkness. Large clusters of sensuous blooms on strong, straight, nearly thornless stems hold their color even in hot sun. 25 to 30 petals. Low, vigorous shrub, 4 to 6 feet tall. Zones 4–9.

Classic and Modern Shrub Roses
(continued)

■ **'Distant Drums'** Shrub, mauve, 1985, Buck. Large rose-purple blossoms in sprays of 2 to 10 florets. Myrrh fragrance; leathery foliage; vigorous, erect bush. 5 to 6 feet. Zones 4–9. RIR=8.0.

■ **'Earth Song'** Grandiflora, deep pink, 1975, Buck. Long urn-shaped buds open to large flowers with strong fragrance. 25 petals. 4 to 6 feet tall. Zones 3–9. RIR=8.2.

■ **Electric Blanket ('KORpancom')** Shrub, coral pink, 2002, Kordes. A self-maintaining ground cover. Glowing coral pink flowers (25 to 30 petals) are borne in small clusters. Foliage is glossy dark green. Repeat bloom is extremely fast. Space 4 feet apart for ground cover. Zones 4–10.

■ **English Garden ('AUSbuff')** Shrub, apricot blend, 1990, Austin. Large, fully double cupped flowers (40 petals, 4 inches wide) of apricot-yellow with a wonderful old-fashioned form and fragrance. Upright plant grows 4 to 5 feet tall; needs pruning to keep from growing too tall in warm climates. Zones 4–9. RIR=7.9.

■ **'Erfurt'** Hybrid musk (shrub), pink blend, 1939, Kordes. Very fragrant, single-petaled flowers (10 petals) are pink with a yellow base. Spreading bushy habit, 6 feet tall. Zones 4–9. RIR=8.5.

■ **Evelyn ('AUSsaucer')** Shrub, apricot blend, 1992, Austin. Large apricot-yellow flowers (40+ petals) are shallow-cupped, gradually building to a beautiful rosette shape at maturity. In warm-weather climates the color is more pink than apricot. Very prominent fragrance. Vigorous, upright-growing, 4- to 6-foot bush. Zones 5–10. RIR=7.7.

■ **Fair Bianca ('AUSca')** Shrub, white, 1983, Austin. Fully double, cupped, pure white flowers with attractive small green pip in center. Strong myrrh aroma. 4 to 5 feet. Zones 5–9. RIR=7.8.

■ **'Felicia'** Hybrid musk, pink blend, 1928, Pemberton. Fragrant flowers all summer. Grow as 5-foot-tall pillar or shrub. Disease-resistant. 15 to 20 petals. Zones 6–9. RIR=8.5.

■ **'F. J. Grootendorst'** Hybrid rugosa, dark red, 1918, Grootendorst. Vigorous, hardy, and disease-resistant. Unusual serrated petals, reminiscent of carnations. Zones 3–9. RIR=7.7.

■ **First Light ('DEVrudi')** Shrub, light pink, 1998, Marciel, AARS. Delicate single-petaled solid pink blooms with contrasting burgundy stamens. Scent is mild and spicy. Compact rounded plant presents a natural wild-rose effect. 3 to 4 feet. Zones 5–9. RIR=7.8.

■ **Flower Carpet ('NOAtraum')** Shrub, deep pink, 1989, Noack. Huge clusters of deep pink flowers. 2 to 3 feet high, 4 to 5 feet wide. Zones 4–9. RIR=7.7.

■ **Flower Girl ('FRYyeoman')** Shrub, light pink, 1999, Fryer. Huge soft pink trusses loaded with blossoms (8 to 15 petals). Grows more like a hydrangea than a rose. Zones 5–9. RIR=8.2.

■ **'Frau Dagmar Hartopp'** Hybrid rugosa, medium pink, ca. 1914. Fragrant single flowers (5 petals) bloom continuously on 4-foot plants. Foliage is rich green and wrinkled. Large crimson hips in fall. Zones 3–9. RIR=8.5.

■ **Geoff Hamilton ('AUSham')** Shrub, medium pink, 1999, Austin. Crowded petals produce an attractive old-fashioned quartered bloom. Flowers are a rose-pink with the outer petals fading to white. Fragrance is strong. Best in warm climates; rain and wind can damage stems. Grows 4 to 6 feet tall with light green matte foliage; highly disease-resistant. Zones 5–10. RIR=7.5.

■ **'Gartendirektor Otto Linne'** Shrub, deep pink, 1934, Lambert. Big clusters of small double pink blooms that repeat well. Unscented. 5 to 6 feet. Zones 4–9. RIR=8.9.

Classic and Modern Shrub Roses
(continued)

■ **Gertrude Jekyll ('AUSbord')**
Shrub, medium pink, 1986, Austin. Rich, glowing pink, old-fashioned blossoms. Deliciously fragrant. In cool, mild climates it can get tall (5 to 6 feet or more) and somewhat lanky; best if pruned to a height of about 2 to 3 feet. Zones 5–10.

■ **Golden Celebration ('AUSgold')**
Shrub, deep yellow, 1993, Austin. Large blooms are more golden than yellow. Fully double flowers (40+ petals) are produced in clusters. Strong rose fragrance. Plant grows upright 5 to 8 feet tall with dark green foliage. Zones 4–10. RIR=7.8.

■ **'Golden Unicorn'** Shrub, yellow blend, 1985, Buck. Large cupped double flowers (28 petals, slight fragrance) in clusters. Yellow with orange-red edges. Foliage is dark olive-green and leathery. 4 to 5 feet. Zones 4–9.

■ **Glamis Castle ('AUSlevel')**
Shrub, white, 1994, Austin. The finest white English rose with a wonderful myrrh fragrance. Florets (50+ petals) are cupped and appear through the season. Compact, 3 to 4 feet tall. Zones 5–10. RIR=7.9.

■ **Graham Thomas ('AUSmas')**
Shrub, deep yellow, 1983, Austin. Deeply cupped florets (50+ petals). 6 to 8 feet tall. Gains height and density in warm climates. Zones 4–9. RIR=8.2.

■ **'Gruss an Aachen'** Floribunda, light pink, 1909, Geduldig. Orange-red and yellow buds open to flesh pink blooms that fade to creamy white (40 petals, 3 to 4 inches wide, sweet fragrance). A small plant with rich, leathery, disease-resistant foliage and nodding stems. 3 to 4 feet. Zones 5–9. RIR=8.3.

■ **'Hansa'** Hybrid rugosa, medium red, 1905, Schaum & Van Tol. A classic hardy rose with wrinkled, dark green foliage and large red double blooms (30 petals, 3 inches wide). Clove-rose fragrance. Striking red hips. 4 to 5 feet. Zones 3–9. RIR=8.4.

■ **'Henry Hudson'** Hybrid rugosa, white, 1976, Svejda. Double white flowers with hint of pink at tip of petals. Good fragrance. 3 to 4 feet. Extremely hardy. Zones 2–9. RIR=9.2.

■ **'Henry Kelsey'** Hybrid kordesii, medium red, 1984, Svedja. One of the hardiest of all climbers. Clusters of semi-double dark red flowers (28 petals) with bright yellow stamens are produced all summer. Spicy fragrance. Can be trained as a climber, 6 to 8 feet high. Dense foliage is glossy green. Needs little winter protection even in severe northern climates. Zones 3–9.

■ **Jacqueline de Pre ('HARwanna')** Shrub, white, 1988, Harkness. Clusters of semi-double milk white blooms with ruby stamens. Musk fragrance. 4 to 6 feet. Zones 4–9.

■ **Jean Giono ('MEIrokoi')** Hybrid tea, yellow blend, 1996, Meilland. A Romantica-series rose, with glowing orange-yellow quartered flowers (100 petals). Habit like a grandiflora, 4 to 5 feet tall. Disease-resistant, vigorous. Zones 4–9. RIR=7.6.

■ **'Jens Munk'** Hybrid rugosa, medium pink, 1974, Svejda. Semi-double soft pink flowers with a hint of lilac. Yellow golden stamens. 5 to 6 feet. Zones 2–9. RIR=8.8.

■ **'John Cabot'** Hybrid kordesii, medium red, 1978, Svedja. Semi-double, 2- to 3-inch flowers, medium red to dark orchid-pink, bloom all summer. Vigorous with large, arching, thorny canes; can be trained as a 6- to 10-foot climber in Zone 5 and south or as a 4- to 5-foot hedge in the North. Extremely hardy. Zones 3–10. RIR=8.9.

■ **Kaleidoscope ('JACbow')** Shrub, mauve, 1999, Walden, AARS. Unusual complementary colors in tan, mauve, orange. 3 to 4 feet tall. 35 to 40 petals. Zones 5–11. RIR=7.3.

■ **'Kathleen'** Hybrid musk, light pink, 1922, Pemberton. Richly fragrant small blooms in large clusters resemble apple blossoms. Orange hips provide a show in fall. 6 to 12 feet. Zones 5–9. RIR=8.7.

■ **Knock Out ('RADrazz')** Shrub, red blend, 1999, Radler, AARS. Virtually impervious to black spot, this genetic breakthrough sets the standard for the new generation of care-free shrub roses. Single, deep cherry red flowers (5 to 7 petals, 3 inches wide) blanket the plant all summer. Light tea scent. Mounded plant with purplish-green foliage. 4 to 6 feet. Zones 4–10. RIR=8.6.

Classic and Modern Shrub Roses
(continued)

■ **Lavender Dream ('INTerlav')**
Shrub, mauve, 1985, Interplant.
Masses of 2- to 3-inch semi-double
blossoms all summer. Tends to throw
out arching canes 5 feet tall by 5 feet
wide. 16 petals. Zones 4–9. RIR=8.4.

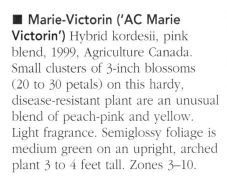

■ **Leonard Dudley Braithwaite
('AUScrim')** Shrub, dark red, 1993,
Austin. Red-to-crimson old-fashioned
blooms are symmetrical and round,
borne one to a stem, with some
clustering in cool climates. Blossoms
are weather-resistant, last long on
the bush and when cut. Fragrance
is strong and pleasing. Grows 4 to
6 feet tall. Zones 5–10. RIR=7.9.

■ **Marie-Victorin ('AC Marie
Victorin')** Hybrid kordesii, pink
blend, 1999, Agriculture Canada.
Small clusters of 3-inch blossoms
(20 to 30 petals) on this hardy,
disease-resistant plant are an unusual
blend of peach-pink and yellow.
Light fragrance. Semiglossy foliage is
medium green on an upright, arched
plant 3 to 4 feet tall. Zones 3–10.

■ **Mary Rose ('AUSmary')** Shrub,
medium pink, 1983, Austin. Rose-
pink blooms in tight clusters perch
on slightly arching stems. In warm
climates the petals shed a few days
after the blooms fully open. Strong
old-fashioned rose scent. Vigorous,
disease-resistant. 4 to 6 feet tall.
Zones 4–11. RIR=8.3.

■ **Molineux ('AUSmol')** Shrub,
deep yellow, 1994, Austin. Repeating
rosettes (50 to 60 petals) in a
delicate glowing yellow with heavy
tea-rose scent. Bushy, upright habit
is ideal for a small garden.
3½ feet tall. Zones 5–11.

■ **Linda Campbell ('MORten')**
Hybrid rugosa, medium red, 1990,
Moore. Tall, arching canes 8 to
10 feet tall covered with huge sprays
of semi-double red flowers (20 to
25 petals). Repeat bloomer. Likes
heat. Zones 4–11. RIR=7.9.

■ **'Martin Frobisher'** Hybrid
rugosa, light pink, 1968, Svedja.
Very hardy, vigorous, upright rose
with blush pink semi-double blooms.
Slightly fragrant. Habit is open and
sparse. 5 to 6 feet. Zones 2–11.
RIR=7.3.

■ **Moore's Classic Perpetual** (**'MORclassic'**) Shrub, deep pink, 1999, Moore. Large, very double pink blossoms (50 to 60 petals) on a dwarf hybrid perpetual only 2 to 3 feet tall. Zones 4–11.

■ **Moore's Pink Perpetual** (**'MORpinkper'**) Shrub, pink blend, 1999, Moore. This dwarf hybrid perpetual is a repeat bloomer with strongly fragrant large flowers (40 to 50 petals) in loose sprays throughout the summer. Very thorny; makes a great dwarf hedge 16 to 24 inches tall. Zones 5–10.

■ **'Morden Amorette'** Shrub, deep pink, 1977, Marshall. Large double flowers (28 petals) on medium-size bush. Slight fragrance. Glossy dark green foliage. 2 to 3 feet. Zones 3–10.

■ **'Morden Blush'** Shrub, light pink, 1988, Agriculture Canada. Held in sprays of 2 to 5 blooms, the small double flowers (about 50 petals) open light pink and fade to ivory, lasting for weeks on the bush. Plants reach 2 to 5 feet tall with medium green foliage. A Parkland Rose from the Morden Research Center in Manitoba, Canada; extremely hardy. Zones 2–10.

■ **'Morden Snowbeauty'** Shrub, white, 1998, Agriculture Canada. Capable of withstanding very cold winters. Pure white flowers are single-petaled and borne in clusters throughout the summer. Superior hardiness; excellent resistance to black spot. 3 to 4 feet. Zones 3–9.

■ **Napa Valley** (**'POUlino'**) Shrub, medium red, 1995, Olesen. Bright crimson blooms on a small, compact, 2-foot plant. Zones 4–9.

■ **Natchez** (**'POUllen'**) Shrub, medium pink, 1994, Olesen. Abundant small pale pink blooms in dainty clusters. Easy-care. Zones 4–9

Classic and Modern Shrub Roses

(continued)

■ **Newport ('POUlma')** Shrub, medium pink, 1994, Olesen. Large double blooms on compact, 2- to 3-foot plant. Zones 4–10.

■ **'Nymphenburg'** Hybrid musk. Orange-pink, 1954, Kordes. Abundant, fragrant, large flowers (20+ petals) in large clusters all summer. Pillar or upright bush 8 to 10 feet tall. Disease-resistant. Zones 4–10. RIR=8.5.

■ **Oranges 'n' Lemons ('MACoranlem')** Shrub, orange blend, 1994, McGredy. Dramatic flowers with stripes of pure yellow splashed onto bright orange. Plants can be trained as pillars or climbers 6 to 8 feet tall. Prefers cool climates. Zones 4–9. RIR=7.6.

■ **Othello ('AUSlo')** Shrub, medium red, 1990, Austin. Color varies with climate from a deep to a clear medium red. Use as a large shrub or a low climber, 6 to 7 feet tall. Needs protection from mildew. 50+ petals. Zones 4–11. RIR=7.4.

■ **Out of Yesteryear ('MORyears')** Shrub, white, 1999, Moore. Quartered antique-looking flowers (40 to 60 petals) bloom in clusters non-stop all summer. Disease resistant with dark green glossy leaves. Grows 4 to 5 feet tall with spreading habit. Zones 4–9.

■ **Outta the Blue 'WEKstiphitsu')** Shrub, mauve, 2001, Carruth. A new-generation rose that captures the look of antique roses. Produced in many big clusters, the flowers (25 to 30 petals) are many-toned, with rich magenta to lavender-blue hues spiked with yellow. Strong clove-and-rose fragrance. Plant is upright to slightly rounded, 3 to 4 feet tall. Zones 5–10. RIR=7.7.

■ **Pat Austin ('AUSmum')** Shrub, orange blend, 1997, Austin. Large double blooms are a vivid combination of colors from rich copper on the topside to pale coppery yellow on the underside. Fruity old-rose fragrance. 5 to 6 feet tall; spreading habit. Zones 5–9. RIR=7.7.

■ **Perdita ('AUSperd')** Shrub, apricot blend, 1983, Austin. Blooms (50+ petals) change from hybrid tea form to quartered cups and finish as neat rosettes. Needs a season to establish. 4 feet tall. Zones 4–9. RIR=7.8.

■ **Peter Beales ('CLEexpert')**
Shrub, medium red, 2000, Clements.
Clusters of rich crimson-red blooms
(5 petals) with a golden-yellow eye.
4 to 5 feet. Zones 4–10.

■ **Pillow Fight ('WEKpipogot')**
Shrub, white, 1999, Carruth. Bright
white flowers (about 35 petals) in
large trusses. Strong honey-and-rose
scent. A shrublet that grows 2 to
3 feet tall, with glossy dark green
foliage and strong upright stems.
Best in dry climates. Zones 4–9.
RIR=8.1.

■ **'Pink Grootendorst'** Hybrid
rugosa, medium pink, 1923,
Grootendorst. Masses of small florets.
(20+ petals) with frilled edges.
Wrinkled foliage, 6 feet tall. An
excellent hedge. Zones 4–9. RIR=7.8.

■ **Pink Meidiland ('MEIpoque')** Shrub, pink blend,
1985, Meilland. Deep pink single-petaled flowers
(5 petals) with a bright white eye provide electric color
on medium-size spreading bushes; small, semi-glossy
leaves. Zones 5–10. RIR=8.6.

■ **'Prairie Flower'** Shrub, red blend, 1975, Buck. Single-
petaled cardinal red flowers (7 petals, 2 to 3 inches
wide) with a white eye appear in small clusters. Light,
old-rose fragrance. Erect bushes reach 5 to 6 feet tall,
with leathery, dark green foliage. Bred to withstand
harsh winters, it needs little or no protection. Zones 3–9.

■ **'Prosperity'** Hybrid musk, white,
1919, Pemberton. Recurrent flowers
in large clusters. 20 petals. Vigorous.
Train as a tall pillar. Very fragrant.
Zones 4–9. RIR=8.5.

■ **'Prairie Harvest'** Shrub, light
yellow, 1985, Buck. Large blossoms
(4 inches wide) with 40+ petals,
singly or in sprays of up to 15
florets. Moderate fragrance, leathery
foliage, upright plant. 4 to 5 feet.
Zones 3–9.

■ **Purple Simplicity ('JACpursh')**
Shrub, mauve, 1998, Zary. The latest
color for the series. Deep raspberry-
purple flowers hold color in hot sun.
5 to 6 feet. Zones 5–10. RIR=7.5.

Classic and Modern Shrub Roses
(continued)

■ <u>Queen Margrethe ('POUlskov')</u>
Shrub, light pink, 1995, Olesen. Heavily quartered old-fashioned blooms (50 petals or more) in heavenly pink pastels. Lovely apple fragrance. Round compact bush grows 4 to 5 feet tall. Disease-free. Zones 5–10. RIR=7.8.

■ **Radio Times ('AUSsal')** Shrub, medium pink, 1997, Austin. Rich, bright pink rosettes age gracefully, with the petals recurving back. Strong fragrance and short bushy growth only 3 feet tall. 60+ petals. Zones 4–9.

■ <u>Red Flower Carpet ('NOAre')</u>
Shrub, medium red, 2001, Noack. Waves of red single blooms all summer on 2½-foot arching shrubs. Glossy leaves, good disease resistance. Excellent for containers. Zones 5–11. RIR=8.1.

■ **Redoute ('AUSpale')** Shrub, light pink, 1994, Austin. Old-fashioned, soft, delicate pink blooms in smallish clusters on upright plant. 4 to 5 feet. Zones 5–9.

■ **Red Meidiland ('MEIneble')**
Shrub, red blend, 1989, Meilland. Brilliant red single blooms (5 petals) with white eyes cover this low (2 to 3 feet) spreading groundcover in spring and again in late summer. Dark, semi-glossy leaves, excellent disease resistance. Abundant red hips in fall. Very hardy. Zones 4–10. RIR=7.2.

■ <u>Red Ribbons ('KORtemma')</u>
Shrub, dark red, 1998, Kordes. A low-care rose used in street plantings. Small bright red flowers (17 to 25 petals, 2 inches wide), usually in small clusters, have a light, fresh scent. Plants grow about 2 to 3 feet tall and can spread 4 to 5 feet. The glossy, bright green foliage is impervious to disease. Zones 4–10. RIR=8.3.

■ **Red Simplicity ('JACsimpl')**
Shrub, medium red, 1991, Zary. Colorfast, deep red blooms (15 to 25 petals) in small clusters. Needs no maintenance. 5 to 6 feet. Zones 5–10. RIR=7.1.

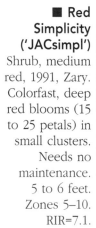

■ **Rockin' Robin ('WEKboraco')**
Shrub, red blend, 1999, Carruth. Profusion of red-, pink-, and white-striped 2-inch blooms (40 to 45 petals) in large clusters that last almost a month. Mild apple scent. A shrublet that grows 2 to 3 feet tall in warm climates, shorter in cool areas. Foliage is glossy green. Remove spent blooms to quicken the repeat-bloom cycle. Zones 4–9. RIR=7.5.

■ 'Roseraie de l'Hay' Hybrid rugosa, dark red, 1901, Cochet-Cochet. Big, open, perfectly flat flowers (30+ petals), crimson-purple with creamy white stamens. Distinct fragrance of cloves and honey. Repeat-blooming. 5 to 6 feet. Zones 4–9. RIR=8.9.

■ Royal Bonica ('MEImodac') Shrub, medium pink, 1994, Meilland. This sport of Bonica bears rich pink flowers (15 to 25 petals, 2 inches wide) in small clusters. Fragrance is slight but stronger in cool climates. In warm climates bushes can grow 3 feet tall and spread about 4 feet. Remove spent blooms to quicken the repeat-bloom cycle. Zones 5–10. RIR=7.7.

■ 'Sally Holmes' Shrub, white, 1976, Holmes. Can spread rapidly to reach 10 feet high and wide in warm climates. Arched canes are covered with large clusters of blooms reminiscent of a gigantic hydrangea. Buds open into large creamy white flowers that fade to pure white (creamy pink in cool climates). Glossy leaves. Zones 4–10. RIR=8.9.

■ Scepter'd Isle ('AUSland') Shrub, light pink, 1997, Austin. Large double blooms (35 to 40 petals) of delicate pink color have a wonderful scent, good repeat cycle. 3 to 4 feet tall. Good disease resistance. Zones 4–9. RIR=8.1.

■ 'Sea Foam' Shrub, white, 1964, Schwartz. Double flowers of glistening white. Delicate fragrance. Blooms hold up well through bad weather. Excellent disease resistance. A good variety to train as weeping tree rose. 2 to 8 feet. Zones 5–10. RIR=8.1.

■ Sevillana ('MEIgekanu') Floribunda, orange, 1978, Meilland. Solid mass of fiery orange-red blooms in late spring; showy red hips in fall and winter. 4-foot plants have bronzy-green foliage, excellent disease resistance. Zones 6–11.

■ Sharifa Asma ('AUSreef') Shrub, light pink, 1989, Austin. Shallow, gently cupped blooms (40 to 50 petals) age to perfectly formed rosettes with good fragrance. Plant is a low grower, 3 feet tall. Zones 4–10. RIR=7.9.

■ Sir Edward Elgar ('AUSprima') Shrub, medium red, 1992, Austin. Blooms open to three-dimensional pompons (50+ petals) too heavy for stems to hold upright. 4 to 5 feet tall. Zones 5–10.

Classic and Modern Shrub Roses
(continued)

■ **Sophy's Rose ('AUSlot')** Shrub, red blend, 1997, Austin. Reddish purple dome-shaped flowers are quite double (80 to 90 petals) with an old-fashioned look and moderate fragrance. Vigorous bushes grow 3½ feet to 5 feet tall, with semi-glossy leaves. Zones 5–10. RIR=8.3.

■ **Starry Night ('ORAwichkay')** Shrub, white, 2002, Orard, AARS. Nearly always in bloom. From late spring through fall this groundcover rose bears huge clusters of single-petaled, bright white flowers (5 petals) with golden stamens reminiscent of flowering dogwood. Slight fragrance. Spreads 4 to 6 feet. Zones 4–10.

■ **'Sunny June'** Shrub, deep yellow, 1952, Lammerts. Single-petaled (5 to 7 petals), brilliant deep yellow blooms cover polished, dark leaves. Good repeat blooms. Grow alone or train on a trellis, 8 feet tall. Vigorous. Zones 5–10. RIR=7.7

■ **Sweet Juliet ('AUSleap')** Shrub, apricot blend, 1989, Austin. Lightly cupped, repeat flowering blooms (50 to 100 petals) are a delicate pale peach. Vigorous, upright, graceful plants, 4 feet tall. Zones 5–10. RIR=7.6.

■ **Tamora ('AUStamora')** Shrub, apricot blend, 1987, Austin. Deeply cupped, long-repeating blooms (40 to 50 petals) have a strong myrrh fragrance. Rich apricot-yellow color. Very thorny. 3 to 4 feet. Zones 4–9.

■ **The Pilgrim ('AUSwalker')** Shrub, medium yellow, 1991, Austin. Fragrant, glowing yellow flowers (50 to 100 petals) are strong and well shaped, age until outer petals are near-white. Grows 3½ feet tall. Zones 4–9. RIR=7.6.

■ **The Prince ('AUSvelvet')** Shrub, dark red, 1993, Austin. Rich deep crimson to royal purple petals form a shallow, very full rosette (100 petals, 4 inches wide). Old garden rose fragrance. Does not grow much above 2 to 3 feet tall. In dappled shade its deep red roses look stunning while its foliage remains healthy and disease-free. Zones 4–9. RIR=7.6.

■ **'Therese Bugnet'** Hybrid rugosa, medium pink, 1950, Bugnet. Good rose for the coldest climates. Large, old-fashioned, ruffled double blooms of lilac pink with a light fragrance. Disease-resistant. Dark green foliage, 5 to 6 feet. Zones 2–9. RIR=8.4.

■ **Topaz Jewel ('MORyelrug')** Hybrid rugosa, medium yellow, 1987, Moore. Rare recurrent-blooming yellow rugosa. 25+ petals. Fruity fragrance. Disease-resistant, hardy, vigorous, 4 to 6 feet tall. Zones 6–9. RIR=7.3.

■ **What a Peach ('CHEwpeachdell')** Shrub, apricot blend, 2002, Warner. Flowers grow in large clusters of long-lasting florets blending from deep to light peach hues. Mild fruity fragrance. Upright plants grow to 3 feet tall. Foliage is glossy green, new growth is reddish plum. Zones 5–10.

■ **White Meidiland ('MEIcoublan')** Shrub, white, 1986, Meilland. Large double white blooms. A ground-cover, 1 to 2 feet high, 4 to 5 feet wide. Zones 5–10. RIR=8.2.

■ **White Simplicity ('JACsnow')** Floribunda, white, 1991, Jackson & Perkins. All the same traits as the pink Simplicity: 5 to 6 feet tall, blooms freely, and is tidy, self-cleaning, and thrives on neglect. The double flowers are satiny white with a touch of gold in the center when fully open. Plant 2 to 3 feet apart for a hedge. Zones 5–10. RIR=7.9.

■ **William Baffin** Hybrid kordesii, deep pink, 1983, Svedja. Extremely hardy. Semi-double blooms are strawberry pink with a touch of white toward the brilliant yellow stamens at the center. Florets grow in clusters with up to 30 blooms per stem from summer to autumn. Little fragrance. Tall, upright plants (10 to 12 feet tall) with slightly arching stems are covered with glossy, disease-resistant foliage. Zones 2–9. RIR=8.9.

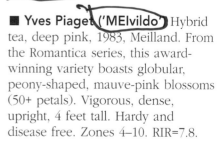

■ **Yellow Simplicity ('JACyelsh')** Shrub, deep yellow, Zary, 1997. Deep yellow 3-inch semi-double blooms (12 to 16 petals) are borne in profusion atop tall upright plants, ideal to plant as a hedge. Light fragrance. Foliage is dark green and glossy. Zones 5–10.

■ **Yves Piaget ('MEIvildo')** Hybrid tea, deep pink, 1983, Meilland. From the Romantica series, this award-winning variety boasts globular, peony-shaped, mauve-pink blossoms (50+ petals). Vigorous, dense, upright, 4 feet tall. Hardy and disease free. Zones 4–10. RIR=7.8.

Old Garden Roses and Species

Old garden roses and species (wild) roses range from dainty to huge. They're perfect for such diverse uses as hedges, coverings for walls and arbors, fragrance gardens, borders, and flower arranging.

There are more than 200 species roses in the world, with about 35 native to the United States and Canada. Many wild roses can spread by suckering and layering 30 to 50 feet in every direction. Species roses have 5 petals; other old garden roses can be quartered, cupped, imbricated, reflexed, globular, or compact. After an initial spring bloom cycle, many varieties stop producing flowers but put on colorful displays of rose hips, which add a different kind of beauty to the garden.

The American Rose Society defines old garden roses as those existing before 1867, when the first hybrid tea was introduced. The oldest rose to be identified is *Rosa gallica*. Old garden roses, famous for their heady fragrance, are grouped into the following classes:

ALBA: Very hardy (Zone 3). Generally upright, often climbing, with dense, disease-resistant, blue-green foliage. Fragrant flowers.

BOURBON: Blooms repeatedly. Ranges from 2 to 15 feet tall in warm climates. Zones 6–10.

CENTIFOLIA: Zones 4–9. Flowers, with 100 petals, bloom once in late spring. 4 to 8 feet.

HYBRID CHINA: Small plants, 2 to 3 feet tall. Repeat blooming. Tender, Zones 7–10.

DAMASK: Plants 3 to 6 feet tall with heavy fragrance; most bloom once, some repeatedly. Moderately hardy, Zones 6–10.

HYBRID FOETIDA: Tall, vigorous plants. Species has unpleasant odor, while hybrids are usually quite fragrant. Blooms once in spring. The source of yellow color in modern roses; descendents are also highly susceptible to black spot. Zones 3–9.

HYBRID GALLICA: Small plants 3 to 4 feet tall that bloom once in late spring. Zones 4–9.

MOSS: Some varieties bloom repeatedly; plants grow 3 to 6 feet tall. Hardy to Zone 4.

NOISETTE: Large sprawling plants, up to 20 feet tall. Fragrant. Tender, Zones 7–11.

HYBRID PERPETUAL: Plants grow 6 feet tall; flowers are fragrant and bloom repeatedly. Hardiness varies.

PORTLAND: Blooms repeatedly; 4 feet tall. Moderately hardy, Zones 6–10.

HYBRID SPINOSISSIMA: Vigorous shrubs, 3 to 5 feet tall, good for barriers because of their many thorns. Abundant flowering—some varieties bloom once, some repeat. Small ferny leaves with many 9-leaflet sets. Zones 3–9.

TEA: Small to medium plants, 4 to 5 feet tall, with droopy flowers that bloom repeatedly. Tender, Zones 7–11.

'Ispahan' is an extremely fragrant damask that dates to before 1832. Blooming once in late spring or early summer with a massive display that pervades the garden with delicious scent, the arching plants reach 5 to 6 feet high.

(continued)

■ **Apothecary's Rose (Rosa gallica officinalis).** Species, deep pink, before 1600. Semi-double blooms have four rows of petals that change gradually from bright crimson to purple with golden stamens. Intense fragrance; ideal for potpourri. Once-blooming. Grows 3 to 4 feet tall, with dark green foliage. Attractive hips in the fall. Zones 4–10. RIR=8.6.

■ **'Archduke Charles'** Hybrid china, red blend, prior to 1837, Laffay. Recurrent bloomer all summer. Deep pink intensifies to crimson with age. Disease-resistant. Vigorous bush, 2 to 3 feet tall. Intense fragrance. 30 to 40 petals. Zones 5–10. RIR=8.4.

■ **Austrian Copper (Rosa foetida bicolor)** Species, red blend, prior to 1590. Blooms once in the spring but the display is dazzling, covered with brilliant orange-scarlet single flowers (5 petals) that have a yellow reverse. Grows 4 to 12 feet tall (tallest in warm climates). Zones 4–11. RIR=7.7.

■ **'Autumn Damask' (also know as Quatre Saisons).** Damask, medium pink, 1819. Large florets (35 to 40 petals) with sometimes crumpled petals on 4-foot-tall plant. Flowers best in spring and late fall. Highly fragrant. Zones 5–11. RIR=8.2.

■ **'Baron Girod de l'Ain'** Hybrid perpetual, red blend, Reverchon, 1897. Repeat blooming. Bright red petals have ragged white deckle edge. Healthy looking 4-foot bush. Fragrant. 30 to 40 petals. Zones 5–10. RIR=7.3.

■ **'Baronne Prévost'** Hybrid perpetual, medium pink, 1842, Desprez. Durable rose-pink flowers (100 petals) in small clusters on strong straight stems. 3 to 6 feet. Recurrent. Zones 7–10. RIR=8.7.

■ **'Blush Noisette'** Noisette, white, before 1817. Nearly thornless bush with delicate soft pink flowers (30 petals) in clusters of 6 to 12. Lush, dark foliage. 6 to 7 feet. Zones 7–10. RIR=8.4.

■ **'Cardinal de Richelieu'** Hybrid gallica, mauve, Laffay, 1847. One bloom cycle on 4- to 5-foot plant during the spring and summer but worth the rich, dark purple display. Sweet fragrance. 40 to 50 petals. Zones 4–9. RIR=7.8.

■ **'Catherine Mermet'** Tea, light pink, 1869, Guillot et Fils. Blooms spring through fall with shapely flesh-pink florets (25 to 30 petals). Flower size can vary with climate. Light fragrance. Plants grow 4 feet tall. Coppery-tinged foliage is disease resistant. Zones 7–10. RIR=7.8.

■ **'Celestial'** Alba, light pink, Kew, prior to 1797. Blooming once in the spring, the large, double, blush-pink blooms (25 to 30 petals) open to reveal golden stamens. Gray-green foliage. Intensely fragrant, vigorous, 6 feet. Zones 5–9. RIR=8.5.

■ **'Celsiana'** Damask, light pink, before 1750. Semi-double blooms tend to nod. Strong musk fragrance. Blooms once in early summer. 3 to 4 feet. Zones 4–10. RIR=8.8.

■ **'Celine Forestier'** Noisette, light yellow, 1858, Leroy. Quartered pale yellow blooms with dark green button at center; spicy fragrance. 5 to 6 feet. Zones 7–10. RIR=8.8.

■ **'Charles de Mills'** Hybrid gallica, mauve, before 1746. Ranging from dark red to crimson to rich purple, the quartered flowers are huge, up to 5 inches wide. Blooms once in late spring. Prone to mildew. Grows 4 to 6 feet tall. Zones 4–10. RIR=8.4.

■ **'Comte de Chambord'** Portland, pink blend, Robert et Moreau, 1860. Attractive quartered-flower form in lilac-pink, with heavy old rose perfume. Disease-resistant. Blooms constantly. Vigorous; medium height. 40 to 50 petals. Zones 5–9. RIR=8.3.

■ **'Crested Moss'** Moss, medium pink, 1827, Vibert. Also known as "Chapeau de Napoleon." One bloom cycle in late spring or early summer. Buds resemble cocked-hats. In warm climates can be grown as small climber, 5 to 6 feet tall. Very fragrant. 35 to 40 petals. Zones 5–9. RIR=8.7.

■ **'Duchesse de Brabant'** Tea, light pink, Bernéde, 1857. Ample supply of shapely soft rose-pink florets late spring into fall. Small, well-foliated bush with a spreading habit, 3 to 4 feet tall. Strong fragrance. 45 to 50 petals. Zones 5–11. RIR=8.6.

■ **'Enfant de France'** Hybrid perpetual, light pink, Lartay, 1860. Huge, satiny, silvery pink blossoms from spring to fall. Small dense bush, 3 feet tall. Very fragrant. 40 to 50 petals. Zones 4–9. RIR=8.6.

■ **'Felicite Parmentier'** Alba, light pink, 1834. Light flesh-pink blossoms are very double (40 to 50 petals) with reflexing petals, powerful fragrance. Tidy bush to 4 feet tall with dark grayish green foliage. Zones 5–9. RIR=8.7.

Old Garden Roses and Species
(continued)

■ **'Ferdinand Pichard'** Hybrid perpetual, red blend, Tanne, 1921. One of the few striped old garden roses to repeat bloom. Flowers are streaked with pink and scarlet. Tall, upright plant with disease-resistant foliage, 6 feet tall. Distinct fragrance. 25 petals. Zones 4–9. RIR=7.4.

■ **'Great Maiden's Blush'** Alba, white, before 1738. Fragrant blush pink flowers on a large arching shrub with grayish foliage. 4 to 6 feet. Zones 3–9. RIR=9.0.

■ **'Harison's Yellow'** Hybrid foetida, deep yellow, about 1830. Small, spectacular, bright yellow blooms appear briefly once in spring. Wonderful fragrance. Attractive hips are bristly, oval, and black. Vigorous, 10 to 12 feet tall. Zones 3–9. RIR=8.2.

■ **'Henri Martin'** Moss, medium red, 1862, Laffay. Claret red to crimson blooms in large clusters open flat on large shrub. 5 to 6 feet. Zones 3–9. RIR=8.7.

■ **'Irene Watts'** China, white, 1896, Guillot. Blooms all summer with clusters of pompon-like florets (35 to 40 petals), soft apricot-orange with a golden eye. Foliage is dark green margined with purple. Vigorous, 3 feet tall. Zones 7–9

■ **'Ispahan'** Damask, medium pink, before 1832. Double flowers are consistently bright clear pink with a powerful old-rose fragrance. 4 to 6 feet. Zones 3–9. RIR=8.4.

■ **'Konigin von Danemark'** Alba, medium pink, 1816. Tight, stubby buds open into large, flat flowers (3 to 4 inches across) packed with bright, flesh-pink petals, darker at the center. Blooms once in spring in heavy clusters that bend stems. In wet regions blooms do not open fully, but the fragrance is exquisite. Grows 5 feet tall; deep bluish-green leaves. Zones 3–10. RIR=8.6.

■ **'La Belle Sultane'** Hybrid gallica, deep red, ca. 1795. One-time display of semi-double florets (7 to 15 petals), open deep crimson, age to violet with yellow stamens. Upright, 5 to 6 feet. Zones 4–10. RIR=8.1.

■ **'Louise Odier'** Bourbon, deep pink, 1851, Margottin. Full cupped flowers of warm pink; rich perfume. 6 to 8 feet. Zones 4–9. RIR=8.5.

■ **'Maréchal Niel'** Noisette, medium yellow, 1864, Pradel. Large golden yellow florets (35 to 40 petals) appear in clusters, very fragrant. Dark coppery green leaves. Vigorous climber to 15 feet tall; weak stems are easy to wrap on supports. Prefers heat. Zones 5–11. RIR=7.7.

■ **'Mme Alfred Carrière'** Noisette, white, 1879, Schwartz. Large, globular, pale pinkish-white blooms with just a touch of yellow at base of each petal. 5 to 6 feet. Zones 4–10. RIR=9.0.

■ **'Mme Pierre Oger'** Bourbon, pink blend, 1878, Oger. Full double flowers (35 to 40 petals) are blush pink with a rosy-lilac reverse. Very fragrant. Recurrent bloomer. Hardy, vigorous, and disease-resistant. 5 feet tall. Zones 6–10. RIR=8.0.

■ **'Marchesa Boccella'** ('Jacques Cartier') Hybrid perpetual, light pink, 1842, Desprez. Fragrant blooms, about 3 inches wide, on tight clusters. Good repeat flowering. 3 to 4 feet. Zones 4–10. RIR=9.1.

■ **'Mme Hardy'** Damask, white, 1832, Hardy. One of the most beautiful whites, with attractive green pip in center of bloom. Nonrecurrent, but spring show is outstanding. 6 to 7 feet. Zones 3–11. RIR=9.0.

■ **'Mrs. B.R. Cant'** Tea, medium pink, 1901, Cant. Medium-size double flowers are rich red and silvery rose, tinged with blush at base of each petal. 4 to 6 feet. Zones 7–9. RIR=8.9.

■ **'Mermaid'** Hybrid bracteata, light yellow, 1918, Paul. Large, fragrant, single-petaled blossoms (5 petals) appear spring to fall, creamy yellow with dark golden stamens. Beautiful climber, reaching 20 to 30 feet tall in mild climates. Watch out for thorns! Tender in cold climates. Zones 5–11. RIR=8.6.

■ **'Mme Isaac Pereire'** Bourbon, deep pink, 1881, Garcon. Huge, full, richly fragrant blooms are deep rose-pink and usually appear in sprays. In autumn, blooms develop purple tint. Flower form is sometimes cupped, sometimes quartered, depending on climate. Exceptionally vigorous plant grows to 7 feet tall. Canes can either be pegged down or trained as climbers to achieve maximum bloom production. Best in warm climates. Zones 5–10. RIR=8.5.

■ **'Mutabilis'** China tea, yellow blend, before 1894. Single-petaled flowers mature from sulfur yellow to orange, copper, red, and finally crimson. 4 to 6 feet. Long flowering period. Zones 7–10. RIR=8.9.

Old Garden Roses and Species
(continued)

■ **'Old Blush'** China, medium pink, 1752, Parsons. Semi-double white flowers (25 to 30 petals) blushed with pink. Light fragrance. Upright, thornless, recurrent bloomer to 4 feet tall. A climbing form for Zones 8 to 10 is available. Zones 7–9 (with protection). RIR=8.7.

■ **'Reine Victoria'** Bourbon, medium pink, Schwartz, 1872. Slender, erect bush with perpetual supply of rich pink cupped florets (25 to 30 petals), usually in small clusters. Light fragrance. 4 to 5 feet tall. Zones 6–9. RIR=8.2.

■ **'Rose de Rescht'** Portland, deep pink, very ancient. Heavily scented fuchsia-red blooms in small tight clusters on short stems. Color can show signs of purple and is often paler in hot climates. 2 to 3 feet. Zones 3–10. RIR=8.9.

■ **'Paul Neyron'** Hybrid perpetual, medium pink, 1869, Levet. Massive, flat, pure pink to rose-pink flowers (50+ petals) on strong, straight stems. Flowers last for weeks. Fragrance is moderate. Vigorous, tall (4 to 5 feet), and upright. Zones 5–10. RIR=8.2.

■ **'Reve d'Or'** Noisette, medium yellow, 1869, Ducher. Shapely buff yellow blossoms (25 to 30 petals) can have a tinge of pink in cooler climates. Some recurrent blooming. Very fragrant. Vigorous climber, 12 feet tall. Zones 7–9. RIR=9.4.

■ **'Rose du Roi'** Portland, medium red, Lelieur, 1815. Bright red flowers (25 to 30 petals) shaded with violet. Dwarf, compact; 3 feet tall. Recurrent blooming, very fragrant. Prefers mild climates. Zones 6–9. RIR=7.7.

■ **'Reine des Violettes'** Hybrid perpetual, mauve, 1860, Millet-Malet. Unusual very double violet blooms (75 petals) appear spring to fall, shatter easily after a few days. Upright climbing plant with few thorns, 6 to 8 feet tall. Great fragrance. Zones 5–9. RIR=8.2.

■ **'Rose de Meaux'** Centifolia, medium pink, 1789. Fragrant flowers have frilly petals and pompon form (25 to 30 petals). Blooms once in early summer. Dwarf with erect stems, 3 feet tall. Zones 4–9. RIR=7.3.

■ **Rosa glauca** Species, medium pink. Small, single-petaled, starlike flowers (1 inch wide) appear once in late spring. Soft lilac-pink color. Striking grayish-purple foliage and attractive hips in the fall. Ideal as dense hedge. 5 to 8 feet. Zones 2–9. RIR=8.8.

■ **Rosa Mundi** Species (Rosa gallica versicolor), pink blend, before 1581. This sport of the Apothecary's Rose is the oldest striped rose known. Semi-double blooms 4 inches wide display red and pink stripes against a white background, accented by golden-yellow stamens. Blooms once in spring. Grows 3 to 4 feet tall with a sprawling habit. Zones 4–9.

■ **'Salet'** Moss, medium pink, 1854. Large, full, rose-pink flowers are flat, 2 to 3 inches across, and bloom intermittently. 4 to 5 feet. Zones 4–10. RIR=8.2.

■ **'Stanwell Perpetual'** Hybrid spinosissima, white, 1838, Lee. Has habit and foliage of a Scots Rose (small and ferny with lots of 9-leaf sets), with the repeat flowering of autumn damasks. Flowers are pale blush pink, double, quartered, and quilled, with a delicious fragrance. Canes are covered with thorns. Remove old wood each year. Grows 3 to 5 feet. Zones 3–9. RIR=8.6.

■ **Rosa rugosa alba** Species, white, prior to 1800. The white form of Rosa rugosa, with the same hardiness, lovely hips, and vigor. 5 petals. Zones 3–10. RIR=9.0.

■ **'Sombreuil'** Climbing tea, white, 1850, Robert. One of the few tea roses that climbs. White blooms often have creamy centers when first open that quickly turn to pure white. Flowers are flat, quilled, quartered, and very double (80 to 100 petals). Blooms continuously all summer. Strong tea-rose fragrance. Climbs 6 to 12 feet. Zones 7–10. RIR=8.9.

■ **'Tuscany Superb'** Hybrid gallica, mauve, prior to 1837. Large dark purple blooms (35 to 40 petals) with contrasting golden yellow stamens appear once in summer. 4 to 5 feet tall. Zones 4–10. RIR=8.4.

■ **Rosa rugosa rubra** Species, mauve, before 1854. Large, single (5 petals), scented flowers are magenta-purple with contrasting golden stamens, appearing early spring through summer. Lavish fall display of large round red hips. Dense shrubs grow 8 feet high with prickly canes and dark, semiglossy wrinkled leaves. Zones 2–9. RIR=9.2.

■ **'Souvenir de la Malmaison'** Bourbon, light pink, 1843. Flat, quartered blooms (35 to 40 petals) with spicy fragrance. Hates rain. 4 feet tall. A climbing counterpart is available. Zones 6–9. RIR=8.7.

■ **'Zéphirine Drouhin'** Bourbon, medium pink, 1868, Bizot. Thornless variety that produces masses of fragrant, cerise-pink blooms all season. 30 to 35 petals. 8 to 12 feet. Zones 5–9. RIR=8.0.

Climbing Roses

Climbing roses add height and density to a garden. Their long, flexible canes, when trained to a vertical support, bring flowers to eye level where you can easily enjoy them. Climbing roses can enhance a plain brick or dry-stone wall and cover an unsightly chain link or barbed-wire fence, transforming utilitarian eyesores into objects of natural beauty.

Climbing miniatures reach a height and width of 3 to 6 feet; large-flowered climbers can be 4 to 12 feet tall, and ramblers grow 20 to 30 feet in every direction. In nature, what we call climbing roses are shrubs with long, arching canes that sprawl and lean on vertical surfaces and other plants for support, sometimes "grabbing on" with their prickles. The long canes bloom at almost every leaf junction, blanketing them with flowers and making them ideal in the garden for training on walls, fences, trellises, pillars, posts, arches, arbors, pergolas, and up through trees. Training is the key word here; long-caned roses are not vines and do not climb. Left to themselves they would mound and sprawl.

Climbers on walls

When you train a rose to cover a long, low wall, choose the same variety to repeat over the length of the wall. Space climbers 5 to 6 feet apart; ramblers need even more room. Spacing the plants is crucial for success, because adjacent plants should interlock canes to provide a uniform, hedgelike final structure.

There are several ways to train a rose on a wall. The simplest is to attach a trellis to the underlying support. A trellis has the advantage of holding the rose away from the wall so air can circulate around the canes to prevent disease. Or you can train the rose on heavy wire fed through eye screws attached to the wall in a vertical, horizontal, or fan-shaped pattern. The wires should be anchored to the wall every couple of feet and pulled taut. Tie the stems to the wires with flexible fabric, garden twine, or raffia.

Small climbers for small spaces and containers

Short climbers provide a blaze of color in an upright growth pattern without invading nearby plants. This tidy behavior makes them ideal for small spaces. With grooming, some ground-cover roses can also be trained to grow vertically in a small area.

Cultivate them in decorative 15- to 20-gallon pots and tubs, and provide a simple lattice to support the canes. The lattice should be rectangular and about 3 to 4 feet wide, or fan-shaped and about 5 feet wide at the top.

Pillars and posts

Rose pillars make a big impression in a small space. But not all climbers flower on a pillar. Most climbers bloom profusely only when the canes are horizontal. But pillar roses are climbers that bloom freely at the leaf nodes when trained on a vertical plane. Trained pillar-rose canes should resemble a spiral staircase that loops around a central post until it reaches its final height. Direct the long, flexible canes in an ascending spiral, spaced evenly apart around the column. By intertwining the canes, you create a solid visual mass along the post. To keep the canes in place, use flexible fabric, garden twine, or raffia attached to hooks or bolts in the structure. As the rose canes grow, you may need to trim some side stems to preserve the columnar effect. Cut back stout side stems by two-thirds and weaker side stems by three-fourths.

Arbors and pergolas

Envelop yourself in flowers by growing a climber on an arch, arbor, or pergola. The best roses to grow on these structures flower from ground level to the tips of their long canes. They bloom equally well on vertical and horizontal planes and produce canes at least 12 to 15 feet long, so that two plants can overlap and intertwine at the midpoint of the arch or pergola. Choose a self-cleaning rose that doesn't require constant grooming. Look for fragrant climbers to heighten your pleasure. For optimal foliage density and flowers, plant roses 6 feet apart and on both sides of a pergola.

At right, Eden Climber (called Pierre de Ronsard in Europe) ascends a cast-iron support.

Climbing Roses
(continued)

■ **'Aloha'** Climbing hybrid tea, medium pink, 1949, Boerner. Elegant rose-pink blooms with darker reverse. Sweet rose fragrance. 6 to 10 feet. Zones 3–9. RIR=7.8.

■ **Altissimo ('DELmur')** Climber, medium red, 1966, Delbard-Chabert. Huge china-lacquer-red, single-petaled blooms (5 to 7 petals) with bright yellow stamens are flat and broad, looking like large red saucers. Vigorous, 10 to 12 feet tall. Scent is light. Zones 6–10. RIR=8.5.

■ **America ('JACclam')** Climber, orange-pink, 1976, Warriner, AARS. Salmon-pink blooms (30 to 35 petals) have perfect form and rich dianthus perfume. 8 to 10 feet. Zones 4–10. RIR=8.3.

■ **Angel Face, Climbing** Climbing floribunda, mauve, 1981, Haight. Small climber with magnificent display of mauve flowers all summer. Zones 5–10.

■ **'Autumn Sunset'** Shrub, apricot blend, 1986, Lowe. Warm apricot-gold blooms (20 to 25 petals) exude strong, fruity fragrance. Excellent resistance to black spot. Zones 5–10. RIR=8.1.

■ **Berries 'n' Cream ('POUlclimb')** Climber, pink blend, 1999, Olesen. Flowers are swirled with old-rose pink and creamy white (more white in cool temperatures), and held in clusters on strong, upright stems suitable for cutting. Canes can grow almost 10 to 12 feet (in mild climates, even longer) and have few thorns. Large, glossy, light green leaves. Zones 5–10. RIR=7.8.

■ **Blaze Improved ('Blaze')** Climber, medium red, 1932, Kallay. Solid scarlet-red flowers (20 to 25 petals) in large clusters on strong stems all along the length of its thick canes. Blooms all summer. Light tea fragrance. Canes generally grow 12 to 14 feet long. Zones 5–10. RIR=7.2.

■ **Cal Poly, Climbing ('MORclpoly')** Climbing miniature, medium yellow, 1997, Moore. Just like its bush counterpart, this plant has bright yellow flowers (20 petals) and handsome foliage. 4 to 6 feet. Zones 5–11. RIR=7.9.

■ **'Candy Cane'** Climbing miniature, pink blend, 1958, Moore. Classic miniature climber. Semi-double blooms (13 to 15 petals) striped with deep pink and pure white. Massive clusters of up to 20 flowers arch on canes to form candy-cane shape. 4 to 6 feet tall. Susceptible to black spot in humid climates. Zones 5–11. RIR=8.2.

■ **Chick-a-dee, Climbing ('MORclchick')** Climbing miniature, medium pink, 2000, Moore. Double pink blossoms in profusion on this climbing descendant of Chick-a-dee. 3 to 4 feet. Zones 5–10.

■ **'Circus, Climbing'** Climbing floribunda, yellow blend, 1961, House. Yellow blooms blend into tangerine. 6 to 8 feet. Zones 6–10.

■ **Constance Spry ('AUSfirst')** Shrub, light pink, 1961, Austin. Double cup-shaped blooms are a luminous soft pink. Myrrh fragrance. Often grown as a climber, the sprawling plant reaches 4 to 8 feet tall and wide. Not a true repeat-flowering rose, but the bloom cycle is long, stretching well into the summer months. Zones 4–9. RIR=8.5.

■ **'Don Juan'** Climber, dark red, 1958, Malandrone. Velvety double dark red blooms (30 to 35 petals) all summer. Strong rose fragrance. Warm temperatures at night produce best color. Glossy dark foliage. Canes can grow 12 to 14 feet; average length is 8 to 10 feet. Can suffer from frost damage during cold winters but will recover. Zones 5–10. RIR=8.2.

■ **'Dortmund'** Hybrid kordesii, medium red, 1955, Kordes. Large single-petaled flowers (5 to 7 petals) with light scent. Small clusters. Needs deadheading to initiate next cycle. Red hips. 8 to 10 feet. Zones 4–10. RIR=9.2.

■ **Double Delight, Climbing ('AROclidd')** Climbing hybrid tea, red blend, 1985, Christensen. The climbing version of the popular hybrid tea. Zones 7–10. RIR=7.5.

■ **Dream Weaver ('JACpicl')** Climbing floribunda, orange pink, 1998, Zary. Small clusters of long-lasting, bright coral-pink rosettes (30 petals) with a slight old-rose scent. Good repeat bloom. Foliage is dark and glossy. Canes can grow 10 to 12 feet long. Zones 5–10. RIR=7.9.

■ **Dublin Bay ('MACdub')** Climber, medium red, 1975, McGredy. Large, fully double, cardinal red flowers. Excellent repeat flowering. Can achieve cane lengths of 10 feet in second season. Dark green foliage is glossy, disease-resistant. Zones 4–10. RIR=8.6.

■ **Earthquake, Climbing ('MORshook')** Climbing miniature, red blend, Moore, 1990. Double flowers (40 petals) are striped bright red and yellow, with yellow reverse, in profuse small clusters of 3 to 5 florets. Repeat bloom is somewhat reduced in cool climates, but striping is more pronounced. 4 to 6 feet tall. Zones 6–10. RIR=8.3.

■ **Eden Climber, Pierre de Ronsard ('MElviolin')** Climber, pink blend, 1987, Meilland. Abundant, large, old-fashioned flowers (40+ petals) in blend of pastel pink, cream, and yellow. Dark green foliage is dense to the ground. 12 feet. Zones 5–10. RIR=8.1.

Climbing Roses
(continued)

■ **First Prize, Climbing ('JACclist')** Climbing hybrid tea, pink blend, 1976, Reasoner. Huge blooms (20 to 30 petals) have a lighter silvery pink reverse. Very thorny canes. Mild tea fragrance. Zones 5–10. RIR=7.6.

■ **Flutterbye ('WEKplasol')** Floribunda, yellow blend, 1999, Carruth. Large clusters of single-petaled blossoms (5 to 8 petals) with different colors at the same time (yellow, coral, tangerine, and pink). Strong 6- to 8-foot canes, especially in warm areas. Zones 5–9. RIR=7.7.

■ **Fourth of July ('WEKroalt')** Climber, red blend, 1999, Carruth, AARS. Big sprays of long-lasting striped blooms (10 to 15 petals) with apple-and-rose fragrance. Excellent disease resistance. 10 to 14 feet. Zones 5–11. RIR=8.1.

■ **'Golden Showers'** Climber, medium yellow, 1956, Lammerts, AARS. Masses of cheerful daffodil yellow flowers (25 to 30 petals) with sweet licorice fragrance. Self-cleaning with good repeat. Vigorous; grows 10 to 12 feet. Best in cool climates. Zones 6–10. RIR=7.3.

■ **Handel ('MACha')** Climber, red blend, 1965, McGredy. Double blooms (20 to 30 petals), white heavily edged in red. Canes grow 10 to 12 feet long with dark olive-green foliage. Best in cool climates. Zones 5–9. RIR=8.0.

■ **'Henry Kelsey'** Hybrid kordesii, medium red, 1984, Svedja. One of the hardiest climbers. Semi-double dark red flowers (28 petals) with bright yellow stamens are produced all summer. Spicy fragrance. Grows 6 to 8 feet tall with dense, glossy green foliage. Zones 3–9.

■ **High Hopes ('HARyup')** Climber, medium pink, 1994, Harkness. Small clusters of elegant pointed buds open to rose-pink, double, high-centered flowers. Sweet strawberry fragrance. Self-cleaning with dark green foliage; canes can grow 10 to 12 feet long. Protect from black spot in humid climates. Zones 5–10.

■ **'Iceberg, Climbing'** Climbing floribunda, white, 1968, Cant. The same classic pure white flowers on a climber as on the popular floribunda, 6 to 12 feet tall. Zones 5–10. RIR=8.6.

■ **'Joseph's Coat'** Climber, red blend, 1969, Armstrong & Swim. Clusters of double flowers (23 to 28 petals) in hues ranging through red, pink, orange, and yellow. Light tea scent. Canes grow 8 to 12 feet long with glossy apple-green foliage. Needs protection in northern climates. Zones 6–10. RIR=7.4.

■ **'Jeanne LaJoie'** Climbing miniature, medium pink, 1975, Sims, AOE. Nonstop blooms start with clusters of long pointed buds that open to nonfading, medium pink, miniature flowers (35 to 40 petals) of exquisite hybrid tea form. Light fragrance. Strong canes grow 6 to 10 feet long. Dark green glossy foliage. Vigorous and hardy. Zones 4–11. RIR=9.2.

■ 'Lavender Lace, Climbing'
Climbing miniature, mauve, 1971, Rumsey. Lavender-pink blooms open fast to reveal golden stamens. Canes reach 4 to 6 feet long. Zones 5–11.

■ 'Lavender Lassie' Hybrid musk, mauve, 1960, Kordes. Delicate rose-pink with a hint of lavender, the large trusses of double rosettes (60+ petals) appear in abundance. Light fragrance. Canes reach 6 to 10 feet long, with disease-resistant foliage. Zones 4–9. RIR=8.1.

■ Mary Marshall, Climbing ('MINico') Climbing miniature, orange blend, 1983, Williams. Fast-repeating blooms (20 to 25 petals) are orange-pink with a yellow base. Moderate fragrance. Canes reach 4 to 6 feet long with dark, leathery, disease-resistant foliage. Zones 5–10.

■ 'Mlle Cécile Brünner, Climbing'
Climbing polyantha, light pink, 1894, Hosp. Large, airy clusters of pointed, eggshell white buds open to silvery pink blooms with spicy, sweet scent. 30+ petals. Canes can grow 20 feet. Zones 6–10. RIR=8.3.

■ 'New Dawn' Climber, light pink, 1930, Van Fleet, WFRS Rose Hall of Fame. Large, full, cameo-pink flowers (40 to 45 petals) with a sweet rose fragrance appear all summer. Very vigorous and hardy; canes can reach 12 to 20 feet, with glossy, dark-green, disease-resistant foliage. Zones 4–10. RIR=8.6.

■ 'Newport Fairy'
Rambler, pink blend, 1908, Gardner. This hybrid wichuraiana bears small, single-petaled, rose-pink blooms with white centers in enormous clusters. Large plants sprawl 20 to 30 feet in all directions. Spring bloom is spectacular; repeat can be slow in cool climates. Zones 5–10. RIR=8.6.

■ Paprika ('MEIriental')
Climber, orange-red, 1997, Meilland. Semi-double flowers (20 to 25 petals) are bright orange-red. Light fragrance. Dense foliage is dark green. 8 to 10 feet tall. Zones 5–10.

■ 'Paradise, Climbing' Climbing hybrid tea, mauve, 1985, Weeks. Double well-formed hybrid tea flowers; petals are silvery lavender at the base blending to ruby red at the edge. Foliage is lush, dark green. Best in cool mild climates. Zones 5–8. RIR=7.7.

■ 'Paul's Himalayan Musk Rambler'
Hybrid musk, light pink, 1916, Paul. Clusters of small, fragrant, pale lilac-pink rosettes droop from threadlike stems for a massive display once in spring. Large, hardy, can sprawl 30 feet in every direction. Ideal for climbing up and through mature trees. Zones 4–9.

■ 'Paul's Lemon Pillar' Climbing hybrid tea, light yellow, 1915, Paul. Cabbagelike blooms with broad overlapping petals are creamy white in bud opening to reveal light yellow centers that quickly turn almost white. Lemony fragrance. Blooms cannot withstand rain. Zones 5–10.

Climbing Roses
(continued)

■ **'Peace, Climbing'** Climbing hybrid tea, yellow blend, 1951, Kordes. The climbing version of the beloved hybrid tea. Canes each 8 to 10 feet. Blooms only on old wood; not for cold climates. Zones 8–11. RIR=6.3.

■ **Playgirl, Climbing ('MORclip')** Climbing floribunda, medium pink, 1995, Moore. Single flowers (5 petals) in clear pink on a 10-foot climber. Zones 5–10.

■ **Rainbow's End, Climbing ('SAVaclena')** Miniature, yellow blend, 1999, Saville. Profuse, small clusters of blooms (35 petals, unscented) are deep yellow with red edges, aging gracefully to deeper reds. Foliage is dark green. Grows 8 feet tall. Zones 5–11. RIR=7.9.

■ **Pearly Gates ('WEKmeyer')** Climber, medium pink, 1999, Meyer. Well-formed, symmetrical flowers (35 petals) are pure pastel pink, shading to lighter tones. Fragrance is sweet and spicy. Blooms all summer. Canes can reach 12 feet. Zones 5–10. RIR=7.7.

■ **Polka ('MEItosier')** Climber, apricot blend, 1996, Meilland. Large fluffy old-fashioned flowers (30 to 35 petals) in dramatic copper-salmon fading to light salmon-pink with deep copper at center. Fragrance is strong and pervading. Canes grow 10 to 12 feet long with healthy dark green foliage. Zones 5–10. RIR=7.8.

■ **'Piñata'** Climber, yellow blend, 1978, Suzuki. Bright yellow flowers (25 to 30 petals) edged in fiery orange-red. Strong, fruity aroma. 6 to 10 feet. Zones 6–10. RIR=7.4.

■ **'Queen Elizabeth, Climbing'** Climbing grandiflora, medium pink, 1960, Whisler. The climbing form of the beloved grandiflora, with sprays of luminous pink flowers. Zones 6–11. RIR=6.3.

■ **'Renae'** Climbing floribunda, medium pink, 1954, Moore. Floriferous small climber with canes that bend to the ground. 4 to 6 feet. Zones 5–9. RIR=6.7.

■ **Renny ('MOReny')** Miniature, medium pink, 1989, Moore. Profuse pink flowers with old-fashioned fragrance and form. Thornless canes. 3 to 4 feet. Zones 5–11. RIR=8.1.

■ **'Red Cascade'** Climbing miniature, dark red, 1976, Moore, AOE. The deep red 1-inch flowers (40 petals) appear along full length of the canes. Light fragrance. Fast repeat. Small leathery leaves. Needs full sun and good air circulation. Excellent for hanging baskets. 3 to 4 feet. Zones 5–11. RIR=7.4.

■ **Rosa banksiae lutea** Species, light yellow, 1824. Abundant clusters of small, double, bright yellow flowers produced once in spring. Can grow up to 30 feet in all directions, with trunks the size of small trees. Excellent on high walls or in mature trees where support is very sturdy. Zones 7–10. RIR=9.1.

■ **'Royal Sunset'** Climber, apricot blend, 1960, Morey. Deep apricot blooms can be high-centered or cupped (30 to 35 petals), with a rich fruity fragrance. The color fades to light peach as blossoms mature in midsummer heat; they can appear a bit blowsy at times. Canes grow 8 to 10 feet long. Leathery foliage is dark copper-green. Zones 5–10. RIR=8.9.

■ **Summer Wine ('KORizont')** Climber, deep pink, 1985, Kordes. Small clusters of big, single, coral pink flowers (5 petals) with red stamens and a light yellow eye appear all summer. Fragrance will permeate the entire garden. An excellent cut flower. Vigorous plants grow 12 feet tall with glossy dark green foliage. Ideal for training on pillar, arbor, or pergola. Zones 5–10.

■ **'Sunsprite, Climbing'** Climbing floribunda, deep yellow, 1989, Kroeger. A sport of the classic and beloved floribunda, Sunsprite, with long canes that can be trained as a climber 6 to 8 feet tall. Same disease resistance and colorfast deep yellow double blooms as its parent. Zones 6–11. RIR=7.8.

■ **'Westerland ('KORwest')** Shrub, apricot blend, 1969, Kordes. Underappreciated for 30 years, this variety is now highly regarded for its blended bright apricot-orange blooms (18 to 25 petals) with a strong spice and rose fragrance. Blooms have a ruffled look due to their serrated petals. Repeat blooming is fast. In mild climates canes reach 12 to 14 feet and will cover a house wall in only a few seasons. Zones 5–10. RIR=8.1.

■ **S.W.A.L.K. ('SEAwalk')** Climbing miniature, medium red, 1999, McCann. Rusty red double flowers (26 to 40 petals). Plants can be trained on a trellis or fence with canes that reach 6 to 7 feet long. Foliage is dark green and glossy. Zones 6–10. RIR=8.2.

■ **White Dawn 'White Dawn'** Large-flowered climber, white, 1949, Longley. This large climber is a proven performer that displays pristine white, gardenia-shaped, ruffled blooms from spring to fall. The sweetly fragrant, double flowers (30 to 35 petals) are weatherproof in sun and rain. Vigorous and disease-free, 10 to 12 feet tall, with glossy, dark green foliage. Performs well in all climates, although more tender than its parent, 'New Dawn'. Zones 6–9. RIR=7.6.

■ **Work of Art ('MORart')** Climbing miniature, orange blend, 1989, Moore. Short buds open to elegant, urn-shaped orange blooms with undersides that are blended with yellow, maturing to a range of orange hues. Blooms are double (35 petals), held in small tight clusters on strong stems. Flowers are long-lasting. Vigorous; in warm climates plants reach 4 to 6 feet in the first season. Zones 5–10. RIR=7.3.

Rose Gardens You Can Visit

Bellingrath Gardens
12401 Bellingrath Gardens Rd.
Theodore, AL 36582
251/973-2217

Berkeley Rose Garden
1200 Euclid Ave.
Berkeley, CA 94708
510/981-5150

Inez Parker Memorial Garden
Balboa Park
2525 Park Blvd.
San Diego, CA 92101
619/235-1100

Huntington Botanical Gardens
1151 Oxford Rd.
San Marino, CA 91108
626/405-2100

Rose Hills Memorial Park
3888 South Workman Mill Rd.
Whittier, CA 90601
562/699-0921

Walt Disney World
Lake Buena Vista, FL 32830
407/934-7639

The State Botanical Garden
2450 South Milledge Ave.
Athens, GA 30605
706/542-1244

Atlanta Botanical Garden
1345 Piedmont Ave NE
Atlanta, GA 30309
404/876-5859

University of Hawaii
Maui City Research Station
424 Mauna Place
Kula, Maui, HI 96790
808/878-1213

Chicago Botanic Garden
1000 Lake Cook Rd.
Glencoe, IL 60022
847/835-5440

Cantigny Gardens
1 South 151 Winfield Rd.
Wheaton, IL 60187
630/668-5161

Dubuque Arboretum
3800 Arboretum Road
Dubuque, IA 52001
563/556-2100

American Rose Center
8877 Jefferson Paige Rd.
Shreveport, LA 71119
318/938-5402

Jacob L. Loose Memorial Park
51st Sreet and Wornall Road
Kansas City, MO 64112
816/784-5300

Missouri Botanical Garden
4344 Shaw Blvd.
St. Louis, MO 63110
314/577-5100

Memorial Park Rose Garden
6005 Underwood Avenue
Omaha, NE 68132
402/444-5955

Reno Municipal Rose Garden
2055 Idlewild Dr.
Reno, NV 89509
775/334-2270

Albuquerque Rose Garden
8205 Apache Ave. NE
Albuquerque, NM 87111

New York Botanical Garden
Bronx River Parkway at
Fordham Road
Bronx, NY 10458
718/817-8700

Brooklyn Botanic Garden
1000 Washington Ave.
Brooklyn, NY 11225
718/623-7241

United Nations Rose Garden
42nd St. at the East River
New York, NY 10017

Biltmore Estate
One Biltmore Estates Drive
Asheville, NC 28803
800/543-2961

International Rose Test
   Garden
400 Southwest Kingston Ave.
Portland, OR 97201
503/823-3636

Hershey Gardens
170 Hotel Rd.
Hershey, PA 17033
717/534-3492

Longwood Gardens
U S Route 1, Box 501
Kennett Square, PA 19348
610/388-1000

Morris Arboretum
100 Northwestern Avenue
Philadelphia, PA 19118
215/247-5777

Memphis Botanic Garden
Audubon Park
750 Cherry Rd.
Memphis, TN 38117
901/685-1566

Mabel Davis Rose Garden
Zilker Botanical Garden
2220 Barton Springs Rd.
Austin, TX 78746
512/477-8672

Fort Worth Botanic Garden
3220 Botanic Garden Blvd.
Fort Worth, TX 76107
817/871-7676

Houston Municipal Rose
   Garden
1500 Hermann Dr.
Houston, TX 77004
713/284-1986

Woodland Park Rose Garden
5500 Phinney Ave. North
Seattle, WA 98103
206/684-4863

Boerner Botanical Gardens
9400 Boerner Drive
Hales Corners, WI 53130
414/525-5601

Resources

Gardeners who enjoy growing roses often need help and assistance as well as want to share their experiences. The American Rose Society (ARS) is a national nonprofit organization composed of a network of about 400 local rose societies in cities and towns throughout the United States. Headquartered in Shreveport, Louisiana, the ARS maintains a 118-acre park known as the American Rose Center, which is dedicated to roses. With more than 22,000 members, the ARS offers many services to promote rose growing:

■ Provides access to more than 2,800 experts who offer personal rose-growing assistance.

■ Lists affiliated rose societies in your area.

■ Publishes an annual *Handbook for Selecting Roses,* which rates new roses.

■ Publishes a 42-page, full-color monthly magazine, *The American Rose.*

■ Publishes the *American Rose Annual,* a 160-page, full-color volume containing the latest information on roses.

■ Publishes four publications on specialized subjects: *Miniature Roses, Old Garden Roses, Rose Arrangements,* and *Rose Exhibiting.*

■ Maintains a lending library of books, videos, and slides that can be borrowed.

■ Holds annual national conventions and rose shows featuring lectures, garden tours, and a chance to meet with fellow rose growers from all over the nation.

For more information, call 800-637-6534 or write to: American Rose Society, P.O. Box 30,000, Shreveport, LA 71130-0300.

Exploring the Internet for rose information

The following rose societies and organizations have web pages crammed full of color photos, and information on new roses and rose growing:

■ All-America Rose Selection (www.rose.org) provides lists and photos of all award winners from 1940 to the present. It also has a search feature that allows visitors to access a list of rose gardens by state.

■ American Rose Society (www.ars.org) offers features such as "Rose of the Month," articles by experts on selected topics, links to local rose societies, answers to frequently asked questions, where to buy roses, and much more. It also includes various links to associated websites.

■ Canadian Rose Society (www.mirror.org/groups/crs) lists current events and shows, public gardens, instructions on how to plant roses, explorer roses.

■ World Federation of Rose Societies (www.worldrose.org) provides a global perspective on roses, plus the Rose Hall of Fame. Site lists "Coming Events" with worldwide conferences and conventions, and editorials from their newsletter, *World Rose News.* Also includes links to national rose societies.

■ Royal National Rose Society (www.roses.co.uk) offers the benefits of membership plus an insight into rose gardens in the United Kingdom, rose care information, events, publications, and more.

Selected mail-order sources

The following are a few of the many mail order companies that carry roses:

Edmunds' Roses
6235 S.W. Kahle Rd.
Wilsonville, OR 97070
888/481-7673

Jackson & Perkins
1 Rose Lane
P.O. Box 1028
Medford, OR 97501
800/292-4769

Johnny Becnel Show Roses
8910 Highway 23
Belle Chasse, LA 70037
504/394-6608

Wayside Gardens
1 Garden Lane
Hodges, SC 29695
800/845-1124

Heirloom Roses
24062 N.E. Riverside Dr.
St. Paul, OR 97137
503/538-1576

Pickering Nurseries, Inc.
670 Kingston Rd.
Pickering, Ontario
Canada L1V 1A6
905/839-2111

Vintage Gardens Antique Roses
2833 Old Gravenstein Hwy S
Sebastopol, CA 95472
707/829-2035

Bridges Roses
2734 Toney Road
Lawndale, NC 28090
704/538-9412

Nor'East Miniature Roses, Inc.
902 Zenon Way, PO Box 1510
Arroyo Grande, CA 93420
800/426-6485

USDA Plant Hardiness Zone Map

This map of climate zones helps you select plants for your garden that will survive a typical winter in your region. The United States Department of Agriculture (USDA) developed the map, basing the zones on the lowest recorded temperatures across North America. Zone 1 is the coldest area and Zone 11 is the warmest.

Plants are classified by the coldest temperature and zone they can endure. For example, plants hardy to Zone 6 survive where winter temperatures drop to –10° F. Those hardy to Zone 8 die long before it's that cold. These plants may grow in colder regions but must be replaced each year. Plants rated for a range of hardiness zones can usually survive winter in the coldest region as well as tolerate the summer heat of the warmest one.

To find your hardiness zone, note the approximate location of your community on the map, then match the color band marking that area to the key.

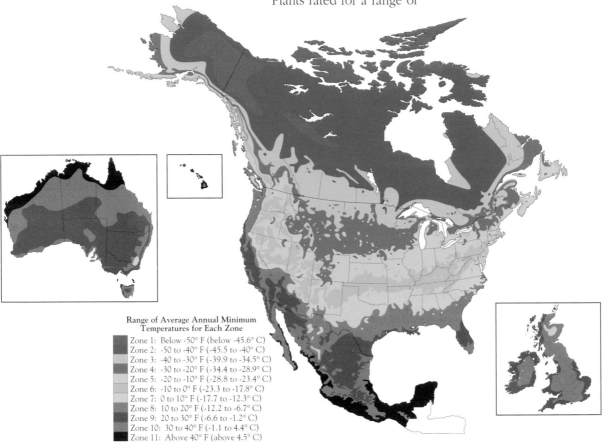

Range of Average Annual Minimum Temperatures for Each Zone

Zone 1: Below -50° F (below -45.6° C)
Zone 2: -50 to -40° F (-45.5 to -40° C)
Zone 3: -40 to -30° F (-39.9 to -34.5° C)
Zone 4: -30 to -20° F (-34.4 to -28.9° C)
Zone 5: -20 to -10° F (-28.8 to -23.4° C)
Zone 6: -10 to 0° F (-23.3 to -17.8° C)
Zone 7: 0 to 10° F (-17.7 to -12.3° C)
Zone 8: 10 to 20° F (-12.2 to -6.7° C)
Zone 9: 20 to 30° F (-6.6 to -1.2° C)
Zone 10: 30 to 40° F (-1.1 to 4.4° C)
Zone 11: Above 40° F (above 4.5° C)

METRIC CONVERSIONS

U.S. Units to Metric Equivalents			Metric Units to U.S. Equivalents		
To Convert From	**Multiply By**	**To Get**	**To Convert From**	**Multiply By**	**To Get**
Inches	25.4	Millimeters	Millimeters	0.0394	Inches
Inches	2.54	Centimeters	Centimeters	0.3937	Inches
Feet	30.48	Centimeters	Centimeters	0.0328	Feet
Feet	0.3048	Meters	Meters	3.2808	Feet
Yards	0.9144	Meters	Meters	1.0936	Yards

To convert from degrees Fahrenheit (F) to degrees Celsius (C), first subtract 32, then multiply by ⅝.

To convert from degrees Celsius to degrees Fahrenheit, multiply by ⅖, then add 32.

Index

Note: Page references in **bold regular type** indicate gallery entries and always include a photograph. Page references in **bold italic type** indicate other photographs, illustrations, or text in captions.

Plant index

Formal rose gardens, 48, *48*, *49*, 50, *170*
Fortune, Robert, 14
Fragrance
    best roses for, 39
    inheritance of, 155
    potpourri, 150–151, *150*, *151*
    as rose selection criteria, 38–39, 54, *55*
France, history of rose culture, 12–13
Fremont, Captain John Charles, 15
Fryer, Gareth, 23
Full flowers, *168*
Fully opened flowers, *168*
Fungicides
    applying, *116*, 120–121
    lime-sulfur, 123
    Ortho® Garden Disease Control, 127
    Ortho® Orthenex Garden Insect & Disease Control, 123, 124
    Ortho® RosePride Rose & Shrub Disease Control, 123
    See also Pesticides

G

Gerard, John, 9
Globular flowers, *168*
Grafting, 17, 26, 35, *164*
    See also Budding
Gravel, as mulch, 91
Greece (ancient), rose culture, 6, 8
Groundcovers, 67
Growth buds. *See* Bud eyes
Guillot (rose breeder), 21
Gypsum (calcium sulfate), 74, 99

H

Harkness, Philip and Robert, 23
Harkness Roses, 23
Harmony, color, 36–37
Harvesting commercial roses, 167
Heirloom Roses, *103*
Herbalists, historical use of roses, 9
Herball, 9
Herbicides, 92–93, *92*, 118
High-centered flowers, *168*, 170
Hips, 26, *27*, 115, *155*, *159*
History of roses, 6–23
    20th century, 19–21
    ancient world, 6, 8
    Asia, 11
    Dark Ages, 9

fossil evidence, 6
modern roses, early, 14–17
Napoleonic empire, 12–13
New World, 10, 11
Hogarth curve floral arrangements, 140, *141*
Horace, 8
Hoses, about, 89
Hot climates, 40, 86
Humidity, as site-selection criteria, 67
Hybridizing (rose breeding)
    about, 154
    for color, 155
    commercial, 164–167, *164*
    for fragrance, 39, 155
    history, 10
    techniques, *154*, 156–157, *156*, *157*

I

Ile de Bourbon (Réunion), 14
India, rose culture, 11
Informal rose gardens, 48, *48*, *49*, 50, *51*
Insecticidal soap, 119, 125
Insecticides
    about, 119
    applying, *116*, 120–121
    contact vs. systemic, 119
    See also Pesticides
Insecticides, specific
    acephate, 126
    carbaryl, 126
    Ortho® Bug-B-Gon Multi-Purpose Insect Killer, 122, 124, 125, 126
    Ortho® Orthenex Garden Insect & Disease Control, 122, 124
    Ortho® Pruning Sealer, 127
    Ortho® Ready-To-Use Rose & Flower Insect Killer, 126
    Ortho® Rose & Flower Insect Killer, 122, 125
    Ortho® Systemic Insect Killer, 122, 124, 125, 126
    pyrethrin, 119
Insect pests
    about, 116
    controlling, 118–119
    as disease carriers, 118
    examples, *118*, *119*
    in native soils, 81
    problem solver, 122–127

weed control and, 92
    See also specific insects
Insects, beneficial, 119
International Registration Authority for Roses (IRAR), 25, 165
Iron
    about, 99
    deficiency symptoms, *99*
Irrigation. *See* Watering; Watering systems

J

Jackson & Perkins Company, 23, *152–153*, 165
James Alexander Gamble Fragrance Award, 39
Japan, *Rosa rugosa* history, 15
Jefferson, Thomas, 11
Josephine, Empress, 12–13
Judging roses. *See* Exhibiting and judging roses

K

Kordes, Reimer, 18, 34
Kordes, Wilhelm, 23

L

Labeling roses, 79
Ladybugs, 119
Landscaping with roses
    about, 46
    arbors, 56–57, *57*
    borders and beds, 50–51, 58–59
    colors, 36–37, 60–61, *60*, *61*
    containers, 62–63, *62*, *63*
    formal gardens, 48, *48*, *49*, *170*
    fragrance, 38–39, 54, *55*
    groundcovers, 53, *53*
    hedges, 52, *52*, 68
    informal gardens, 48, *48*, *49*
    mass plantings, 51
    mixed plantings, 58–59, *58*, *59*
    screens, 53, *53*
    selection criteria, 24
    small spaces, 56, 234
    view enhancement, 55
Latin names, 25
Lawrance, Mary, 9
Layering (propagation), 162–163
Leaf axils, 26
Leaf cutter bees, *118*
Leafhoppers, *118*, 124, *124*
Leaflets, 26, *27*

Ortho's Complete Guide to Roses

Executive Editor, Gardening: Michael McKinley
Contributing Editors: Janet Goldenberg, Catherine Hamrick
Contributing Technical Consultants: Phil Edmunds,
 Michael D. Smith
Contributing Writers: Dr. Tommy Cairns, Ann Reilly
Senior Associate Design Director: Tom Wegner
Assistant Editor: Harijs Priekulis
Copy Chief: Terri Fredrickson
Copy and Production Editor: Victoria Forlini
Editorial Operations Manager: Karen Schirm
Managers, Book Production: Pam Kvitne,
 Marjorie J. Schenkelberg, Rick von Holdt, Mark Weaver
Contributing Copy Editor: Barbara Feller-Roth
Contributing Proofreaders: Mark Conley, Lorraine Ferrell,
 Terri Krueger, Jodie Littleton, Margaret Smith
Contributing Map Illustrator: Jana Fothergill
Contributing Prop/Photo Stylist: Rosemary Kautzky
Additional Contributors: Tim Abramowitz, Janet Anderson
Indexer: Ellen Davenport
Editorial and Design Assistants: Kathleen Stevens,
 Karen McFadden

Additional Editorial Contributions from
Art Rep Services

Director: Chip Nadeau
Designers: lk Design
Illustrator: Michael Surles

Meredith® Books

Editor in Chief: Linda Raglan Cunningham
Design Director: Matt Strelecki
Executive Editor, Gardening and Home Improvement:
 Benjamin W. Allen

Publisher: James D. Blume
Executive Director, Marketing: Jeffrey Myers
Executive Director, New Business Development:
 Todd M. Davis
Executive Director, Sales: Ken Zagor
Director, Operations: George A. Susral
Director, Production: Douglas M. Johnston
Business Director: Jim Leonard

Vice President and General Manager: Douglas J. Guendel

Meredith Publishing Group

President, Publishing Group: Stephen M. Lacy
Vice President-Publishing Director: Bob Mate

Meredith Corporation

Chairman and Chief Executive Officer: William T. Kerr

In Memoriam: E.T. Meredith III (1933–2003)

Thanks to Cathy Long, Diane Witosky

Photographers

(Photographers credited may retain copyright ©
 to the listed photographs.)
L = Left, R = Right, C = Center, B = Bottom, T = Top
American Rose Society: 142; **Rich Baer:** 5B, 21C, 22TR, 31TC, 31CR, 82, 88BL, 144, 145, 151, 171C, 171BR, 172-173, 174TL, 174CL, 175TL, 175TR, 175CR, 175BC, 177TL, 177TC, 177CR, 177BL, 178C, 180TL, 180C, 181BC, 182TL, 183TL, 184TL, 184C, 185BC, 190CL, 190C, 190BL, 192TC, 192CR, 193BL, 194BC, 196TR, 200TL, 200CL, 200BL, 200BC, 202BR, 203C, 204TR, 205TL, 205CL, 205CR, 205BR, 206CR, 206BL, 207TR, 207C, 211BR, 212BL, 214TL, 215CR, 215BR, 216TR, 216BR, 217CR, 221TL, 221BC, 221BR, 224TL, 225TR, 230TC, 236CL, 236C, 240TL, 240RCT, 241TL, 241CR; **Bridges Roses:** 201TL, 201C; **The British Library:** 9; **Karen Bussolini/ PositiveImages:** 129; **David Cavagnaro:** 228TR; **Conrad-Pyle Company/Star Roses:** 42R, 43B; **Crandall & Crandall:** 178CR, 194BL; **Irene J. Cross/Positive Images:** 170; **R. Todd Davis:** 197C, 218TR; **Alan & Linda Detrick:** 10R, 15CR, 16T, 19T, 30CR, 31TL, 34CL, 182C, 183TR, 201CL, 202CL, 216BL, 217CL, 218CR, 229CR, 230TR; **John E. Elsley:** 20TR, 22TL, 22T, 22BC, 179CR, 185TL, 185CL, 185BR, 188CL, 189TR, 193TR, 194CR, 195BL, 195BR, 201BR, 206BC, 210TL, 211BL, 212TL, 212CL, 212BR, 213TL, 213CL, 213C, 213CR, 213BL, 213BR, 214CR, 215TCL, 216CL, 216C, 216CR, 217TR, 218BR, 219TL, 219TC, 219BL, 220TC, 220C, 221TR, 222TC, 223CL, 222CL, 223BC, 224CL, 224C, 224CR, 224BL, 225BR, 228C, 228BR, 229C, 231TR, 238TC, 239BL, 240CL, 241CL; **Derek Fell:** 12-13, 15B, 16B, 19B, 41T, 43T, 53T, 73B, 178CL, 179TC, 189C, 192BR, 207CL, 218TL, 222TR, 236BL, 241BL; **John Glover:** 4T, 7, 12L, 31C, 35TL, 63B, 102, 192TR, 215BCL, 223BR, 230TL, 231BL, 233BC; **John Glover/Garden Picture Library:** 231TC; **Harry Haralambou/Positive Images:** 69B; **Lynne Harrison:** 31BR, 58T, 174TC, 217TC, 220CL; **Marijke Heuff/Garden Picture Library:** 211CL; **Saxon Holt:** 15L, 17T, 20TL, 21T, 49BL, 56, 78, 86, 88BR, 90, 106T, 111BL, 115B, 146, 147, 148, 154, 156, 157, 159, 164L, 166, 167, 214BC, 217BL, 228CR, 229TC, 230CR, 231CL, 231C, 233CL, 236BC; **Horticultural Photography:** 189BL, 229TL; **Jerry Howard/Positive Images:** 40L; **Jackson & Perkins:** 197BR, 225BL, 237CR; **Rosemary Kautzky:** 149T; **Andrew Lawson:** 4C, 19C, 48 (Designer: Anita Pereire), 62BR, 106B, 223TL, 231BR, 236TL; **Janice Lee:** 195C; **Peter Lindtner:** 31CL, 179TL, 215BL; **Kathy Longinecker:** 33R, 182BR, 185CR, 193C, 201CR, 202TR, 203BR, 206TL, 212TR, 220BR, 232TR, 232C; **Janet Loughrey:** 171BL, 178TC, 191TR, 206BR, 222TL, 229BC, 230BC; **David McDonald:** 14C, 18T, 30TL, 41B, 53B, 57B, 180BL, 181CR, 181BR, 190CR, 190BC, 192TL, 194C, 201TC, 204TC, 205TC, 212CR, 221BL, 228BC, 229BR, 230C, 233BL, 238BR, 239TR, 239BCR; **Heidi Mitchell:** 192C; **Clive Nichols:** 230CL; **Arthur N. Orans/Horticultural Photographer:** 229TL; **Jerry Pavia:** 14L, 15TR, 33L, 70T, 180TC, 185C, 188CR, 191C, 191CR, 196TL, 211TL, 228BL; **Diane A. Pratt/Positive Images:** 34TR; **Laslo Puskas/Garden Picture Library:** 190TR; **Ann Reilly/Positive Images:** 197CL, 206C, 223CR; **Howard Rice/Garden Picture Library:** 84-85, 232BL; **John Saville/Noreast Miniature Roses, Inc.:** 203CR; **Ron Shaw:** 1, 174BL, 174BR, 176BL, 177CL, 178BL, 179TR, 179BL, 180CL, 181BL, 182TR, 182CR, 183CL, 183CR, 184TC; **Richard Shiell:** spine, 11, 14R, 22BR, 25, 30TR, 30BR, 31TR, 52, 71, 171TL, 175CL, 175C, 176C, 179BR, 180CR, 181CL, 184BL, 188BR, 189CR, 189BR, 191CL, 193CR, 193BR, 194CL, 195TL, 196BL, 197BC, 200TC, 201TR, 201BL, 201BC, 202CR, 203TL, 203BR, 204CL, 204BC, 205C, 205BC, 207CR, 207BL, 207BR, 214BR, 219TR, 219BR, 220TL, 220TR, 225TL, 226-227, 228TC, 229TR, 229BL, 230BR, 231TL, 232TL, 232CL, 232BC, 233TC, 233CR, 237TL, 237TC, 237BCR, 238TL, 240BC, 240RCB, 240BR; **J. S. Sira/Garden Picture Library:** 69T; **Meleah T. Spinell/ Horticultural Photographer:** 189BL; **Albert Squillace/Positive Images:** 10C, 221CL, 230BL, 232CR, 240TR; **Friedrich Strauss/Garden Picture Library:** 63T; **Michael S. Thompson:** 6, 8L, 10L, 31BL, 31BC, 33T, 45, 58BL, 62BL, 72, 103, 150, 152-153, 155T, 191TL, 194TR, 197TC, 197CR, 200CR, 203CL, 204BR, 207TL, 210CR, 214TR, 223BL, 228CL, 231BL, 238CL, 239TL, 239TC, 239CL; **Tracey Treloar/Treloar Roses:** 206TC; **Deidra Walpole:** 35TR, 177TR; **Weeks Roses:** 169Row4#1T

On the cover: Hot Princess Rose, photograph by Ron Shaw

All of us at Meredith® Books are dedicated to providing you with the information and ideas you need to enhance your home and garden. We welcome your comments and suggestions about this book.
Write to us at:
 Meredith Gardening Books
 1716 Locust St.
 Des Moines, IA 50309–3023

If you would like to purchase any of our gardening, home improvement, cooking, crafts, or home decorating and design books, check wherever quality books are sold. Or visit us at: meredithbooks.com

If you would like more information on other Ortho products, call 800/225-2883 or visit us at: www.ortho.com